A Young Fisherman's Dream Come True

A Young Fisherman's Dream Come True

Captain Bill Harrison

Copyright © 2016 Captain Bill Harrison
All rights reserved.

ISBN: 069270809X
ISBN 13: 9780692708095

Contents

Chapter 1	Born in Miami ·	1
Chapter 2	Cozumel, Mexico, June 20, 1965 · · · · · · · · · · · · ·	3
Chapter 3	The Old Pier 5, Miami, Florida · · · · · · · · · · · · · ·	11
Chapter 4	Bimini on the Charter Boat *Queen B* · · · · · · · · ·	36
Chapter 5	Pier 5, Miami, Florida, February 3, 1969 A Perfect Day to Troll the Reef · · · · · · · · · · · · · ·	45
Chapter 6	Pier 5, Miami, Florida, September 13, 1969 Catching Eleven Warsaw Groupers in One Day ·	53
Chapter 7	Pier 5, Miami, Florida, February 10, 1970 Trolling the Reef with Buddy Carey · · · · · · · · · ·	59
Chapter 8	Pier 5, Miami, Florida, November 7, 1970 The Hialeah Funeral Home · · · · · · · · · · · · · · · ·	66
Chapter 9	Miami Beach, Florida, November 13, 1970 The Speigle Family of South Beach · · · · · · · · · · ·	72

Chapter 10	Pier 5, Miami, Florida, November 20, 1970 Timmy Thomas from the Sir John's Night Beat Hotel ·	79
Chapter 11	Pier 5, Miami, Florida, March 9, 1971 The Giant White Marlin · · · · · · · · · · · · · · · · · ·	86
Chapter 12	Pier 5, Miami, Florida, March 12, 1971 Catching a 496-Pound Jewfish · · · · · · · · · · · · · · ·	92
Chapter 13	Pier 5, Miami, Florida, September 19, 1971 Fishing with Bob and Rolan · · · · · · · · · · · · · · ·	98
Chapter 14	Pier 5, Miami, Florida, October 16, 1971 Captain Red Hagen Mates on the *Sea Boots* · · ·	104
Chapter 15	Pier 5, Miami, Florida, November 6, 1971 Fat Fredy Works the Cockpit · · · · · · · · · · · · · · · ·	110
Chapter 16	Bimini, Bahamas, May 8, 1972 The First Bluefin Tuna of the Year · · · · · · · · · · ·	117
Chapter 17	Pier 5, Miami, Florida, April 16, 1973 The Mysterious Mr. Jones and Mr. Smith · · · · · ·	125
Chapter 18	Bimini, Bahamas, April 14, 1975 The First Bluefin of the Season · · · · · · · · · · · · · ·	133
Chapter 19	St. Thomas, US Virgin Islands, July 1975 Harry Tellam's Greatest Day · · · · · · · · · · · · · · · ·	139
Chapter 20	St. Thomas, US Virgin Islands, August 20, 1975 The Four Anglers from the Great State of Texas ·	144

Chapter 21	St. Thomas, US Virgin Islands, August 8, 1975 Jim Lambert's First Blue Marlin · · · · · · · · · · · · · 152
Chapter 22	St. Thomas, US Virgin Islands, August 20, 1975 The Crazy Texans · · · · · · · · · · · 159
Chapter 23	St. Thomas, US Virgin Islands, August 23, 1975 The Miami Garden Group · · · · 168
Chapter 24	Pier 5, Miami, Florida, November 17, 1975 Ronald, the Stretch Limo, and the Three Kids · · 174
Chapter 25	Pier 5 Miami, Florida, December 1, 1975 Fishing the Russian · 183
Chapter 26	Bimini, Bahamas, May 21, 1976 Yohannes and the Record Bluefin Tuna · · · · · · · 190
Chapter 27	Bimini, Bahamas May 9, 1978 Reverend Pinder and Our Fish · · · · · · · · · · · · · 207
Chapter 28	St. Thomas, US Virgin Islands, August 18, 1978 Dee's Six Blue Marlin in One Day · 214
Chapter 29	St. Thomas, US Virgin Islands, August 19, 1978 The *Belama* Catches Seven Blue Marlin in One Day · · · · · · · · · · · · 223
Chapter 30	Pier 5, Miami, Florida, April 1, 1980 Vicky's Good Friday Amberjack · · · · · · · · · · · · · 230
Chapter 31	Pier 5, Miami, Florida, April 13, 1981 JC Dobson and the Amberjack · · · · · · · · · · · · · 237

Chapter 32	St. Thomas, US Virgin Islands, August 18, 1986 Ray Rosher and Monty Padilla	243
Chapter 33	St. Thomas, US Virgin Islands, September 13, 1986 Roy's Best Blue Marlin Day Ever!	250
Chapter 34	St. Thomas, US Virgin Islands, September 14, 1986 A Great Blue Marlin Day on the *Pescador*	256
Chapter 35	The Great Barrier Reef, Australia, November 5, 1986 Raul's Thousand-Pound Black Marlin	263
Chapter 36	St. Thomas, US Virgin Islands, September 7, 1987 The Great Captain Mike Benitez	272
Chapter 37	The Great Barrier Reef, Australia, October 31, 1989 Sam's Winning Black Marlin	279
Chapter 38	Captain Buddy Carey	288
Chapter 39	Captains Who Have Influenced My Life	300
Chapter 39-A	Dude Perkins	306

Preface

I want to thank Carla Boccuti, my girlfriend, for the many hours she spent proofreading the text. I want to thank Dude Perkins for his advice and memories of people from the past; Allen Merritt for his great memory of his tuna stories and mine; Jan Fogt for her continual support to keep me charging ahead; and Mike Hoffman, marine artist, for his eagerness to offer any painting from his extensive collection of great marine art.

I need to thank the many captains and mates from around the world who fished with me during a lifetime of catching fish, whether the fish were one thousand pounds or just a couple of pounds. Also, there were the thousands of people who paid money to go fishing and contributed the great experiences that added up to the contents of this fun book.

Through my lifetime I took notes, some careful and clear, some not so clear. Thanks to the thousands of pictures I took and saved over the years, I was able to remember the locations, the boats, the fish and their weights, and the names of the anglers. Unfortunately I did need to change a few names from the past.

A Young Fisherman's Dream Come True is only a small select number of the great days of my life that I choose to share. There have been so many more.

• • •

CHAPTER 1

BORN IN MIAMI

332 pound jewfish with Bill Harrison at Weeche's Dock, Bimini. June 1959.

      Bill Harrison was born in Miami, Florida, and grew up in a small section just south of the downtown area, called Coconut Grove. At that time the waterfront of Coconut Grove had a small commercial fishing fleet with lots of mullet, mackerel, lobster, and stone crab boats along with a half dozen bay shrimpers all tied up side by side against the seawall. Going to elementary school just up the street from the docks, Bill soon started working on a variety of these commercial fishing boats.

His first real job was working for the Miami Seaquarium at age thirteen. Not long after that, he visited the charter boat dock at Pier 5 in downtown Miami. This was the most famous charter boat dock in the world. Seeing the excitement surrounding the boats, the people, and the massive numbers of fish put on the dock every day, he knew where his future lay. Bill started his fishing career in Miami, Florida. In the early 1960s, he started marlin fishing in the Bahamas and then fished the famous San Juan, Puerto Rico, blue marlin tournament in 1966.

When he first fished the North Drop of St. Thomas in 1969 for blue marlin, his desire to tag and release these beautiful fish started. In 1986 the NOAA (National Oceanic and Atmospheric Administration) gave him an award for tagging the most blue marlin of any captain. He has always believed in and supported the tagging and releasing of giant bluefin tuna and marlin (black, blue, stripped, and white).

Bill has fished the Gulf of Mexico; the Sea of Cortez; and the Atlantic, Pacific, and Indian Oceans. Some of his most enjoyable adventures were twelve trips to lower Africa, four seasons on the Great Barrier Reef of Australia, and many trips to Panama, Costa Rica, Guatemala, Cabo San Lucas, El Salvador, Ecuador, the Galapagos, Colombia, and Venezuela.

When asked about his fishing off Northern Canada and New England for giant bluefin tuna, he said, "I don't like the cold." Today he still enjoys releasing marlin in the Bahamas and bluefin tuna off of Cat Cay.

CHAPTER 2

COZUMEL, MEXICO, JUNE 20, 1965

266 pound blue marlin. The first blue marlin caught out of Cozumel, Mexico. Angler Louie DeHoyos, captain Bill Harrison and mates Bayto, Jose and Louie. June 20, 1965

This was my second year flying from Miami to the city of Merida, located on the north part of the Yucatan Peninsula of Mexico. I was searching for bluefin tuna and giant marlin that the local fishermen reported seeing in the late spring and early summer between Cozumel and the Mexican coast. After I landed and cleared customs, I took a bus loaded with the usual array of Mexican families, with their numerous bags and cages containing chickens, pigs, and dogs, all headed down a costal road to who knew where.

I was going to get off at Puerto Azul, which was due west of the island of Cozumel. The young Mexican mother sitting next to me on a piece of plywood nursing her baby kept a nonstop dialogue going in Spanish for several hours. I politely smiled and wondered if the rotund baby would ever finish his dinner as she switched him from left breast to right breast and back again without stopping her one-sided conversation with me. This was 1966. The thirty-year-old bus we were riding in had no air conditioning, some floorboards, and no muffler.

When the bus reached Puerto Azul, I bid good-bye to my talkative lady friend and her still-nursing baby and disembarked. With some help from the locals, I found the commercial dock where a local-made single-diesel-engine boat with a small sail, called *Pez Vela*, was waiting. I knew Captain Baytoe from the previous year. He and his mate, Jose, loaded my bags onboard the *Pez Vela*, and we were off to the island of Cozumel. At that time there was no airport on the island, and the marina was being dynamited out of the shoreline. There was room in the small marina for only five boats while the work continued.

Louis de Hoyos had hired me the previous summer to try to catch the first bluefin tuna or blue marlin out of Cozumel. A young Mexican pilot, Tito, had met me in Merida, and we spent two days flying the Mexican coast looking for schools of bluefin tuna that the local fishermen talked about. We flew south to Belize and back up the Mexican coast in hopes of seeing schools of bluefin tuna like I was used to seeing off Cat Cay in the Bahamas.

A YOUNG FISHERMAN'S DREAM COME TRUE

I felt that June was too late for bluefins, since they were being caught in the Gulf of Mexico in April and in the Bahamas in May and early June. Louis went by what the local fishermen said. I pointed out that they had never caught either bluefin tuna or blue marlin. The June bluefin tuna proved to be about as factual as the thirty-foot marlin the local fishermen frequently hooked but never landed.

June 1965 was fun in Cozumel. I was fishing in an aluminum boat with a crow's nest, not a tower. There were big dolphin everywhere along with lots of sailfish. We released all but two sailfish every day; the crew received one each for their families. The large dolphin we caught went to the hotel restaurant.

Since we were targeting bluefin tuna, we fished a 12/0 Fin-Nor reel filled with 130 lb. test Dacron line and an unlimited rod. Using this tackle we were going to easily catch any blue marlin that was dumb enough to eat a swimming mullet. That happened the second day of fishing. Louis wound the marlin to the boat without it taking more than a dozen yards of line from the Fin-Nor reel that was set with 55 pounds of striking drag. The overpowered blue was easily gaffed and put in the boat.

That afternoon we returned to the town dock to unload the marlin. As word spread, hundreds gathered to see us unload this huge blue marlin and put it on a cart pulled by a donkey and two dozen young boys who wanted to be part of the celebration. The downtown destination was a scale on metal wheels, with circular plates that were added as needed to make the weight accurate. With all fairness to the true weight of this blue marlin, we should have subtracted the stack of 2X6 planks that had been added to keep the fish's sagging tail and head from touching the ground. However, this was not done.

The mayor was summoned to read the weight of the first ever blue marlin officially weighed in at Cozumel. I am very skeptical that this was the first blue marlin caught off Cozumel island, but everyone knows how Mexicans are—it takes very little to start a fiesta on a Saturday night! The mayor showed up in a coat and tie and read the official weight as 266 pounds. Then the blue marlin was dragged from the scale to a large tree in the town square where it was hung by its tail for all the towns people to see. I looked at the pile of 2X6s still resting on the scale; the stack weighed eighteen pounds.

At my young, naive age, I felt that the mayor should know about the discrepancy, so I advised his assistant. The police chief and two officers soon arrived to notify me that the mayor was never wrong, and I should concentrate on catching fish and let the mayor do the official weighing. I immediately bought six beers for my three new friends, and after they were consumed the police escorted me through the crowd as a hero.

In 1966, one year later, I arrived in Cozumel in mid-June. I again felt that the bluefin tuna had long since migrated into the Gulf of Mexico and on past the Bahamas. Louis, my sponsor, said the bluefin were still there. Since he was the boss, I smiled and eagerly looked forward to the next day's fishing.

We started early the next morning, heading west to the Mexican coast in the same aluminum boat, with Captain Baytoe and mate Jose. They were eager to see me, since we had caught several more blue marlin last June, leading to huge celebrations in the town square that meant they did not have to work the following day.

After five days of looking for the elusive bluefins and catching only large dolphin and sailfish, Louis got an emergency call from one of his businesses in Mexico City. He had to leave the next morning to solve some kind of problem. I said good-bye as he boarded the *Pez Vela* and headed for Puerto Azul. This left me with at least five free paid days.

A YOUNG FISHERMAN'S DREAM COME TRUE

Two days earlier Pudgy Spaulding, my friend from Pier 5 in Miami, had arrived on the island for his first trip to fish Cozumel and the surrounding areas. He was running a fifty-six-foot wooden Norseman-built boat called the *Play-Bay-B*, owned by Connie Dinkler of the Palm Bay Club in Miami. The boat had three 370 Cummins diesel engines. Unfortunately they lost one engine due to mechanical failure just north of the island on the way from Key West. A longtime friend of Pudgy, Charlie O'Keiffe, was the mate on the *Play-Bay-B*. Since Pudgy was unfamiliar with the area, he hired me to fish with them. This was perfect for me, since I had time to double-dip and fish with old friends.

The charter parties were great because of the cast of characters on the boat. First there was Charlie (known as Killer O'Keiffe), who desperately wanted to be identified with the Mafia. He tried to talk like Al Capone—until he finished the first bottle of rum. Then he couldn't talk at all. Then we had Banner, a big, youthful golden retriever. He was a great dog that slept on the bridge next to his master and best friend, Pudgy, the captain. Once we hooked a fish, Banner became more excited than any first-time charter boat customer. This crazy dog would turn around and then go backward down the bridge ladder to get to the cockpit, so he could look over the covering boards to see whatever we were catching.

Pudgy Spaulding was a second-generation charter boat captain who had a successful operation out of Pier 5 in Miami. Last of all there was me. Back then I loved fishing so much, I would have worked for free, but no one knew that.

On our first day of fishing, we ran from the island of Cozumel over to the coast side of the Yucatan Channel. Although Pudgy had never fished there, he was a natural-born fisherman. He could find fish when no one else could.

In 1966 a fifty-six-foot Norseman was a huge charter boat. It had three chairs in the cockpit and two on the flying bridge. We trolled five lines—two ballyhoo from the long outriggers and two ballyhoo from the short outriggers, with one bonito down the middle from the center rigger. The big rod with the bonito stayed in the large fighting chair in the center of the cockpit.

As the day passed, the huge fish box and the four coolers started to fill. We caught lots of twenty-, thirty-, and forty-pound dolphin plus several big kingfish and a few wahoos. We were releasing all the sailfish. Every time we released one, the lone Mexican we brought along to clean the inside of the boat and make sandwiches cried. He had no idea we were going to give him a cooler filled with filleted dolphin, kingfish, and wahoos at the end of the day.

Late that afternoon sail fishing caught fire. There were man-o'-war birds diving on schools of bait everywhere. We were the only boat fishing, so it was a no-competition day. During the last half hour of fishing, we hooked two big dolphins. Then a large group of sailfish appeared behind the boat, and two sails ate the remaining ballyhoo. I quickly pitched another ballyhoo out, and we had three sails on. I then grabbed a small bait rod and threw another ballyhoo over the transom; a sailfish ate it instantly, so I handed the rod to Pedro, who had no idea what to do with a rod and reel.

A five-foot-long blacktip shark started chasing one of the hooked dolphins and soon ate the bonito that was fished on the center rigger. The shark could not pull any line off the 12/0 Fin-Nor reel, since it had a striking drag of fifty pounds. Banner the dog had descended to the cockpit. The more the dolphin or sailfish jumped, the more Banner barked.

Killer O'Keiffe wanted this day to end as soon as possible, so he could get back to Cozumel and have a rum and Coke or two. Both of the big dolphins were gaffed and put in the fish box. We then started to release the four sailfish that were tangled with the blacktip shark. Finally the lines were untangled, and all the sailfish were released, allowing one angler to wind the shark to the boat.

The Mexican was begging us to keep the shark for his family. Pudgy shouted down to Killer and me to grab the pectoral fin of the shark and throw it in the boat. I might have been young, but I was not dumb; I knew better than to do that. Since we had several gorgeous ladies onboard that day, Pudgy pulled off his shirt, came down the ladder, and pushed Killer and me out of the way. He leaned over the starboard side of the boat, grabbed the blacktip shark by its left pectoral fin, and started to lift. The first slap of the shark's tail sent Pudgy's sunglasses ten feet in the air and into the ocean. The second slap drew a large amount of blood from Pudgy's nose. He quickly released his grip on the shark's fin and returned to the bridge, where he used his T-shirt to try to stop the blood flow from his rearranged nose. Although the girls tried not to giggle at Pudgy's shark encounter, Killer and I couldn't stop laughing.

Since we were using very heavy leader wire and a 14/0 Mustad hook to the bonito, I knew I could easily lift the shark over the covering board. As I balanced with one foot on the transom and the other foot on the starboard covering board, I took a double wrap of the wire and started to swing the sixty-pound blacktip shark into the cockpit. Killer, backing me up, grabbed my belt and steadied me as I swung the shark over the covering board and into the cockpit. Balancing carefully, I walked up the covering board to the tower leg and stepped back into the cockpit.

Banner was barking, and Killer O'Keiffe was screaming. I could not believe what I saw. The shark had landed on its stomach and was flopping wildly, head to tail and tail to head. This knocked Killer's feet out from under him. He fell with his back to the transom in the starboard corner of the cockpit deck. Since the cockpit sole slanted aft, the shark was flopping downhill toward Killer. Banner was doing his best to save him.

The second time Killer kicked the shark in the face, its jaws deeply implanted in the right heel of Killer's new boat shoes. Banner now had the shark by the tail, and the shark had Killer by the heel of his shoe. Within moments the shark had removed the heel from the shoe, and Banner had fallen into the boat's open live-bait well, which was filled with salt water and ten thirty-pound dolphin. Luckily the shark soon tired. Killer, bruised and battered, pulled the wet Banner from the well while Pudgy, with a bloodied T-shirt over his nose, headed the *Play-Bay-B* home to the harbor on Cozumel island.

So started our first day of chartering from the island of Cozumel. So much was to follow.

CHAPTER 3

THE OLD PIER 5, MIAMI, FLORIDA

A good catch of warsaw groupers. Caught onboard the Sea Boots with captain Buddy Carey and mate Red Hagen in the mid 1950's. The Old Pier 5 Miami, Florida

I fished out of the old wooden docks of Pier 5 in the 1960s—those wonderful days when massive numbers of all kinds of fish were laid on the dock day after day. The colorful good old days of killing anything and everything every day of the month, since charter parties were paying money to do exactly that.

This came to an end when the city of Miami closed down the Pier 5 location, which was at the east end of Fifth Street downtown. All the charter boats and head boats (so called because they charged by the head, or per person) were relocated to the west side of Watson Island, where walk-on traffic was nonexistent. Without the added fishing days generated by the walk-on customers, I knew, the charter boat fleet would be smaller when we returned to the new Miamarina in 1970.

Early that year all the boats and their crews were ready and hungry to start making money, months before the parking lot of Miamarina was even paved and painted. Trying to survive the lack of walk-on traffic at Watson Island cost several charter boats and one head boat their livelihoods and their family businesses. The new arrangement of boats was now north-south instead of the previous east-west.

The old Pier 5 was a long wooden pier that started from a parking lot in Bay Front Park and went east, with fifteen slips on the south side and thirteen on the north side. The head boats started at the north end of the new Miamarina. This bordered on the two-lane road heading to the seaport, which had a train bridge and a drawbridge separating Dodge Island from downtown Miami.

Henry Simone owned three head boats—the *Seabreeze I*, the *Seabreeze II*, and the *Seabreeze Jr.* This well-run business took people out for half days and full days off Miami to drift fish. Also, Jud Waterman had the *Reward*, which was the longest-lasting head boat in Miami history, since it kept being sold and resold and then, with plenty of money, reborn with the same name.

Frank Smith had the *Sea Runner*, a head boat that lasted through the Watson Island era. The boat then moved to Miamarina, where Frank

A YOUNG FISHERMAN'S DREAM COME TRUE

struggled to pay the rent. After months of nonpayment, he and his boat were kicked out. The boat eventually returned to Watson Island.

Next on the Miamarina docks came the tour boats, which were long and low, so they could get under the bridges of the Miami River without causing the bridges to open and tie up city traffic. Mike Rogers was the owner and tireless driving force of two of these boats—the *Island Queen I* and the *Island Queen II*. Mike kept both boats going from nine in the morning till midnight seven days a week. I remember him as large and mustached, with dyed black hair and endless energy. He would get to the dock at six in the morning and make sure the boats were immaculate before they started sailing with eager tourists who wanted to see all the Miami River had to offer.

Mike promised the possibility of seeing rumrunners, dope smugglers, alligators, and gunfights. Gunfights in the middle of the day, were more common than the promised drug smugglers, alligators, and rumrunners since most of them appeared well after dark and ended before morning.

Starting south down the new docks, there was the *Prowler*, a forty-five-foot Norseman-built charter boat owned by Robert Christiansen and mated by his father, Chris. The next charter boat was owned by a longtime Pier 5-er named Bing Spaulding—the *Flying Fish*. Bing was the father of Pudgy and Ken Spaulding, who both went into the charter boat industry.

Capt. Bing Spaulding's longtime mate was Eddie Manarski. Eddie's live-in girlfriend, Mazy, would arrive with Eddie at the dock at 5:45 every morning. Mazy's sister, "Sweet Relish," worked across Biscayne Boulevard at the Park Lee Diner, a long-established South Florida dining landmark located on the ground floor of the Park Lee Hotel.

Mazy would walk across Biscayne Boulevard with two steaming pots of hot coffee from her sister's diner every morning for the captains and mates. Whenever we were not booked, the captains and mates would go across the street and order breakfast from Sweet Relish and leave her a big tip for the many mornings that her sister would bring us hot coffee. In the winter, when we were working every day, fishing fifty or sixty days in a row, Mazy and Sweet Relish looked like queens from a sailor's dream at five or six in the morning. Then the sun came up.

The next charter boat was the *Sea Lion*, owned by Joe Chriscolie. He had so many colorful mates. Rick "the Whip" came first, and then there was Jose "the Flare Gunner." Jose received this name when he shot a burglar in the lower area of the stomach with a flare gun as he burglarized the rods and reels off Capt. Joe's boat.

The *Miami Herald* reported that the burglar had the most important parts of his body burned off by the flames caused by the coast guard-approved flare shot from the coast guard-approved flare gun. Jose was later tried in a very expensive multiweek trial for disfiguring this model Miami citizen, who had been arrested forty-six times.

Jose was found guilty in a federal court of law and ordered to pay $2 million to LeRoy, the disfigured man. Unfortunately, two days after the trial was over, LeRoy was shot and killed by the father of a twelve-year-old retarded girl. The father just happened to be carrying a gun when LeRoy dragged the girl to the ground and stole her necklace and earrings. The police followed the blood trail to an overgrown lot where the disfigured LeRoy had collapsed and bled to death while still clutching the necklace and earrings.

Each month the US government flies several federal agents to Miami to collect the $2 million from Jose, who is a homeless man who lives under the Watson Island Bridge. He has no bank account, no home address, no family and only one set of clothes. He does have three pairs of expensive stolen shoes.

Then there was the three-engine Norseman called the *Play-Bay-B*, owned by Connie Dinkler of the Palm Bay Club. She had started with a forty-foot charter boat built by Norseman Boat Yard. She had then built a forty-five-foot Norseman and put it in charter for Pudgy Spaulding to run out of Pier 5. A few years later, Connie built another Norseman that was fifty-five feet long and had three 370 Cummins diesel engines. Pudgy ran all of her boats. He liked this three-engine one the best—it was big and fast.

Pudgy's mate was his longtime friend Killer O'Keiffe. Only Pudgy, with his "nothing bothers me in life" attitude, could put up with Killer's chronic alcoholism, oversleeping, and unsavory friends. I remember one morning when two yellow cabs pulled up behind *the Play-Bay-B* with a rowdy group of guys. It was clear to me they were still partying from the night before. Pudgy frequently fished with several NFL players, and they were as wild as it could get.

Since I had the *Sea Boots* set up to go fishing, I walked north several slips to direct the group to the *Play-Bay-B*. After talking and laughing for a couple of minutes, I noticed the door was open on the *Play-Bay-B*. I jumped onboard to wake Killer and tell him about the early arrival of his charter party.

As I entered the boat, I was shocked to see a naked sixty-year-old prostitute in the middle of the saloon, spread-eagle and asleep. Much scarier than that was seeing a naked Killer next to her, with his wrists loosely tied to a barstool by some of Connie Dinkler's brightly colored scarfs that she was famous for wearing at gala events.

Once I untied Killer's wrists and got him to his feet, he exhaled in my face, and I realized the three bottles of rum he had consumed had not exited his bloodstream or his body. While I was walking out of the *Play-Bay-B*'s cabin, a miracle happened. Mazy shouted to me from two boats down, "Billy, I brought you coffee and sweets."

I jumped off the boat and told the drunken football players, "I have a blonde for you guys." These athletes, who had just downed a couple more beers on top of the previous night's margaritas, looked up and saw Mazy. At twenty yards away, in the predawn darkness, this thin blonde with bright-red lipstick looked great!

Once the guys surrounded her, she became a real tease, even though she had only four teeth. Many times Mazy bragged to me that during her younger days, she knew how to "please a crowd"! Since I was quite young, I thought this must have been a very long time ago.

Before I could take a sip of my hot coffee, I heard someone scream, "I can't swim!" We all looked at the *Play-Bay-B* and saw Killer holding the sixty-year-old prostitute—both still naked—with one foot on the transom of the boat and the other foot on the dock as the distance from the dock to the boat increased. It was like one of those slow-motion films from the past.

The prostitute slowly climbed up Killer's chest as the boat got farther and farther away from the dock. We all ran to save the naked couple as they balanced, but it was too late. At the moment she wrapped her legs around Killer's neck, the two of them tumbled into the dark, cold, seaweed-filled water of Miamarina.

Those NFL guys were strong! They pulled the two out of the water in moments. As luck had it, a yellow cab was slowly passing by the charter boat parking lot in the predawn hours. I gave a loud yell, and the cab driver backed up but refused to take the naked prostitute in his cab. I solved this problem by jumping onboard the *Play-Bay-B* and

A YOUNG FISHERMAN'S DREAM COME TRUE

grabbing the first dress I saw in Connie Dinkler's closet. The guys put the dress over the prostitute's head, pushed her into the cab, and threw the driver two twenties.

Ten minutes later Killer emerged from the boat wearing some clothes he had found in Connie's husband's closet. Pudgy then drove up in his green Chevy El Camino. Looking around, I realized Killer would now be protected by the guy thing that is honored by all males—a total silence about prostitutes. If you are a senator, governor, mayor, or boatmate, all males know nothing and see nothing.

Two months later I learned the dress I gave to the prostitute was one of Connie's favorites. A Chanel dress that had been given to her when she was in Paris.

A new charter boat was added when the dock first opened. Built by the Enterprise Boat Company, the *Quetzal* was owned by Ed Wheeler and captained by JC Dobson. JC had his longtime friend Wayne Eisenhower as a mate. This combination worked well for owner Ed. After two years Wayne moved on to a private job. A guy named Ronnie was then hired as the full-time mate, and he brought several of his loyal charter customers to the *Quetzal*. One was Airplane Annie. We all knew that her stories about flying in World War II were not true, since she had been born in 1935. We could do the math!

All the guys at the dock looked forward to Annie chartering the *Quetzal* twice a month, since she always brought five young women who loved to take off their clothes while they fished. Frequently, once the charter boat fleet was fishing, JC would call me on the radio to give me a heads-up. I would then tell my charter clients to get their cameras ready, and I would troll very close to the *Quetzal* as they were in the process of catching a big dolphin or sailfish.

It never failed—all the girls on the *Quetzal* were so excited, they jumped up and down while wildly waving at us, wearing only suntan lotion!

The next boat was the *Sea Boots*, which was owned by Buddy Carey. It was a Carolina-designed charter boat built by Charlie Allygood's Boat Yard in North Carolina. Buddy was very loyal to the Norseman Boat Yard in Miami. He built three Norseman charter boats in the late 1940s, one in the mid-1950s and one in early 1960.

Norseman Boat Yard was located on the south side of the Miami River, just west of the Fifth Street Bridge. This was the place to go if you wanted to build a charter boat for South Florida waters. These were great sea boats and were seen at the Castaways Charter Boat Dock (Castaways Hotel), Baker's Haulover Charter Boat Docks, Chamber of Commerce Docks located at the southwest end of Miami Beach, Pier 5 in downtown Miami, Bud and Mary's and Whale Harbor docks in Islamorada, and even on Charter Boat Row in Key West.

Buddy made a tough decision not to build another Norseman. He decided to build a larger and wider charter boat and went to North Carolina to build a forty-seven-foot Allygood that would give his clients more comfort and a bigger and wider cockpit area to seat four. At that time we drilled holes in the gimbals and rod butts so we could put pins through them to keep the rods from leaving the chairs. This system of keeping four customers in the cockpit and two on the bridge worked very well.

The bridge had two chairs with drilled gimbals, so we could fish our two long outrigger rods up there, giving everyone onboard a chair and a fishing rod. We used 9/0 Penn Senator reels filled with eighty-pound test line. When I started it was eighty-pound Dacron, and we then went to monofilament shortly after. Mono lasted so much longer and allowed us to mark the long riggers and short riggers, making it easier for the mates.

Back then every Pier 5 boat fished two wire lines from the two chairs in the aft part of the cockpit. Buddy always had two electric reels in those chairs. They were so great for young kids and ladies, who could simply push a button and be able to catch amberjacks, black groupers, and nice-size mutton snapper all day long. When I mated for Buddy, we had so many five- and ten-year-old boys and girls successfully catch one-hundred- or two-hundred-pound warsaw groupers by just pushing the buttons on the electric reels. Teenage girls loved to catch big amberjacks and sharks without cranking the handles on reels.

The new sky-blue Carolina boat had four chairs in the cockpit, with lots of room for the mate to work. Since the boat was much wider, Buddy added a huge live-bait well. Live bait became more important in the late 1940s for all the Miami charter boats that caught so many amberjacks and groupers. They also fished live bait out of the outriggers for sailfish and dolphin.

Once the Pier 5 and chamber of commerce charter boats went out of Government Cut and trolled south, there were no other charter boats to compete with. The reefs south of Fowey Rock Light House were great for trolling wire lines to catch black, gag, and red groupers along with a few mutton snapper. In the winter the reefs produced cero mackerel, barracuda, bar jack, amberjack, and kingfish on the two long outriggers and two short outrigger rods.

The next boat Buddy Carey built was also called *Sea Boots*, but it was designed and built by Tweed Hunter. Although it had the name *Sea Boots* on the transom, everyone called it *Sea Boots II*. Buddy's forty-seven-foot Carolina boat (the first *Sea Boots*) was nine years old, and he wanted a newer charter boat for his youngest son, Mike, to run. It was almost identical to the charter boat *Queen B*, owned by Captain Jimmy O'Neille, who fished out of the Crandon Park charter boat docks. Jimmy's boat rode and fished so well that Buddy built one just like it.

The next boat was the fifty-foot *Sherrie D*, built by Kenny Spaulding after he mated on the *Sea Boots* for many years. It was a Carolina boat that was identical to *Sea Boots* except it was three feet longer. Kenny had a mate named Dick Betteran, also known as PH. This was short for Pecker Head.

Dick's girlfriend, Lotus Blossom rode the City of Miami bus with Dick every morning to the Pier 5 dock. When the charter boats returned in the afternoon, Lotus Blossom would collect the trash from all the charter boats and put the aluminum beer cans in plastic bags, then she would sell the cans to the junkyard for scrap aluminum. She saved any leftover ham, turkey, chicken, and cheese from the box lunches for her family's dinner, and the paper and plastic went to the Dumpster.

After Lotus Blossom had separated the garbage, she took all the bread and chips across the parking lot to Bay Front Park. Lotus had a special bench she visited every afternoon with the "treasures" from the garbage of the charter boats. Once positioned, she would whistle loudly then flap her arms wildly, and hundreds of pigeons would descend to the earth and surround her to dine on the leftovers from the charter boats. Several of the Miami TV stations did specials about the "Bird Lady of Bay Front Park."

Then there was Pappy Peters, the wash-down boy of Pier 5 who lived on the *Sherry D*. Pappy was an old bald-headed man who had spent most of his younger years working for the Ringling Bros. circus. He had great stories to tell to the fishing customers, especially the very young boys.

A YOUNG FISHERMAN'S DREAM COME TRUE

The next slip went to a longtime captain who had owned head boats and charter boats all his life. His name was Vince De Bonas. In his youth he had been a bodybuilder with several Florida all-state championships. Vince built a sixty-foot Beach Boat Slips charter called the *Sea Fox*. Most of the charter boat captains and mates called it the *Sea Box*, since it was made from an eighty-foot mold that was cut off twenty feet too short.

Vince had the great idea of taking twenty people at a time to the Bahamas on three-day trips and making lots of money. In order to qualify for the license and insurance for these trips, Vince had to have a watertight and airtight door in the bulkhead that separated the working area of his charter boat from the living area. When Vince had been finishing the *Sea Fox*, he'd had the opportunity to buy a brand-new walk-in freezer door from a guy who stole stoves from Burger King restaurants as a full-time job and stole freezer doors from the warehouse district as a part-time job.

When the coast guard inspector saw the strange airtight and watertight door, he knew he had to find some way to fail the *Sea Fox* for it. Once he failed the door, the coast guard inspector knew he could come back over and over to reinspect the door and get free fish from Vince during every inspection.

Vince called the Miami Beach coast guard commander and reminded him of all the free trips he and his family had taken over the last ten years on the *Sea Fox*, and the failing report disappeared. The possibility of being transferred to a Maine coast guard station to do boat inspections in the winter caused Vince to receive the best report ever issued from the US Coast Guard commercial boat inspector. The base commander continued to take his family and friends fishing for another year. Now Vince had a boat he could legally use to carry more than six paying passengers to fish the Bahamas.

The Miamarina parking lot was finally paved and painted. Eventually the parking meters and curbs were put in. As the months went by, more boats were added. Captain Charlie had dreamed of being a charter boat captain all his life. He bought a Marine Management hull and spent a year and a half building a charter boat. He took measurements from other Marine Management charter boats and privately owned boats around South Florida and incorporated many interesting concepts into his boat. The *Catch 22* was beautiful, very expensive, and well thought-out.

Charlie's best friend, Dick, dreamed of being a charter boat captain also. Dick owned a bar out on Southwest Bird Road in the South Miami area. He would bring cases of liquor to the dock every afternoon. He then set up a bar behind the *Sherrie D*. By the time the charter boats started docking, Dick was handing out free drinks to all the fish customers who were waiting to see and buy the fish the charter boats brought in.

Having a new guy at the dock who would mix free drinks for all the mates and captains was a bad formula! It did not take long for Dick to meet many of the loyal fish customers. They soon became part of the inner circle and qualified for drinks on the house from Dick. Many of the fish customers got so drunk, they forgot to buy and take home fresh fish for their families.

Once Dick became part of the Pier 5 group, he started showing up every afternoon with an expensively monogramed shirt saying "Capt. Dick" on the left side of his chest. As the months went by, the amount of gold on the shoulders and chest of his shirt increased dramatically, as did the cases of free liquor. He was proud to be known as Captain Dick, even though he had never fished one day as a charter boatman out of Pier 5.

After a year and a half of giving away thousands of free drinks to the captains, mates, and hundreds of fish customers, Captain Dick bought the Knight newspapers boat. It was a Carolina-built boat called the *Rerun*. Captain Dick renamed it the *Prima Donna* after his beautiful blonde wife. This boat would later burn with the Tweed Hunter-built *Sea Boots* during a strange unsolved fire.

Captain Dick had to be the most colorful person at the dock from 1973 on. Even though the Pier 5 charter boats were known for their ability to bring in huge catches of grouper, dolphin, kingfish, snapper, sailfish, bonito, sharks, tarpon, amberjack, etc., Captain Dick announced he was going to be the top captain at the dock. He started his career as a charter boat captain out of Pier 5 by catching almost nothing for the first five days. The next day he caught his first sailfish and celebrated on the way in with the charter clients by consuming two bottles of Bacardi's best rum.

Captain Dick then decided to show the entire dock his boat handling ability. He lined up on the *Prima Donna*'s slip and roared toward the dock with both engines full throttle in reverse. White water flew in the air, Dick's mate grabbed the bowlines as fast as possible. Thinking only of his survival, the terrified mate placed the bowlines over the custom-made bow rail. When the bowlines snapped tight, saving the boat from slamming into the dock, the bow rail compressed and shot two-thirds of the way to the *Natoya*, a yacht docked across the marina, and landed in the dirty water, where the rail disappeared forever.

The next day Dick paid a diver one hundred dollars an hour to spend three unsuccessful hours looking for the bow rail. The day after that, the diver returned with another diver, and they searched for several hours more before giving up all hope of finding Captain Dick's custom-made bow rail. Captain Dick never added another bow rail, and the embarrassing incident was never mentioned again.

Captain Dick was known for his continual patronage of the Miamarina bar, which changed names with the different seasons of the year. It finally became the Blue Dolphin Bar, and Captain Dick would support it by buying round after round of drinks for all the captains and mates and all the girls who liked free drinks. The Bauder Fashion College was about a dozen blocks away, and the attending girls learned quickly that they could drink for free if they joined Captain Dick's group with low-cut shirts or short skirts!

One morning I showed up a little earlier than normal. I needed to put new line on the two long outrigger rods and mark them. Back then the long outrigger and short outrigger rods were carefully marked, making fishing very easy. As I jumped down to the dock and walked toward the boat, Geronimo, who lived on Buddy Carey's boat, was lying on the dock laughing. Geronimo—so nicknamed by Buddy—was a wonderfully funny and talented sixteen-year-old runaway guy who lived on the *Sea Boots* and washed several of the charter boats in the afternoons for a living.

Walking toward the *Prima Donna* in the predawn hours, I saw why Geronimo was laughing. Captain Dick had met a rotund Bauder Fashion College lovely and persuaded her to join him for a romantic evening onboard the *Prima Donna*. The only problem was the exceptionally high tide, which had the boat up and away from the standard boarding area of the Pier5 dock.

After purchasing and consuming a large amount of alcoholic beverages from the Blue Dolphin Bar, Captain Dick and his 260-pound fiancée had tried unsuccessfully to jump to the transom of the *Prima Donna*. Their failed attempt landed them both in the dark water of Miamarina.

Once in the cold winter water, Captain Dick had started screaming, "Geronimo" over and over. This managed to wake Geronimo, who had been sleeping two boats away. Once I arrived and saw Captain Dick's predicament, Geronimo and I managed to pull him out of the water with the Sargassum seaweed draped around his neck like a yellow Santa Claus beard. His fiancée was another story. She was too heavy to pull out of the water and onto the dock.

Luckily the dock's security guard drove by in his golf cart. Captain Dick got a dock line off the *Prima Donna* and tied it around his fiancée's waist. With the golf cart, Geronimo, Captain Dick, and I all pulling, she was rescued from the cold predawn waters of Miamarina.

As the line pulled her body up, it removed her shirt and bra. Lying on the concrete dock on her back, topless, with the line around her wrists, she looked up at Captain Dick and said, "I thought you were supposed to yell 'Geronimo' before we jumped."

• • •

In 1978 Killer O'Keiffe decided to enter the charter boat industry. He showed up at Pier 5 with a forty-five-foot Chris Craft named the *Scuffler*. Since Killer had no money, we all thought about his longtime bluefin tuna fishing out of Bimini while mating for the Chicago gangster Tony "Big Tuna" Acardo. Killer had mated for Tony during his six or seven seasons out of the Bimini Big Game Club.

Big Tuna enjoyed bluefin tuna fishing and always brought three or four "friends" from Chicago with him. These friends called themselves fishermen but all were pasty white and had bulging areas under their sport jackets, which they wore every day on the boat and every evening during the hottest (May to June) Bimini nights. It was common to hear about several people who ended up at the Bimini clinic after getting too close to Big Tuna.

Killer's boat never ran any charters, eventually sank at sea under mysterious circumstances, and was never found.

The next boat was a Stapleton hull with a small tower called the *Grand Slam*. The captain was Freddy Harvey. Freddy had a long Pier 5 history. In the early 1960s, he had mated on one of Red Rainwater's charter boats out of the old wooden Pier 5, the *Papa Sea Gull*. He also ran Warren Schaffer's private boat for sailfish tournaments in the Florida Keys. Warren Schaffer owned the very popular Fisherman's Paradise Tackle Shop in Miami.

Warren's passion in life was fishing all the sailfish tournaments in the Florida Keys. Once Freddy became captain of Warren's boat, the *Fisherman's Paradise*, Warren started winning or placing in almost every tournament.

On the last day of the Islamorada Sailfish Tournament, which Warren was leading, he went down to the boat early to make sure everything was perfect for him to win the most important Keys tournament. He found Freddy sleeping in the cockpit of the gas-engine-powered Scottie-Craft. Freddy was curled up like a cat, wearing only his birthday suit. While the boat was offshore fishing, Warren called his Miami store, the Fisherman's Paradise, and had a driver bring Freddy some Top-Sider shoes, a pair of long pants, and a shirt suitable for the awards banquet while the boat was offshore fishing.

As Freddy's Lucky Streak lasted through the last day of the tournament, Warren Schaffer placed first. I still remember "Fat Freddy" wearing only a hotel towel while he drove the boat all day from the flying bridge. I remember Erwin, the mate, saying how frightening it was to look up at the bridge with Fat Freddy wearing the towel over his right shoulder. The driver did not arrive till noon and waited till Warren's boat docked so Warren could sign for the store merchandise. Warren deducted the full retail price of the shoes, shirt, and pants from Freddy's pay.

A YOUNG FISHERMAN'S DREAM COME TRUE

The *Grand Slam* was owned by Steve, who successfully ran several pawnshops and a bail bond service. This boat would end up being stolen during the Mariel boatlift of 1980. While bringing sixty-six Cubans from Mariel to Florida, the thirty-six-foot boat sank. All sixty-six who were fleeing the Castro regime were then rescued by the US Coast Guard and brought to Miami. The boat is still on the bottom of the ocean somewhere in the Gulf Stream.

• • •

After a few years, the dock started changing as more boats were added to Pier 5. Pudgy Spaulding bought a forty-five-foot Norseman-built boat from a failing charter operation on Key Biscayne. This was the same charter boat he had run in the mid-1960s out of Lucaya, Grand Bahama Island. He renamed it the *Play-Bay-B* after the fifty-five-foot Norseman Connie Dinkler owned. The boat was in sad shape, but Pudgy had the money and the time to give it a new lease on life. He was a magnet for mates who did not have full-time jobs and were willing to work for two or three hours a day and then hang out for the rest of the day smoking free *special* cigarettes.

On a beautiful March day, Pudgy walked down the charter boat dock to the *Sea Boots*, which I was running at the time, and asked if it was OK to use my mate for an afternoon trip. I said yes, since Steve, my mate, was always ready and happy to make a day's pay. I helped them ice the beer on the *Play-Bay-B*, and off they went with only one person, who was wearing a nice suit and dress shoes.

One hour later I was surprised to see the *Play-Bay-B* returning to Miamarina at an exceptionally high rate of speed. Pudgy spun the boat around unusually fast and backed into the slip. As I jogged down three boat slips to help put the lines on the stern cleats of the boat, I was surprised to see only Pudgy and Steve. I immediately thought it was strange that the boat had gone fishing with one paying passenger and was returning with no one onboard.

When I jumped on the covering board of the transom with one of the stern lines, I looked down and saw the man, in his new suit and dress shoes, lying on his back. His wide-open eyes were gazing up into space. His forehead had a hole where a .357 bullet had entered. The bullet had then exited the back of his head, removing the majority of his skull.

Living in Chicago and hoping to make a lot of money in a quick deal, this father of two had arranged a marijuana transaction with a group that had close ties to some Miami people. He had been instructed to fly to Miami with $50,000 in cash and meet a Cuban kingpin. What happened after that was never known. This poor guy cut the labels out of his jacket, his shirt, and even his underwear. He bought a six-pack of Bud Beer and walked across Biscayne Boulevard and Bay Front Park from the Columbus Hotel, where he was staying. He then chartered the *Play-Bay-B* to go fishing. Or so he told Pudgy, the captain.

Steve and Pudgy's story went like this. Once the *Play-Bay-B* reached the Gulf Stream, Pudgy slowed the boat down, and Steve put out the long outrigger bait and got the two wire line rods and reels ready to drop live bait to the bottom to catch amberjacks, a very popular fish that lived around the many wrecks off the Miami coast.

This guy then offered Steve a beer. Steve politely said no, and the guy showed him a .357 pistol and said, "Sit down." Steve agreed, and the guy climbed outside the cockpit and leaned against the side of the outrigger. As he hovered over the water, he placed the barrel of the gun to his forehead. As Steve stood up and reached for him, the stranger pulled the trigger.

We at the dock learned from the FBI that this man had been trying to save his family from financial catastrophe back in Chicago. The FBI interviewed all of us, and we learned that taking large sums of cash to Miami in hopes of making a huge score was the newest and greatest trick for people in Chicago who were on the brink of losing everything.

Another boat was added to the growing number of Pier 5 charter boats. The captain and owner was Tubby Brown. He had dreamed of being a charter boat captain all his life. He bought an Andy Mortensen-built boat that had once been named the *Tiger*. In the past this famous boat had been captained by Don Hardesty.

Captain Tubby hired Captain Joe Criscolie's longtime mate, Rick "the Whip." Tubby was sure Rick would teach him all the secrets the great Captain Joe Criscolie had passed on to him. When Tubby finally booked his first trip, the charter party was sure they had the perfect boat and captain, since Tubby wore black pants and a white shirt with large gold epaulets on the shoulders.

However, the party became suspicious of Captain Tubby when Rick returned to the cockpit after taking off the bow lines, and Tubby confused the throttles and the forward and reverse clutch levers, causing the boat to crash violently into the concrete dock. The damage was extensive and very expensive.

The adventure had just begun! While they trolled past Fowey Rocks Light House, which Captain Tubby thought was an oil rig, one of the wire line rods screamed, as a huge fish had eaten the bait. Captain Tubby had never experienced this, since he had never caught a fish. For the next six hours, he would back south against the north-flowing Gulf Stream. All of us knew Captain Tubby had snagged a lobster trap buoy, since it was lobster season in South Florida, and there were hundreds of lobster traps everywhere.

All the Pier 5 captains and mates laughed as Captain Tubby and Rick the Whip backed into the slip after dark, with the story of the sea monster that had eaten the bait. Almost everyone believed this story except Tubby's charter party, who ran off the boat and jumped into a yellow cab, vowing never to charter a boat for the rest of their lives.

Another boat joined the Pier 5 area at the south end of the dock. This was a Key West-built boat. The owner was a longtime mate who had worked for many of the captains of Pier 5. He had an unlimited budget, since he had worked very hard in Colombia for almost one full year, making enough money to buy several homes, many cars, an airplane, and this fishing boat.

All the charter boats out of Key Biscayne, Pier 5, and Baker's Haulover experienced two exceptionally slow summers of dolphin fishing off Miami and Miami Beach. The spring started with lots of big dolphin, and then the school-size dolphin fishing exploded like no one had ever seen. Everyone was catching hundreds of dolphin every day! One day I fished my commercial boat, *Coconut*, by myself and caught 1,182 pounds of dolphin.

This was nothing compared to what my ex-mate, Dell, caught the same day. Dell bought the same hull as I had. With an unlimited budget, he had a boat yard put two big engines in the hull, then added a tall tuna tower. The skilled woodworkers then added lots of varnished teak trim everywhere. He was lucky—all he had to do was snap his fingers, and a $10,000 fish box would appear. Snap his fingers again and twenty custom-built rods for dolphin fishing, along with the best high-retrieve reels that money could buy, would be delivered to the boat.

Dell took twelve of his business associates out dolphin fishing that day. These guys were the best! After fishing off Miami, they docked at three o'clock at Pier 5 in Miamarina and started lining their catch

A YOUNG FISHERMAN'S DREAM COME TRUE

up for pictures. The twelve athletic guys started throwing the dolphin from the boat onto the hot dock. After taking off their shirts, they prided themselves on who could throw a dolphin highest in the air before the fish landed on the solid concrete dock. One of the guys went over to the Blue Dolphin. He sweet-talked the youngest barmaid with three hundred-dollar bills to bring a round of rum and Cokes over to the boat.

Dell and his friends started placing the dolphin on the hot dock side by side, in neat lines. They made nine rows, each containing one hundred dolphin. Once the lovely barmaid delivered the first round of drinks to the boat, they left the remaining fish in the fish box. Dell and his friends posed for pictures with no shirts and with big smiles!

The barmaid, Naomi, received another hundred-dollar bill. When Vickie, my cute seventeen-year-old blonde fish seller saw this, she ran over to Naomi and said, "The next time you bring a tray of drinks over to these guys, take off your bra and stomp your feet to make your puppies bounce!"

Twenty minutes later Naomi came bouncing and giggling up the dock, with a tray of rum and Cokes for the boys. She made sure to bend over and look at all the fish on the hot dock. For delivering the drinks and bending over to show her braless figure, she received a $500 tip.

On the next delivery of drinks, she made sure to giggle and bounce around while telling all the guys what big muscles they had. For this she received a tip of $1,000. The next time she came back, Dell and his friends were so drunk, they put Naomi on the bar tray and carried her back to the bar, where they stayed till closing.

The homeless community that lived under the Fifth Street bridge on the north side of Pier 5 soon learned that there were hundreds of "fish" on the hot Pier 5 concrete dock. While Dell and his twelve friends drank the night away at the Blue Dolphin Bar, the homeless community grabbed their shopping carts and loaded them to the top with Dell's dolphin. It did not take long for the 11 eleven homeless people to load nine hundred or more dolphin into the Publix shopping carts they kept under the bridge. Thanks to Publix, these fish were rushed off to the Overtown section of downtown Miami, where they were put to good use. The people of Overtown all said, "Thank you, Publix supermarket!"

Naomi stopped by my boat a week later and thanked Vickie and me for the best night of her bartending career—she'd made $6,000! Vickie turned and punched me in the arm, saying, "I told you that would work!" This was in reference to removing Naomi's bra.

Naomi thanked me by pulling up her top so I could see her puppies, and then she kissed me on the cheek. She simply handed Vickie five hundred-dollar bills and winked, saying, "Thanks." She ran off laughing to check in at the bar. All charter boat docks have such colorful people!

Going south on the new Pier 5 dock, a Breuil Enterprise boat came in—the *Sea Quester*. Captain Matty's operation got off to a slow start. His beautiful wife, Loraine, wanted him to be successful at his new job as Captain Matty, charter boat fisherman extraordinaire. He soon hired a mate named Patty. We called her Hurricane Patty, since she had a pair of huge you know whats. These—or, should I say, Hurricane Patty's personality—started booking the boat.

The first week the *Sea Quester* caught next to nothing. Yet the boat returned to the dock day after day with smiling, satisfied clients. This was because Hurricane Patty always wore a very small bikini. Sometime during the fishing trip, her top always fell off at the right time, and the fishermen and fisherwomen took turns taking lots of pictures!

A YOUNG FISHERMAN'S DREAM COME TRUE

Several days later the famous catch occurred. The topless Hurricane Patty harpooned a large sunfish, sometimes called a Mola mola. The huge fish was dragged back to Pier 5 in Miamarina, and a tow truck was summoned to lift the three-thousand-pound sunfish out of the water so the happy charter party could pose for the crews of the channel seven, channel six, and channel four news stations. Hurricane Patty made sure her small bikini top stayed on as she joined the group for pictures.

The downfall of this charter boat operation happened when Hurricane Patty was featured in a famous girlie magazine. She was beautiful and topless as she threw the harpoon into the defenseless sunfish on the front cover of the May edition. The story and pictures were enough for Captain Matty's very jealous wife to sell the boat and file for divorce. Hurricane Patty then moved on to mate on several other Pier 5 boats.

An entirely different boat joined the Pier 5 group next. This was a thirty-five-foot stone crab boat built by Steelcraft. The owner was Marty Crab Claw, and the name of the boat was the *Bamma Buzz*. Marty was a stone crab fisherman with eight hundred crab traps and five hundred crawfish traps. He had a blond Labrador named Lobster. They fished together five days a week and took Saturdays and Sundays off.

Vicky, my fish seller, saved the backbones and heads from dolphin, amberjack, and sharks she filleted. Marty used these leftovers to bait his stone crab traps. The grouper heads were too valuable; Vicky sold these to her loyal fish customers.

When I was a kid selling fish at the dock, all snapper and groupers had been filleted and skinned. As the population dynamics of Miami changed, so did the preparation of the fish we sold. The customers who bought snapper and groupers now wanted them scaled and staked.

Marty Crab Claw and Lobster the dog would come down the dock just after dark to pick up the scraps from Vicky. Marty gave her a garbage can for the discarded skins, gills, tails, and bones and any parts she could not sell. In return Marty frequently gave her bags of stone crab claws or crawfish tails.

It did not take long for Lobster to learn that Vicky would go through the charter boats' box lunches that were thrown in the garbage can, pull out the ham, roast beef, and chicken, and save it for Lobster's afternoon snack. After a long day of watching Marty pull crab traps, the dog would run down the dock wagging its tail to see Vicky for his reward.

The *Bamma Buzz* was continually breaking down in different locations of Biscayne Bay, where Marty fished his crab traps. Once a month someone from the dock would walk down and tell Vicky or me where Marty had broken down. After Vicky had sold out of fish or run out of customers and I had finished cleaning, icing, and fixing the *Coconut*, the two of us would throw off the dock lines, turn on the running lights, and head out to look for the *Bamma Buzz*.

When we neared the last position of Marty's boat, Vicky would go to the bow of my boat with a search light and look for the drifting boat. Marty would wave a flashlight once he saw us, and we would drive over and raft up to hear his problems. Once we were side by side, Lobster would see Vicky and immediately jump ship, leaping into the *Coconut*.

What happened for the next two hours became routine. Vicky would throw a towline to Marty, who would tie the line to the bow Samson Post of the *Bamma Buzz*. She then put the line through the special towing bridle I had made and dropped both loops over the stern cleats. Lobster patiently waited for us to get underway with towing the *Buzz*, knowing that once we did, Vicky would go to the cooler and get his dinner ready.

When it was getting late at night and Lobster had almost finished his meal, Vicky would get a blanket and pillow out and put them down on the engine box. Two minutes later she was asleep. Once Lobster had completely finished his dinner, he would go over to Vicky and snuggle up. For the next hour or two, Marty would sleep on the *Bamma Buzz* as I towed it up Biscayne Bay, and Vicky would wrap her arms around Lobster as the two slept till we got to the dock at Pier 5. Just one more type of adventure that happened all the time at our charter boat dock.

CHAPTER 4

Bimini on the Charter Boat Queen B

300 pound blue marlin caught on the charter boat Queen B with captain Jimmy O'Neille and mate Bill Harrison. Blue Water Marina Bimini

I have fished with captains all around the world and enjoyed almost every day. There are a few captains I can think of who influenced my values, my ethics, how I ran my business, my fishing style, and

A YOUNG FISHERMAN'S DREAM COME TRUE

my life. I was born with a love of fishing, but I was not born with the knowledge it takes to catch all the great fish I did in every ocean of the world. This I learned from these great teachers.

Knowledge and ability come from years of watching, listening, and doing what you are told. All the good captains I respect for their ability have put in time mating for other good captains. When you work the cockpit for a captain who has put in a lifetime at sea, you are going to come out a better fisherman.

Explaining the life and the experiences of working at a big charter boat dock is difficult, because so much is happening around you all the time. Watching new captains join the dock is always interesting, especially when they've never mated before. One thing is certain—their poor judgment will always lead to great stories!

I first met captain Jimmy O'Neille in the mid-'60s, when he had just finished building his forty-eight-foot charter boat, the *Queen B*. I filled in for JC Dobson, who had been with Jimmy from the time he'd launched the boat. Jimmy had mated and captained out of the old wooden Pier 5 dock and had captained several private boats that fished out of the Miami area. He knew from the beginning he needed to build a charter boat for himself first and then start building a fishing business out of Key Biscayne.

The Crandon Park Marina had a small charter boat dock at that time, and Jimmy moved in with the best and newest charter boat. I fished with him out of that dock off and on and then went to work as his full-time mate. Fishing with Jimmy was fun, and we caught lots of great fish.

In order to let me work full-time, Jimmy laid down the law about my hair. I had to cut some of it. This was not exceptionally painful because I knew it would grow back. Sometime before my first day on the job, my girlfriend at the time went to work and changed my life—or so I thought when I looked in the mirror.

Jimmy had just started his charter boat business, so he was taking every kind of trip that paid money. He booked trips to Bimini and Chub Cay whenever possible. One of the best trips I ran with him was an early trip to Bimini. We were going to fish three days for blue marlin. We docked at the Blue Water Marina at noon, and Jimmy rushed us to fill out all the customs and immigration papers so he could go to the customs house and clear everyone. He wanted to go marlin fishing as soon as possible.

Mike Hoffman was a teenager who had just moved to Key Biscayne with his mother at that time. None of us knew he would eventually become one of the greatest wildlife artists ever. Mike's mother wanted to visit Bimini and booked Doc Ludens's charter boat, the *Doc's Out*, for a three-day trip to Bimini the same time as us. Doc Ludens had never been to Bimini, so he relied on Jimmy to tell him everything about the island and fishing.

As we idled out of Bimini Harbor after clearing customs, we passed the *Doc's Out* entering the harbor. Doc Ludens had no idea how to clear customs and immigration in Bimini. He struggled with the paperwork till closing time at five o'clock. Jimmy never told Doc that including a five-dollar bill in the paperwork would have solved all his problems.

We put the marlin bait in the water at two o'clock and started trolling north off the area known as the Pines. On the north end of Bimini, there was a two-mile area of tall *Casuarina* pines that stood out when viewed from offshore.

We fished a Spanish mackerel in one long outrigger attached to a 9/0 Fin-Nor reel and a mullet in the other long outrigger, also on a 9/0 Fin-Nor reel. Both reels were filled with eighty-pound test Garcia brand Dacron braided line, which was made by DuPont in the United States. Jimmy liked to fish two ballyhoo on eighty-pound test line in both short outriggers, so that was what I did.

A YOUNG FISHERMAN'S DREAM COME TRUE

We hooked a nice thirty-pound cow dolphin on one of the short rigger ballyhoos, and as I grabbed the leader wire to gaff the fish, the other short outrigger popped out of the rigger pin with the cow dolphin's thirty-eight-pound mate—a nice bull dolphin. This gave the charter party a good idea of what was going to take place shortly.

Since this charter party had never been fishing before, Jimmy wanted to fish the two 9/0 Fin-Nor reels from the long outrigger chairs in the flying bridge. I was happy with this setup. If a blue marlin ate one of the long outrigger baits and Jimmy dropped back the bait and missed the marlin, he could not blame it on me.

On a picture-perfect afternoon in the Bahamas, a blue marlin came out of the water and ate the Spanish mackerel that was trolling from the left long outrigger. Jimmy free spooled the Fin-Nor reel and wound the slack out of the Dacron line coming tight with the fish. I watched him hook the blue marlin on the first try—Jimmy was good at hooking fish!

Once the marlin was on, Jimmy tossed down from the bridge the safety line that was tied to the rod and reel the jumping marlin was on. I tied it to the chair before he passed me the 9/0 reel and rod. Moments later our angler was sitting in the fighting chair, with the harness snapped onto the reel. Everyone watched the nice-size blue marlin jump two hundred yards behind the *Queen B*.

I was too busy getting the flying gaffs out and fastening the nylon lines to the bridle around the fighting chair base to see any of the twelve spectacular jumps this marlin made. After about a one-hour fight, Jimmy made sure this marlin was so tired I simply wired the lifeless fish up to the right side of the boat and popped its head out of the water. Jimmy left one engine in gear and came down the bridge ladder to open the transom door, and I passed him the marlin's nose.

39

The excited charter party all grabbed the marlin's nose, lower jaw, and dorsal fin, and the marlin easily slid into the cockpit of the *Queen B*.

As I shut the transom door, Jimmy had the boat running toward the Native Cut to weigh and mount this trophy marlin. The Native Cut had been dynamited out of the rocks in 1962 by the Texaco Oil Company, so their fuel barges could get into the Bimini Harbor and supply the island with gasoline and diesel. Mother Nature slowly reclaimed this deep-water channel as the years went by. When we ran through the cut, it was the top of the flood tide (high tide), and the crystal clear water was considerably shallower than it had been in 1962.

We had just tied up to the dock under the weighing scales when Doc Ludens walked by waving his arms and cursing. According to Doc, he had spent four frustrating hours at the customs office, doing the paperwork necessary to clear into the Bahamas over and over till five in the afternoon. When he finally got out of the customs office, the immigration officer was locking the door to his office—he was done for the day. Doc would need to return at nine the next day.

Mike Hoffman and his mother walked up and saw the blue marlin in the cockpit of the *Queen B* before Doc realized we had tied up to weigh the fish. The fact that Doc could not go fishing because of the customs officer and seeing the fish in our cockpit infuriated him even more, and down the dock he stormed, shouting obscenities.

Shorty, the dockmaster at that time, came out and ran the electric winch, lifting the fish out of the boat and up to the scales—three hundred pounds exactly. We moved the marlin over to the gallows, and everyone on the dock took lots of pictures. I took several pictures of Mike as he stood next to the fish—just in case.

The next day was beautiful. About a dozen boats were getting ready to go fishing, with captains and mates busily rigging baits and

A YOUNG FISHERMAN'S DREAM COME TRUE

checking the rods and reels. At nine o'clock in the morning, we were the last boat to leave the dock except for the *Doc's Out*. Doc Ludens was standing behind his boat with passports and paperwork in hand. We waved and wished him good luck. Doc did not wave back; he simply stood with his arms crossed, staring up the dock.

Once out of the Native Cut and across the white sandbar, Jimmy turned north and slowed the boat down on a color change and small seaweed line. We fished exactly as we had the previous day. Just as before, a bull and a cow dolphin attacked the two ballyhoo fished off the short outrigger rods. Each fish was about twenty or twenty-five pounds. A half hour later, a big bull dolphin ate the mullet we were fishing on the right long outrigger. The angler stayed up in the bridge and reeled in the fish on the eighty-pound test outfit.

Somewhere close to noon, the *Doc's Out* came running out and slowed down next to us, finally getting their baits in the water. As we trolled side by side, watching each other, the ballyhoo closest to the *Doc's Out* popped out of the outrigger pin, and I dropped back as Mike watched. Coming tight with the unseen fish, the rod bent over, and up jumped an average-size white marlin. Since Doc was watching also, he angrily spun his boat around and trolled directly away from us. He refused to answer when Jimmy repeatedly called him on the radio.

About an hour later, I heard Doc frantically calling Jimmy on the radio saying something about hooking a blue marlin. Doc had been rewarded for all his aggravation. Mike was in the chair and fighting a jumping marlin. Jimmy turned the *Queen B* around and started trolling south, looking for the *Doc's Out*. It took about forty-five minutes to find them sitting dead in the water, with a marlin five hundred yards straight down.

While we trolled by Doc's boat cheering Mike, Jimmy shouted, "Watch the mackerel on the left long outrigger. There's something behind it." I looked up in time to see the black bill come out of the water, followed by half the body of a large blue marlin. This was one of the classic marlin strikes that take place during a calm day while trolling a splashing mackerel.

Jimmy hooked it on the 9/0 Fin-Nor reel he was fishing from one of the bridge chairs. The marlin jumped over and over while I was getting the two short outrigger baits in the boat. Once the marlin calmed down a little, we moved the rod down to the big fighting chair in the center of the cockpit, and our angler went to work.

Both boats were hooked up to nice-size blue marlin within a quarter mile of each other. Jimmy was a good boat handler, so he did everything he could to tire our fish. In just under one hour, I had the leader wire, and Jimmy put the first flying gaff into the marlin's shoulder and cleated the nylon rope. I put a second gaff in the fish, and all that was left was to pull it through the door. With all the energy and excitement, we had the fish in the boat in moments and were cheering.

Since Doc had been at a standstill for over two hours, with Mike getting ready to give up, Jimmy volunteered to put me off on the *Doc's Out* to help—without telling me. I figured it out quick when he told me to put my fishing pliers back on and get some double gloves as he backed the boat to the bow of the *Doc's Out*. The transfer went well, and Jimmy said, "See you at the dock" then headed the *Queen B* toward Bimini Harbor.

Since I could see there was not enough drag, I pushed the lever a little higher and had Doc idle slowly away. Once we had pulled off about one hundred yards, I had Doc back toward the fish, and Mike reeled in the slack line. This is called planing up the fish. It worked well for us, as Mike continued to retrieve line.

Then I saw the first knot go by as the monofilament changed from green to red. Doc was known to try to save money by saving his old line and tying the different pieces together. As the next knot passed, the line changed to blue, and then to white, and then to pink. By then I didn't care, because Mike had the dead fish close to the boat, so I grabbed the leader wire and gaffed Mike's first blue marlin. Everyone helped me pull the fish in the boat, and we were running full speed toward the weighing station of the Blue Water Marina.

When we tied up behind the *Queen B*, the sixty-two-pound white marlin had been weighed and was being photographed. I was there in time to take a couple of photos and be in some. The next fish took a bit of work. We got it out of the boat and up to the scales. I could see 554 pounds showing on the scales. This marlin was thick and muscular, with a long, beautiful bill.

After the usual cheering, congratulations, and pictures, Jimmy pulled the *Queen B* out of the way, and Doc pulled his boat under the scales so we could weigh Mike's marlin. Shorty, the dockmaster, and Mike were already making bets. Mike said the marlin would be over three hundred pounds, and Shorty said no way. Doc was holding the money as more of the people on the dock got involved in on the betting.

There was quite a crowd that afternoon, since several other marlin had been weighed in earlier. By seven o'clock the rum and Cokes were kicking in, and a casino attitude was happening. Mike went up the ladder to verify the weight with Shorty, and both read the scales the same—295 pounds. Shorty walked over to Doc and took all the money. No one said a word. Shorty was short, but he had biceps bigger than coconuts and shoulders wider than a golf cart!

Mike was the happiest person on the island that night, and his mother was visibly proud. Look what the Hoffman family had accomplished. They had moved down from New York and booked a charter boat to go to Bimini and catch a blue marlin, and that was exactly what they had done. Mike was probably in his midteens, and I was a few years older. I never said anything to him, but I am sure I was the second happiest guy on the island. I had weighed a sixty-two-pound white marlin, a 295-pound blue marlin, and a 554-pound blue marlin. And, most important, I did it with a great captain: Jimmy O'Neille!

CHAPTER 5

PIER 5, MIAMI, FLORIDA, FEBRUARY 3, 1969 A PERFECT DAY TO TROLL THE REEF

Captain Buddy Carey's charter boat Sea Boots in front of Fowey Rock Light House. Miami, Florida. Painting by Mike Hoffman, Marine Artist.

I was running the forty-seven-foot *Sea Boots* for the owner, Buddy Carey. He had jury duty, and I was going to take Mr. Shephard out to troll the reefs for grouper with Buddy's full-time mate, Bobby

Jenkins. Geronimo worked the cockpit with Bobby the three days a week that Mr. Shephard chartered the boat each winter. Buddy owned two charter boats named *Sea Boots* that fished out of Miamarina in downtown Miami, Florida.

Buddy had built his first charter boat in 1935 and named it *Sea Boots*; he then kept the same name for all six boats he built. The boat I was running that day had been built in North Carolina by Charlie Allygood Boat Works and was forty-seven feet long. The newer and longer boat Buddy had just built was designed and built by Tweed Hunter and was forty-eight feet. Buddy was one of several Miami second-generation charter boat captains. He had started working for his dad, Oliver Carey, at age thirteen and stayed in the business till he retired at age seventy-seven.

The three days a week that Mr. Shephard chartered the *Sea Boots* each winter ran like military clockwork. The Old Man, as we on the Pier 5 dock called him, walked from the Park Lee Hotel, where he rented the penthouse every winter, to the boat each morning. The Park Lee was located on the west side of Biscayne Boulevard, about two blocks from where the *Sea Boots* docked. Mr. Shephard arrived at 6:20 each morning—not 6:19 or 6:21. Buddy had the engines running, and Bobby had the dock lines off the stern cleats at exactly 6:20. I had to do the same.

Mr. Shephard was in his late seventies, so he dozed off while I ran the *Sea Boots* down Biscayne Bay and west of Cape Florida Light House toward Fowey Rocks Light House. Bobby and Geronimo set up the cockpit with two rods with electric reels filled with wire line. I fished two 12/0 Penn Senator reels with a twelve-volt electric motor Bud had adapted to the handle sides of the reels.

About a quarter mile before we reached a great grouper area of the shallow reef south of Fowey Rocks Light House, I slowed the boat to trolling speed. Bobby and Geronimo instantly had a four-ounce trolling feather and a double-hooked ballyhoo in the water and going out to the short mark on the electric reel wire-line rods. Next they put out the rods we fished in the short outriggers. They each had small jap trolling feathers with 6/0 hooks. The long outrigger rods were up in the bridge chairs with me, and Geronimo had the small ballyhoo I liked to use for bait in the water and out to the marks in record time. The lines were then snapped into the pins and pulled to the tops of the long outriggers.

Right away we were off to a great start, with a doubleheader of small black groupers biting the feathers and baits on the wire lines. As I went back to trolling speed, one of the long outrigger baits popped out of the rigger pins with a jumping barracuda, so I reeled it in without slowing the boat.

I could see schools of ballyhoo showering a half mile ahead of the boat. Sometimes several hundred or even thousands of ballyhoo jump into the air to flee the predators that live on the shallow reefs. This causes a showering effect, with the shiny ballyhoo in the air while barracuda, kingfish, cero mackerel, mutton snapper, and groupers all try to eat the fleeing baitfish, which are their main food fish on the reef.

Once we got to this ballyhoo-rich area called Long Reef, both electric rods and reels bent, with the clickers screaming. Geronimo jumped in one of the wire line chairs while Bobby waited to see if Mr. Shephard wanted to catch the other grouper. Mr. Shephard pointed to the empty chair, and Bobby jumped into it to catch the grouper. Mr. Shephard was a man of very few words and preferred to point rather than speak. Of all the times I worked with him, he never went to the bridge to ride or even catch a fish. I do not remember one time that he ever caught a fish on one of the short outrigger rods either.

As we trolled south over Long Reef, the groupers kept biting, and the ballyhoo continued to shower on all sides of the *Sea Boots*. Doubleheader after doubleheader of groupers came in. Mr. Shephard would stand between Bobby and Geronimo in the cockpit as they pushed the buttons on the wire line reels and shout, "Get him, get him!" He loved watching the boys catch groupers.

The amount of marine life on top of Long Reef that day was incredible. We caught red groupers, black groupers, mutton snapper, cero mackerel, yellow jack, bar jack, blue runners, amberjacks, kingfish, and even a lizard fish. The wintertime ballyhoo congregation on the many areas of the shallow reef attracted huge numbers of predators every winter.

When Mr. Shephard looked up at me and pointed toward Pacific Reef Lighthouse, I knew it was time to leave this area and troll south. We were now headed for my favorite gag grouper hole that Buddy had taught me about over the years. It was south of the Pacific Reef Lighthouse and produced several hundred gag groupers for Bud and me each winter.

Mr. Shephard loved this area because we would frequently hook two gag groupers—a doubleheader—on the electric reels. As we reeled the two groupers to the boat, several other gags would follow them up and eat the ballyhoo on the long outriggers. Sometimes, if the gags were schooled in big numbers, they would eat the short outrigger baits also. Catching four or five ten- to twenty-pound gag groupers at the same time was a rare but exciting accomplishment.

After catching a dozen gag groupers, I headed for the Whistle Buoy, located off the Ocean Reef Club on Key Largo. We caught some black groupers and big cero mackerel while we trolled south. I knew Mr. Shephard would let us catch ten or twelve barracuda, which always lived around this large red buoy anchored on the shallow reef.

A YOUNG FISHERMAN'S DREAM COME TRUE

After making four passes by the big red buoy and catching three or four 'cudas each time, Bobby walked to the back of the cockpit and pointed north. Mr. Shephard knew we sold the barracudas and gave us five or ten minutes to catch as many as we could, but when he pointed his finger north, the *Sea Boots* better turn and troll north with two wire lines dragging a feather and a bait on each outfit.

On our way north, I had time for one pass through the half-mile-long gag hole, and we managed to catch three gags. We then went by Pacific Reef Lighthouse in ten feet of water and caught a double-header of four-pound black groupers. They were hardly worth slowing the boat for, but this size grouper sold the best at our retail fish market behind the boat.

The next marker we passed was Beacon A. At that time it was a big, red floating buoy that was anchored in different depths of water since it kept breaking away from its mooring each winter, making the US Coast Guard reanchor it several months later. Having no GPS at that time, the USCG would guess where to drop the giant block of concrete, which was what was used to anchor most buoys. The big red Beacon A buoy would be in fifteen feet of water one winter and eighty feet the next winter.

With Mr. Shephard, arriving at the Pier 5 dock at 3:00 in the afternoon was as important as departing at 6:20 in the morning. Looking at my watch while we passed Beacon A, I knew we needed to move offshore and get into the northbound flow of the Gulf Stream. The added four miles per hour would get us back to Miami on time.

Bobby and Geronimo switched the short outrigger baits to ballyhoo and kept the electric reel baits out with a feather and a ballyhoo for bait. Now that we were in the Gulf Stream, I saw two man-o'-war birds hovering over some fleeing flying fish. As we went under these beautiful birds, the two short outrigger baits popped out of the rigger pins. Two female (cow) dolphin were hooked. As these fish jumped, the man-o'-war birds dived down and ate the flying fish that came out of the dolphins' stomachs when they jumped.

As I watched from the controls in the flying bridge, I saw several more big dolphin following the two cows. The left long outrigger bait popped out, and I went over and wound the slack line tight as the *Sea Boots* idled ahead. Another big cow dolphin was on. Geronimo saw a big bull dolphin following the cow that Bobby was getting ready to gaff and threw a rigged ballyhoo to the hungry fish. The bull ate the ballyhoo, and Geronimo wound the slack out of the line and hooked the fish.

While Mr. Shephard slept, Buddy's great team of Bobby and Geronimo caught all eight of the big dolphin swimming behind the boat. The bull weighed forty-four pounds. The *Sea Boots* was again moving north in the Gulf Stream and was passing Fowey Rocks Light in 240 feet of water when I saw a sailfish behind the right short outrigger bait. I shouted to Bobby, and he hooked the fish on the first try. Geronimo was jumping into the short rigger chair when I heard the right long outrigger pin pop out. I dropped back and hooked another unseen sailfish.

Bobby woke Mr. Shephard, asking if he wanted to catch a fish. The Old Man asked, "Is it a grouper?" When Bobby said no, Mr. Shephard went back to sleep. Bobby then came up the flying bridge ladder and started winding in the sailfish that was on the right long outrigger rod. Since Geronimo had his sailfish almost to the side of the boat, I went down the bridge ladder, grabbed the tired sailfish by the bill, and swung it into the fish box.

Bobby did not take long to catch the thirty-five-pound sailfish on the eighty-pound test Ande monofilament line we used on all four outrigger rods. Geronimo grabbed the sailfish by the nose and quickly put it in the fish box. I had the *Sea Boots* again trolling north in 240 feet of water, on schedule to get Mr. Shephard to the dock on time.

With about two miles to go till we reached the Miami Sea Buoy, I saw a group of forty or fifty small tuna birds diving over some splashes on the surface of the water that meant something was feeding in this area. Passing through the diving birds produced nothing on the four outrigger baits. As the two wire line baits passed through the activity six hundred feet later, both rods bent over with drags screaming. This woke Mr. Shephard.

The Old Man jumped out of his special chair and started cheering Geronimo and Bobby on as they pushed the electric reel buttons. As the two electric reels moaned and groaned, Mr. Shephard looked over the side of the *Sea Boots* and realized we were in deep water. Knowing these two fish were not groupers, he pointed toward the Miami skyline. To translate this quickly, it means, "Get the boat running now!"

Both Bobby and Geronimo had their yellowfin tuna to the tip of the wire line rods and were wiring the two seventy-five-pound fish as Mr. Shephard walked out the second time and pointed toward Miami. As I increased the speed, Geronimo fell to his knees, holding on to the leader wire as the tuna bounced behind the boat. Bobby was not doing any better, with his tuna flopping in the wake also. I ran down the bridge ladder and gaffed Geronimo's tuna in the face, and we both were laughing so hard we could not pull the fish over the transom.

Sometimes things work out for the best, and this was a good example. Geronimo and I pulled his yellowfin tuna over the transom and into the cockpit and ran to help Bobby, who was out of gas. He was on his knees, with his armpits hooked over the transom. He was not going to give up this valuable fish! The three of us pulled his yellowfin tuna over the transom and into the boat then collapsed on the cockpit deck, laughing as the *Sea Boots* ran west toward Miami with no one at the helm.

We arrived at Pier 5 with four minutes to spare. Mr. Shephard sat in his special chair staring at his watch while I filleted, skinned, and deboned one of the smallest groupers. This rich old Canadian loved trolling down the reefs catching groupers with Buddy, Bobby, and Geronimo more than anything.

At exactly 3:00 Mr. Shephard's foot hit the concrete dock, and he took the bag of filleted grouper from me without saying a word. I watched the Old Man shuffle away, headed west on Fifth Street toward the Park Lee Hotel, walking all alone.

CHAPTER 6

Pier 5, Miami, Florida, September 13, 1969
Catching Eleven Warsaw Groupers in One Day

260 pound warsaw grouper with captain Bill Harrison. Caught on the Sea Boots with captain Bill Harrison and mate Steve Tellam. Pier 5 Miami, Florida September 11, 1969

I was running Buddy Carey's second boat, the *Sea Boots*, out of Pier 5 in downtown Miami. Mating for me that day was Steve Tellam. He was a Key Biscayne kid who loved to bottom fish the different wrecks off Miami. I enjoyed doing this, since we had a great fish market behind our boats, and we could sell everything we caught.

There was a huge city-run parking lot directly behind the Pier 5 dock where the twenty charter and commercial fishing boats backed in stern first. Hundreds of people came down every day to the dock to see the fish the charter and commercial boats brought in. Many of these people were there to buy fresh fish for their families.

This Saturday Bob Daniels had promised to take his two granddaughters deep-sea fishing. Bob had a huge landscaping company in Miami and enjoyed getting away on the boat so he couldn't be contacted or bothered. He liked to sit on the flying bridge with me, drink beer, eat roast beef sandwiches, and watch his granddaughters catch fish. Carla was twelve, and Dorothy was ten. Both loved fishing.

I fished two long outrigger rods from the flying bridge chairs. This worked out well because I had Bob up with me handling the rods if he wanted to catch a fish, and the two short outrigger rods were attached to the short rigger chairs in the cockpit for the girls. The girls loved using the electric wire line outfits we fished from the other two chairs in the back of the cockpit, near the fish box.

When we were trolling, the wire line rods were almost horizontal and pointed a little outboard of each cockpit corner. They were pinned into the chairs, so there was no way they could be pulled overboard. Once a fish was on, all the girls had to do was push the buttons, and the wire lines would be wound in. If we hooked a big fish, the brake washers in the reel slipped, and the fish pulled line off the reel. The motor worked exactly like a handle on any fishing reel. Instead of having a ten-year-old girl try to crank a big, bulky fishing reel, she simply pushed a button, and the electric motor wound the fish in.

A YOUNG FISHERMAN'S DREAM COME TRUE

Since this was a half day, I had to plan it carefully. Bob liked only dolphin to eat and always left me all the amberjack and warsaw groupers we caught while fishing the deep-water wrecks. As we trolled down the 120-foot edge off Miami, the bonitos were biting fast and furious. Bonitos love to eat a #3 1/2 Drone Spoon. If a color change is visible, the bonitos will be on the dirty- water side of the edge (the west side), and the dolphin will be on the blue- water side.

The girls were catching doubleheaders of big bonitos as fast as Steve could get the fish unhooked and then let the bait back out to the correct mark. The bonitos were a blessing for us in the summer and fall because we cut strips out of their sides, and the kingfish, dolphin, and sailfish loved eating them. Every year I caught a couple of small blue marlin and a half dozen white marlin on bonito strips.

By the time we got to Fowey Rocks Light House, we had thirty big bonitos and ten small kingfish in the fish box. As I headed the boat offshore to try bottom fishing on one of my favorite deep-water wrecks in about 320 feet of water, Steve rigged several warsaw grouper baits. I liked to use fifteen feet of #15 piano wire and a 12/0 Mustad hook. We started with a side of a bonito that had been trimmed to twelve or fourteen inches long and was thin enough to slither through the water. These baits were only an hour or two old and worked so well we called them "lollipops."

With no loran or GPS at that time, all of us charter boat captains used land ranges and Fathometers to find our favorite spots. The color Fathometers and bottom machines had not yet been invented. We had a stylus that went round and round, leaving a mark on a paper as it sparked. Once a week we had to wipe clean the black dust the sparks left, so we could see the image on the paper.

The Gulf Stream is almost always moving north off Miami, so some skill was needed to line up the land ranges and move far enough south to drop the bait in position for a warsaw grouper to see and eat. It is hard to believe now, but many days when I was mating or captaining on charter boats, I would drop two wire lines and catch two warsaw groupers at a time! I am talking about warsaw groupers that were one hundred or two hundred pounds and sometimes much heavier.

Steve loved warsaw grouper fishing. He had the bait ready to go, and ten-year-old Dorothy was going to be the first in the chair to push the button on the electric reel. All young kids loved catching warsaws, amberjack, and sharks on the electric reels. As I went over the wreck, I noticed the Fathometer marked an exceptionally high cloud of fish. Most of the time, I had to guess the depth because the stylus, as it wore down, showed the wreck getting deeper and deeper.

Passing over the wreck, the Fathometer showed a big cloud on the paper. I went south of the wreck about one quarter mile, so Steve would have time to let the bait sink all the way to the bottom and wind it up the equivalent of twenty cranks. If the bait tangled in the wreck, we would lose the hook, the leader, the snaps, and some very expensive Monel wire. It was rare, but sometimes the big warsaws got back in the wreck, and we ended up breaking them off.

I watched Steve drop the bait to the bottom, and he then pushed the button to bring the bait up to the proper height. Right away the rod started to bounce, so I put one engine in gear. Steve and I had done this hundreds of times with amberjack and warsaw groupers, so there was no need for talking between us. He left the rod horizontal on the transom and pushed the button. The rod bent over, and Dorothy squealed.

As Bob sat with me in the flying bridge, he said, "Seeing this gal so happy is a granddad's dream." Carla was jumping around the cockpit

A YOUNG FISHERMAN'S DREAM COME TRUE

cheering as Steve lifted the front of the rod, and Dorothy pushed the button on the way down. It was not long before a two-hundred-pound warsaw grouper popped up on the surface behind the *Sea Boots*. Big groupers float as they get close to the surface because the pressure down deep is much greater.

I helped Steve put the warsaw grouper in the boat and started trolling back to the wreck. I went down to the cockpit and helped Steve set up two baits, one for each electric reel. Dorothy would be in one chair, and Carla would be in the other. The *Sea Boots* had a steering wheel and two clutches and two throttles on the left (port) side of the cockpit. This was better than a third mate.

Once I had lined up on the wreck and saw its silhouette on the Fathometer, I trolled about a quarter mile south and went down the bridge ladder to the cockpit, so Steve and I could drop two baits at once. We both pitched the bonito baits over the stern and put the two-pound lead bank weights in the water. We then pulled the brake levers back on the electric wire line reels and dropped the two baits at the same time. Dorothy and Carla sat in the chairs and waited with excitement. My bait was the first to be eaten, so I reached over to the cockpit controls and put one engine in gear. Dorothy pushed the button, and the rod bent over.

Steve had a bite moments later and gave the warsaw a little drop back. He free spooled the reel for ten or twelve feet to let the big grouper eat the bait as the boat moved forward. Once the boat was moving forward, Steve pushed the button, and the rod bent over. Carla was hooked up to a big grouper. Bob watched his granddaughters laughing, squealing, and having so much fun. Dorothy's warsaw grouper popped up on the surface first and weighed about a hundred pounds. Carla's was a bit larger, weighing about 125. Steve and I lifted the fish into the boat and put the groupers in the different boxes that were half filled with ice.

As I lined up the boat again, Steve and I did the same thing. I was driving the boat using the cockpit controls and dropping the bonito bait to the bottom. My rod bounced first, so I put one engine in gear. The rod bent over, and Dorothy had another warsaw hooked. Steve hit the button, and Carla was also hooked up. Bob was up on the bridge drinking a beer, eating a roast beef sandwich, and laughing.

We caught eleven warsaws that morning, one larger than 250 pounds, before I started trolling north toward downtown Miami. I stayed in about three hundred feet of water to get the extra speed the northbound Gulf Stream provided. Trolling in this depth provided us with six nice dolphin before we reached the Miami Sea Buoy.

Once we tied up the *Sea Boots*, I filleted three of the six dolphin for Bob. He did not want to lay any of the fish out on the dock. He was a quiet and reserved kind of guy. Bob knew Steve and I would sell the fish and make a great day's pay. He still tipped both of us, and he and his granddaughters thanked us for the fun day. I had so many great fishing clients who were both friends and customers.

CHAPTER 7

Pier 5, Miami, Florida, February 10, 1970 Trolling the Reef with Buddy Carey

It was a Tuesday, and I was going to mate for Buddy Carey because his full-time mate, Bobby Jenkins, had his yearly physical scheduled for that morning. Bobby rarely took a day off because Buddy kept his charter boat, the *Sea Boots*, fishing thirty days a month. All winter Bobby made more money than the next three mates on the dock combined because Buddy had a rich Canadian who booked the *Sea Boots* for three days a week during the winter months every year and loved to troll the reefs off Miami for groupers. Mr. Shephard, or the Old Man, as we all called him, was from Canada and loved to troll the reefs off Miami for groupers fishing the reefs with Buddy and Bobby Jenkins.

Buddy liked me to fill in on the very few days Bobby took off. I had mated for Buddy, so he knew I was good—but, as Mr. Shephard said, "Not as good as Bobby." Even though I tried to be the fastest ever in the cockpit of the *Sea Boots*, Mr. Shephard would tell Buddy the next day they fished, "That young guy with the big mustache and long blond hair was not as good as Bobby! He doesn't let the grouper baits out fast enough, he doesn't gaff the groupers fast enough, he doesn't wind in the cutoff baits fast enough. and he doesn't wash the boat fast enough." Buddy was nice enough to share this information with me with a laugh, since we were great friends, and I was captaining his other boat at the time.

When Mr. Shephard was onboard, Buddy always ran down Biscayne Bay by Cape Florida Light and started to troll the reefs just south of Fowey Rocks Light. The coral reefs in this area of twenty to forty feet of water were teaming with ballyhoo, blue runners, bar jacks, kingfish, and four different kinds of groupers. Buddy was the king of the South Florida area because he knew every foot of the reef. Trolling wire lines over the reefs from Miami to the Florida Keys every winter for fifty years every winter gave him an understanding of where the groupers liked to stay and where the baitfish and ballyhoo swarmed like honeybees.

Instead of slowing the *Sea Boots* just to the west of Fowey Rocks Lighthouse on that Tuesday, Buddy ran to the next lighted buoy fifteen minutes south, called Beacon A. At that time Beacon A was a big red buoy anchored in sixty feet of water just north of the end of Long Reef.

When trolling the reef with Mr. Shephard onboard, the two electric reels that were filled with wire line, were the most important fishing outfits, since they caught most of the groupers, which were the only kind of fish the "Old Man" enjoyed catching. Buddy liked to start fishing with a white three-and-a-half-ounce feather on each wire line rod. One wire line outfit would have a red skirt behind the feather, and the other rod would have a green skirt between the feather and the bait. Buddy liked to use two 3407 9/0 Mustad hooks with either a split-back ballyhoo or a mullet strip for bait. If one color outfished the other, I would switch to the more productive color.

Once the two electric reels were out, I snapped two ballyhoo on the long outrigger rods and let them out. Buddy fished them from the long rigger chairs on the flying bridge. I put out a small white feather in both short riggers and doubled up on the rubber bands we wrapped around the wooden clothespins we used on our outriggers.

These small white feathers caught mostly cero mackerel along with blue runner and bar jack.

Buddy never slowed the boat down when he caught a barracuda, kingfish, or cero mackerel on the two bridge rods. As I looked back and watched the wire line rods for a grouper strike, I would see a fish bouncing on top of the water as Bud wound it to the back of the boat. Buddy used eighty-pound test monofilament on all our trolling rods. The short rigger rods I had in the cockpit were pinned to the chair gimbals, so all I did was wind in the cero mackerel or jack from a standing position.

Since a cold front had just passed, the wind was very light out of the northwest, and the sky was blue—perfect for trolling the reefs. Everything was biting that day. By the time we passed Pacific Reef Lighthouse, we had eight black groupers and forty small jack, mackerel, barracuda, and kingfish in the fish box. Everywhere you looked on the reef, there were cero mackerel diving and ballyhoo fleeing from all the predators.

As we approached one of Buddy's favorite gag grouper holes, he had me switch the small white feathers I was fishing on the short outrigger rods to ballyhoo. The gag groupers would school up to spawn during the winter months in different areas along the reefs off the Florida coast in large numbers. Bud knew every spot where they spawned from Miami to Key West.

Buddy used a small flashing Fathometer to read the depth and land ranges to know where his gag hole started. It did not take long for us to hook a doubleheader of gag groupers on the two electric reels. Mr. Shephard pushed the button on one wire line rod, bringing in a gag grouper as I did the same on the other electric reel. As the groupers got close to the boat, some other gags followed the two hooked fish and swallowed both of the long outrigger baits. Now we had four nice-size groupers on at the same time. While I was pulling in the leader wire on a grouper, one of my short outriggers popped out of the pin with a hungry gag grouper trying to pull line off the reel. Bud kept one engine in gear so the groupers could not get back into the reef.

What a way to start fishing the gag hole—catching five groupers at the same time. On that day all the gag groupers averaged fifteen to twenty-five pounds. Buddy had the boat moving again at trolling speed, and as I let the wire line out a gag grouper grabbed the feather and bait, so I pushed the drag lever up, and the fish was hooked. A happy Mr. Shephard pushed the button and said, "We are doing good!" I snapped a ballyhoo on the left long outrigger that Buddy fished from the bridge chair and was hand lining the eighty-pound test off the reel to get the bait out as fast as possible when I felt something grab the ballyhoo.

Buddy engaged the drag lever, and we had a doubleheader of gag groupers on. The only other bait in the water was the ballyhoo on the short outrigger that had not been eaten when we'd caught five fish at the same time, so I snapped it out of the outrigger pin and free spooled the reel. As the ballyhoo drifted past the gag Mr. Shephard was bringing in, something ate it, and we had three gag groupers on at the same time.

Once we were trolling again, both Buddy and the Old Man expected six good baits out instantly, so I let out one electric reel to the mark and then the other as fast as possible. Two hookups occurred moments apart, with Mr. Shephard growling about me not having six baits out and fishing. Gag groupers are always hooked so well that I just took a double wrap of leader wire and swung the fish into the fish box. Pulling the hook on a grouper was extremely rare.

I felt the *Sea Boots* turning around, so I knew Bud was going to line up and make another pass on the mile-long gag hole. I quickly put out two fresh ballyhoo on the long outriggers and two on the short riggers. The wire lines had to be let out when the boat was going straight, so there was no chance of tangling the baits.

Once I had the wire line baits out to the proper marks and all four ballyhoo up in the outriggers, I looked over at Mr. Shephard and said, "Are you ready to do it again?"

The "Old Man" growled at me saying, "Bobby would have had the baits out twice that as fast.".

We trolled about two hundred yards farther and had another doubleheader. When Mr. Shephard and I reeled our gags up toward the boat, both of Bud's long riggers popped out of the pins. We had four gags on at once.

Buddy made a big loop so I could get all four of the outrigger baits out, and he then lined up for our next one-mile troll. I let out both electric reel grouper baits to the marks and waited. This time we had only one strike and caught a nice gag grouper. Bud then kept the boat heading south toward the Whistle Buoy, which was off of Key Largo and the Ocean Reef Club. We caught two nice thirty-pound black groupers before we got to the Whistle Buoy, and Bud turned the *Sea Boots* inshore to fish the shallow reefs on our way back to Miami.

No one knew as much about those ten- and twelve-foot reefs as Buddy, and it always amazed me how he steered the boat between coral heads, catching so many small black groupers and mutton snapper. He always wanted to have a bunch of small black groupers and mutton snapper to sell to his loyal fish customers when we backed into Miamarina in the afternoon.

When trolling this very shallow water, Bud would not slow the boat down after hooking a five-pound grouper, since they never got off the double hooks on the wire line. We stopped fishing the outrigger baits because the small groupers were biting so fast. Mr. Shephard moved from one electric wire line reel to the other, catching small mutton snapper, red groupers, and black groupers.

As we passed a long distance west of Beacon A, Bud told me to wind up the baits on the electric reels. Before I could get both leaders and baits in the boat, he had the *Sea Boots* running at seventeen knots. He ran way to the west of Fowey Rocks Light House and a half mile inside Bug Light. When I looked over the side of the boat, I saw scary water that was less than six feet deep.

Bud always arrived at the dock at three o'clock with Mr. Shephard. I liked this forty-minute run home because Mr. Shephard dozed off, and I could clean the cockpit and get the boat ready for Bobby to go fishing the next day. Bobby left me with six grouper leader wires rigged with feathers, skirts, and razor-sharp hooks. I wanted to have the same number of rigs ready for him, with a bait box of perfectly cut mullet strips and split-back ballyhoo. I had only a couple of minutes to go to the flying bridge and tell Bud the cockpit was cleaned and I had organized and iced the bait box for Bobby. I glanced down to the helm where Buddy kept score with an old pencil he sharpened with a bait knife—we'd caught forty-four groupers, the most groupers I had ever caught in one day.

As Buddy Carey backed the *Sea Boots* into the slip and up to the dock, Mr. Shephard was already walking toward the fish box. I rushed to put the step in place so he could put one foot on the step box; the next foot went on the fish box; the next step he made was on the transom; and the final step Mr. Shephard made was on the concrete dock. I then put the dock lines on the stern cleats of the *Sea Boots*, and Bud shut the engines down. Mr. Shephard then walked west on

Fifth Street and across Biscayne Boulevard, back to his penthouse at the Park Lee Hotel.

Several days later, when Steve and I were getting Buddy's second boat ready to go fishing, Buddy came down laughing and said, "Mr. Shephard told me if Bobby had been working the cockpit, we would have caught three times as many groupers. Here's a twenty he wanted me to give you!"

I said to Bud, "I thought Mr. Shephard never tipped till the end of the winter."

As Bud started to walk back to his boat, he laughed and agreed that for the last five years, Mr. Shephard had never tipped any mate till he got ready to go back to Canada at the end of winter. I said to Bud that I did not understand.

Buddy stopped, turned around, and smiled while saying, "That's right. He liked fishing with you."

CHAPTER 8

PIER 5, MIAMI, FLORIDA, NOVEMBER 7, 1970 THE HIALEAH FUNERAL HOME

It was a Tuesday, and I was running the *Sea Boots* out of Pier 5. Ronnie was mating for me that day. The owner of a group of Hialeah funeral homes would charter me three times a year to take out the hundreds of urns and cardboard boxes that contained the remains of the people he had cremated.

Alejandro Martinez -Garcia- Rodriguez was a funeral director and looked exactly like one. Alejandro had chalk- white pastyie skin and black eyes, with jet- black dyed hair that was slicked straight back. I think he had seen too many Elvis Presley movies, because he combed his hair in a similar way.

He had three funeral plans for the predominantely hispanic clientele he catered to. The Deluxe or Platinum Plan gave the family a hand painted urn that would be made by a skilled Egyptian pottery artist and hand-painted by an elderly Michelangelo trained Italian artist.

Alejandro promised to have a priest accompany the urn to the clear, clean Gulf Stream water, where the family's favorite verse from the Bible would be read. The priest would then, gently place the urn in the clear water and wave some religious and historic gold cane as the urn slowly sank to its final resting place in the ocean depths. Alejandro also promised that a special boat would take the beloved out, with no one onboard but the priest and the well-trained boat crew. All this could be had for $5,000.

Alejandro's next plan was the gold plan, which promised another custom-painted, somewhat smaller urn and a boat that had only the specially trained crew, who would gently place the remains in the clear, clean Gulf Stream water after reading a family-selected verse from the Bible. All this could be had for $2,000.

His next plan was the silver plan. Alejandro promised to place the loved one in a smaller hand-painted urn. He then gave the same speech about the trained crew and the clear, clean water. Then he would put his hands together, as if he was going to pray, and say, "Your loved one will share the boat with only one other departed soul." This way he could justify the $1,000 price.

On one of our trips, after we had disposed of all the ashes of the three-hundred-plus people, I asked Alejandro about all the cardboard boxes that had gold painted crosses and Spanish names on the tops. Alejandro placed his palms together, looked up at the heavens, and said, "I am a good negotiator." I guessed there was a fourth or fifth plan also.

This day Alejandro arrived, like always, at 3:00 a.m. driving a rented truck. He immediately went to the north end of the dock and walked under the bridge, offering some of the many homeless men living there twenty-dollar bills if they helped move some boxes for an hour or two.

Once he returned with ten or twelve guys who were half asleep or still drunk from the night before, Alejandro started a chain gang or assembly line where each person would receive a box and then pass it to the next person. Alejandro had the box truck filled with urns and cardboard boxes. The boxes had been put in the truck first and the urns last.

Alejandro wanted the urns to be taken out of the rented truck while it was still dark, so no one would witness what was happening. The colorful urns were placed far forward in the bow area, where they could not be seen. We filled the bow, both bathrooms, and the area belowdecks with urns. The men then unloaded over three hundred cardboard boxes from the truck and stacked them throughout the boat, since they were square.

This unloading procedure never went as smoothly as Alejandro wanted. Several of the bleary-eyed homeless always dropped three or four of the cheap Mexican-made urns on the concrete dock, where they shattered, spilling ashes everywhere. Alejandro would get the wash-down hose and turn it on high. He would start at the back of the dock and wash the broken pottery and black ashes forward till everything had been pushed into the marina water around the boat. He always said the same thing: "It's only mud."

After the truck was empty, Alejandro gave every homeless person a twenty-dollar bill and told them to meet the boat at two in the afternoon. He then moved the rented truck far away and left it in the parking lot.

We usually finished unloading by 5:00 a.m., but Alejandro had a record number of urns and boxes that day—556 in all. We finished by five thirty, and the dock was empty except for the old Cuban security guard Alejandro had given a fifty-dollar bill to go all the way around to the other side of the marina and not come back till the boat was out of sight.

The *Sea Boots* departed Miamarina and went under the Dodge Island Bridge, entering Government Cut. Alejandro and Ronnie

A YOUNG FISHERMAN'S DREAM COME TRUE

immediately started with the cardboard boxes. They would peel the gold crosses off the fronts of the boxes and throw the crosses in one of the many Publix grocery store bags Alejandro had brought. Next they peeled off the labels with the departeds' names and threw them overboard. They dumped the ashes into Government Cut and flattened the boxes so they could be used again. They then placed the flattened cardboard boxes in big black garbage bags, so they would not be visible when we docked at two in the afternoon. The bags would be taken off the boat and stacked in the rented truck.

As I drove the boat, the two of them worked fast and furiously until we reached the US Coast Guard base. This had a well-lit dock, and the boat crews were always looking at boats that went by the base while it was still dark. Once we were a safe distance away, I gave a signal, and the work started again. With more than three hundred boxes to dump overboard, it took the two of them over three hours to finish.

Next came the urns. The cheap Mexican-made urns were very breakable and had to be dumped and then washed out with the washdown hose, so Alejandro could use them again. They dumped and washed the small ones quickly, but the large ones took forever. By eleven in the morning, Alejandro and Ronnie finally sat down and had a couple of Budweisers. It was time to start fishing.

Ronnie had four ballyhoos out and fishing in record time. Two were fished in the long pins of the outriggers, and two were fished from the rods in the short riggers. Alejandro enjoyed catching a couple of small groupers for his family and always let us keep the big groupers. I trolled over a deep-water wreck, and Ronnie dropped one electric rod and reel to the bottom, with two hooks baited with small pieces of bonito. Alejandro saw the rod tip bounce a few times and wound up two small snowy groupers.

Ronnie dropped the second wire line outfit to the bottom, and Alejandro moved to the other chair and brought up two more small snowy groupers. Ronnie already had the first electric reel back down to the wreck and fishing. This time Alejandro caught two deep-water Coney groupers. He had caught enough and went inside to take a nap.

Ronnie attached a rigged bonito to the electric wire line rod as I positioned the boat ahead of the wreck. Once the bait reached the bottom, it did not take long for a warsaw grouper to eat the bonito, and Ronnie hooked him. Fifteen minutes later the fish was floating behind the *Sea Boots*.

We did the same thing again; another warsaw grouper ate the bonito bait and was on and tugging. Fifteen minutes later another big grouper was floating behind the boat. Each warsaw was about 150 pounds, so I started trolling toward downtown Miami. Alejandro wanted to have the rented truck backed up to the dock and open at two o'clock in the afternoon.

Ronnie filleted, deboned, and skinned several small snowy groupers and put the fish in a plastic bag on the ice. Once we got the boat tied up, Alejandro, as usual, wanted to unload the urns and cardboard boxes and get the truck moving in a hurry. The homeless guys were waiting and formed an assembly line to pass the big black bags containing the cardboard boxes and gold crosses to the back of the rented truck. They carefully passed the urns from guy to guy, with a perfect score. They dropped nothing. Alejandro slammed and locked the truck door and paid and thanked the guys.

Alejandro always paid me in cash and always carried a large black briefcase. He called Ronnie over and said, "Instead of tipping in cash, I would rather give you some earrings for your wife or girlfriend." He opened the black briefcase, and there must have been five hundred pairs of every kind of earring known on this earth. Ronnie asked Alejandro how he had gotten so many earrings.

Alejandro explained, "While you're sitting with the grieving family, you put the palms of your hands together." He then demonstrated by looking at Ronnie with black puppy-dog eyes and said, "If you're a good Catholic, you would never take your mother's jewelry away as she is departing for that higher place." Alejandro then turned his head toward the sky as a tear ran down his cheek and he kissed the fingertips of his praying hands.

Since Christmas was the next month, I grabbed a handful of earrings.

CHAPTER 9

MIAMI BEACH, FLORIDA, NOVEMBER 13, 1970 THE SPEIGLE FAMILY OF SOUTH BEACH

It was Friday, and Shelley Speigle had booked almost all of the Miami, Key Biscayne, and Baker's Haulover charter boats for an afternoon fishing trip for one of his many convention trips. Shelley was a morbidly overweight but colorful charter boat captain who worked with the many conventions that were held during the fall in Miami Beach and downtown Miami every year. He handled everything that was needed from the time the charter buses delivered the people to the dock. That meant he booked the boats, arranged the pickups, and supplied them with beer, soda, and box lunches.

Shelley bought hundreds of cases of cheap beer and soda once a year from a large Miami distributer that sold expired beverages and stored the cans in the boat warehouse, so he could use them when needed. All the captains heard the same complaints every trip they ran from the Chamber of Commerce Dockdock: "These are flat!" And that day was no different.

Shelley had a group of Haitians who assembled the cardboard boxes that the lunches would be placed in. Starting one week before the thirty boats were needed for the 180 conventioneers, Shelley had the Haitians start making the 360 sandwiches. One sandwich would be mayonnaise, ham, and yellow cheese. The next would be mayonnaise, bologna, and white cheese. One apple, a single napkin, and a candy cane were then added to each box, and the finished lunches were stacked in the corner of the warehouse on the concrete floor.

When Shelley came by to pick up the number of needed boxes, the Haitians would load them in his green Cadillac convertible, and the rest went into the metal trolley he dragged from the trailer hitch of his Caddie. If there were extra box lunches, they were saved for the next convention a week or so later.

Shelly had found a place in Hialeah that made candy—including Christmas candy canes by the thousands. Mercado, the owner of the small warehouse business, would save all the candy canes that were not good enough to sell in the many retail stores he supplied. Shelly knew that once Christmas had passed, he could get the damaged canes for three cents on the dollar, because they had no value to Mercado. Shelly stored the four hundred pounds of candy canes on the floor of his warehouse, where they stayed till they were used or till the rats ate so many that he had to visit Mercado again.

The Speigles had a family charter boat business with three boats at that time docked on the south side of the Chamber of Commerce dock, located near the southwest tip of Miami Beach. Shelley's father, Woody, and his uncle, Label, ran around the dock and dock area wearing shorts purchased from a secondhand store and no shirts. Their continually exposed backs, shoulders, chests, and legs were seared dark brown by the Florida sun. They were not big men; Woody might have weighed 160 pounds on his best day, and Label was possibly 140 pounds. They both growled when they spoke, and their New Jersey background limited their vocabulary to a group of words that children should never hear. Their South Jersey accents were better than the Hollywood movies ever used.

Shelley weighed in at 360 pounds and was amazingly agile when he climbed the triple-reinforced bridge ladder. He was also a very good fisherman.

I arrived early with the *Sea Boots* so I could tie up and not have to drift near Government Cut till Shelley called the other boats in to pick up their groups of eager anglers. This Friday the thirteenth was not a good day for Shelley. As he walked out to talk to me, he stepped on the end of a dock plank that was not nailed properly to the dock frame. As he stepped on the end of the plank, he started to descend, and the long plank flipped up and hit him in the middle of his back. With a massive splash, Shelley disappeared into the water. By the time I had my boat tied up to the dock, Woody and Label had thrown Shelley a dock line and were calling him a fat bastard. He was yelling back, "You motherfu**ers, get me out of here."

So I just watched as Woody pulled Shelley along the bulkhead to the electric boat lift. Label had run over to the lift and had the hoist at water level, with the lifting straps well below the surface of the water. Shelley sat in one of the huge nylon lifting straps as Label and the two dock boys hoisted him out of the water. Once Shelley was on the concrete dock, he went over to the wash-down hose and sprayed off his gun, then went inside and changed clothes.

For some reason Shelley liked me and enjoyed telling me terrible things about the other captains as they arrived and waited for the buses. He came up with stories I knew were not true, but they kept me continually laughing. Shelley had the ability to find the worst in everyone. I always wondered what he said about me as my boat idled toward Miamarina.

Tommy, my mate, was terrified of Woody and Label. These two old men had long, straggly hair and ran around passing out the boxed lunches and drinks with no shirts, weathered suntans, and

A YOUNG FISHERMAN'S DREAM COME TRUE

knives on their belts. The young mates were frightened to make eye contact. When one of the young charter boat mates said something to Label, he pulled his knife out, reached up, and grabbed the kid—who was over a foot taller and a hundred pounds heavier—by the hair.

By the time I got there, Label had the kid on his knees and was pushing the knife under his left eye, saying, "I'm gonna cut both your eyes out and feed them to the fish." The sixty-five-year-old Label was about as strong as the average four-year-old child, but no one knew that. I grabbed him by the wrist and walked him over to see Shelley. When I walked away, I heard Shelley telling his uncle, "Good going, you scared the sh**" out of him."

As the four large buses arrived, Woody and Label directed them to park close to the charter boats along the side of the road. Both of the brothers pointed out the loading area and instructed the anglers to proceed to the boarding area. They both invited the drivers to watch the fancy boats dock and load the conventioneers. Once the drivers walked over to the water's edge and were in the middle of the crowd, Label went inside the first unlocked bus and found the driver's sunglasses and ball hat. He pushed them into the plastic bag he had brought. Woody was more successful when he entered the second bus. The driver had left his wallet under the seat. The third bus was locked.

Finally all the boats were filled and were off to go fishing. Every one of the captains ran slowly to save fuel or trolled out to the Gulf Stream. That day the kingfish were feeding directly east of Miami, so we all caught several kings for all six anglers who were assigned to each charter boat. Shelley charged the organizers of the conventions top dollar plus 40 percent and paid the cheapest he could to the charter boats. He also included a 10 percent tip for the mates, who never saw a penny of the appreciation. That was why we all traveled

75

at trolling speed on our way out and on our way back to the dock—to save fuel.

If you wanted to take any of Shelley's trips, the charter boat had to pitch in a five-dollar bill for the "kitty," as Shelley called it. Whichever boat caught the largest fish would receive the entire kitty of $150, or so Shelley said. When I returned from fishing and docked the *Sea Boots* a couple of minutes early, I told Tommy not to take any of our kingfish up to the measurement area. Since I was fishing two electric reels filled with Monel wire, I had at least seventy-five small kingfish in the fish box. All were what we called "snakes," since they ranged from two to six pounds and were so skinny that Tommy never had to gaff a single fish. This size fish sold well at our dock market.

We captains who had run fishing trips for Shelley knew he was going to win, so producing a large fish was useless.

Bill McMurray was the captain of a Key Biscayne charter boat named the *Semper Fi*. He was big in stature and someone you did not want to cross paths with once he started drinking. He also knew Shelley carried a gun, because he could see the houlster on Shelley's six-and-a-half-foot leather belt. Alberto was the mate on the *Semper Fi*; he was filling in for Richie, who did not like going on any of Shelley's trips.

As I stood at the measuring area looking down at the eight largest kingfish that were laid on the wooden dock, which was built over the deep-water part of Government Cut, I saw Woody and Label dragging a very large partially frozen kingfish from the dock freezer. They placed it down next to the line of other kings. Once Alberto saw this fish, he and Captain Bill knew they were going to win the kitty with the giant kingfish they had caught. Alberto ran to the *Semper Fi*, grabbed the giant king out of the fish box, and lugged it back to the measuring area.

A YOUNG FISHERMAN'S DREAM COME TRUE

I did not know what was going to happen next but knew it would not be good for Captain Bill and Alberto. Once Alberto carefully placed his giant kingfish alongside Shelly's partially frozen fish that had been caught months earlier, it was clear the *Semper Fi* had won the contest. I watched Shelley slide his left foot under the tail of the larger kingfish. Just as Alberto said, "We won," Shelley raised his foot, and the king fish splashed into the deep water of Government Cut and was never seen again.

The moment Alberto yelled at Shelley, calling him a cheater, Label leaped like a spider on Alberto's shoulders and grabbed his fluffy hair, jerking it to the left as he sank his teeth into Alberto's right ear. Alberto crumbled to his knees in pain. Captain Bill stepped forward to save his mate and was met with the barrel of Shelley's gun. As I watched in disbelief, Shelley said, "Get back on your boat, or I'll blow your guts across Biscayne Bay!"

Bill ran toward the *Semper Fi* while Alberto tried to get Label to let go of his bleeding ear. Woody was kicking Alberto in the ribs too. Alberto had played football for Miami High and was in great shape but could not unlock Label's jaws. Once Label ran out of energy, Alberto sprinted toward the *Semper Fi* as Captain Bill untied the dock lines and pushed the boat off the dock.

Both Woody and Label, with a combined age of 130 years, were standing on the wooden dock shouting at Captain Bill and Alberto as their boat idled away, "If I ever see any of you f**kers from Key Biscayne again, I will crush your heads like grapes!" The heaviest thing that either Woody or Label could lift was a can of beer.

Returning to the *Sea Boots*, I found Tommy hiding on the flying bridge with a pair of binoculars. He had witnessed the entire thing. Once we untied the lines and departed the dock, I headed west down Government Cut for Pier 5, to sell our catch of kingfish. Several days later I learned that Alberto needed to have six stitches put in his right ear to close the wound from Label's teeth.

Another exciting story and a fun day in the life of a charter boat captain.

CHAPTER 10

PIER 5, MIAMI, FLORIDA, NOVEMBER 20, 1970 TIMMY THOMAS FROM THE SIR JOHN'S NIGHT BEAT HOTEL

Timmy Thomas's first sailfish with captain Bill Harrison. Caught on the Sea Boots with captain Bill Harrison and mate Ronnie. Miami, Florida November 20, 1970

CAPTAIN BILL HARRISON

It was Friday, and another beautiful Miami day. I was running Buddy Carey's second boat, the *Sea Boots*, out of Pier 5. Since early November the charter business had started to pick up, with quite a few conventions in the downtown Miami and Miami Beach areas that needed fishing boats. I preferred fishing full days instead of the half days the conventions booked, but these out-of-state people always left the fish for the crew to sell, and there were built-in tips for the mates and captains.

By ten in the morning, I had given up hoping for a walk-up group to jump out of a cab and say, "Let's go fishing." In South Florida it was common for a family to catch a cab and ask to be taken to the closest charter boat dock where they could get on a boat and go fishing. I had fished all or part of the previous six days, and I was preparing to get the sandpaper, paint, and brushes out to repair some of the chips and dings that occur during a fishing day onboard a charter boat.

All the Pier 5 charter boats backed to the dock on the Biscayne Bay side of Bayfront Park. Most of this beautiful park has long since been replaced by groups of retail shops and small restaurants. Since the park at that time was filled with huge trees and had flowers, grass, and lots of benches, it was common to see families, groups, or single people walk across Bay Front Park and look at the charter boats. Sometimes the captains or mates who were not fishing would talk them into going fishing that day or the next day.

I watched an elegantly dressed black man walk through the park and head straight for my boat. I told my mate, Ronnie, "This guy has money." He was wearing a cream-colored wide-brimmed hat with a black satin band, a three-piece cream-colored suit with a black satin ascot, and cream-colored shoes with shiny black spats.

He walked up to me and said, "Are you the captain?" (I was young back then.) He wanted to go fishing but needed some other clothes, like a bathing suit and a T-shirt. I assured him there was a locker up forward on the boat containing various clothing items customers had left onboard, and he would find something that fit him.

His name was Timmy Thomas. He introduced himself to me and said, "This is my first fishing trip. Do I pay you first?" I looked down at the wad of hundred-dollar bills he was holding in his hands, which had more gold on them than most of the Miami jewelry shops had in their display cases.

"No sir!" I said. "We can settle up at the end of the day."

Ronnie had already seen Timmy's gold chains, gold Rolex with diamonds, and gold rings, so he already had both of the caterpillar engines started and running.

About the time the boat was passing the cruise ships, Timmy came up to the flying bridge wearing some plaid shorts and a Joe's Stone Crab Restaurant T-shirt. Ronnie was up the bridge ladder in a flash saying it didn't matter if Timmy went barefoot; Ronnie said he never wore shoes either. I casually looked at Ronnie's feet and saw they had never seen the sun—they were snow white.

Ronnie followed up by saying, "Mr. Thomas wants to mount a sailfish," and then he went to the cockpit to get the sailfish tackle ready. This gave me fifteen minutes to talk about the taxidermy company I represented and how perfectly and beautifully they preserved sailfish, which were their specialty.

Back then very few boats flew fishing kites, so I explained that Timmy could stay up there on the flying bridge and adjust the two 4/0 red-sided Penn Senator reels that were filled with pink thirty-pound test monofilament. Once the fishing kite was up and flying, Ronnie would first put out a small bonito to be fished on the long kite pin and then put a small blue runner on the short pin of the kite.

We crossed a nice blue-water edge in 120 feet of water and put up the kite, with the two baits right on the color change. Ronnie put two wire line rods in the back chairs next to the fish box, with a two-pound lead bank weight and a snapper bait on each rod. I told Timmy we caught a variety of fish on those rigs and sometimes caught the freshest live baits that could be used for catching sailfish. That was half true, but Timmy was dead set on catching and mounting a trophy sailfish. Ronnie caught a mutton snapper right away, so I said the six-pound mutton was too large for a sailfish bait, and Ronnie should put it in the fish box.

Timmy's first fish was a twelve-pound bull dolphin. He thought this was great, because he saw the fish eat the blue runner that was fished on the short kite pin and then watched the brightly colored dolphin jump a dozen times as it swam wildly around the stern of the *Sea Boots*. This was good, because he now had a basic understanding of what was going to happen if we raised and hooked a sailfish.

Ronnie put another blue runner in the short pin of the fishing kite, and another dolphin of about the same size ate it. The next strike was a sailfish, which ate the small bonito on the long kite pin. It jumped off within two minutes. I was somewhat happy, because it was not a big fish.

Rather than watch Ronnie catch muttons on a regular basis and tell Timmy lies, I started to talk to Timmy about his Miami trip. I knew he was not a doctor or lawyer by all the gold jewelry he wore. He told me he was a rhythm and blues singer who was working at Sir John's Knight Beat Hotel and Club for a one-month gig. Everyone knew about this club, but I had never known any of my friends to go there, since it was in the scary part of downtown Miami.

As he was telling me about the songs he had written and recorded, a big sail raised its dorsal fin and started to circle the blue runner

A YOUNG FISHERMAN'S DREAM COME TRUE

on the short kite pin. The sailfish turned darker until its sail was completely black. This was a good sign, because it meant the fish was hungry and going to eat the bait. Timmy was watching the sailfish stalk the blue runner while Ronnie wound up both snapper baits. The big sail ate the blue runner and swam straightaway from the boat at a slow speed. Everything seemed perfect, since the fish was now hooked and running off line from the Penn reel.

Timmy was in the left long flying bridge chair, howling with the rhythm and blues voice he used to record his records. "Captain, my dream has come true"! he shouted.

I thought, *How could a poor black kid who was born in the ghetto of Chicago dream of catching a sailfish?* But it did make me feel good.

After twenty minutes Ronnie moved to the aft corner of the cockpit with the long-handle gaff for the perfect gaff shot. I backed the boat in a circle, shortening the distance between the sailfish and the *Sea Boots*. I could see the sail getting browner by the moment. As a sailfish or marlin becomes exhausted, it turns brown.

I saw the right moment and backed the boat quickly to the tired sailfish, telling Ronnie to take his best shot. He was an exceptionally good mate and made a great gaff shot to the head of the sailfish. He pulled the sail into the cockpit while I ran down the flying bridge ladder and got my camera from the forward locker. I got Timmy to hold the large sail while I snapped a bunch of shots. Timmy slapped Ronnie on the back and thanked me for the greatest day of his life.

Timmy joined me on the flying bridge at two thirty and said, "Captain, if there is anything you want to do for the next hour, go ahead." I told Timmy we sell the extra fish at the dock, and catching a grouper or two would make a big difference in my pay, since I did not own the boat. Timmy said, "Go ahead." I ran down the bridge ladder and helped Ronnie get one of the electric reels out of the rod locker.

Ronnie pulled the hand-crank wire line rod out of the left cockpit chair, and I put the electric reel in the gimbal and pinned the rod in place. Ronnie then attached one of the warsaw grouper baits he had cut and rigged in the morning while hoping for a walk-up charter. Ronnie had everything ready by the time I steered the boat over a small wreck in 350 feet of water.

I trolled south past the wreck, giving Ronnie enough time to let the bait hit the bottom and wind it up twenty feet. While we waited for a bite, I told Timmy about the big groupers and sharks we sometimes caught there and that he might enjoy catching one if we were lucky enough to hook a fish. About the time I finished my explanation, Ronnie gave me a yell, so I put the boat in gear.

As the rod bent over the transom with the wire line being pulled off the reel, Ronnie looked up at Timmy and asked him if he wanted to catch a warsaw grouper. Timmy rushed down the bridge ladder and jumped in the fighting chair, and so the battle started. Fifteen minutes later a 125-pound warsaw grouper was floating behind the boat.

Timmy loved this, so we tried again. I lined up the land ranges and saw the wreck go by on the Fathometer as I trolled south. I gave Ronnie the signal, and he dropped the warsaw bait to the bottom. As he reeled the bait up to the proper distance for grouper, something big ate it. Timmy hollered with pleasure. He had all the fishing techniques down now. He would lift the rod when he could and then push the button on the electric reel as he lowered the rod retrieving line. Twenty minutes later a 175-pound warsaw floated to the surface behind the *Sea Boots*.

Sitting in the wire line chair of the *Sea Boots*, Timmy shouted up to me, "Can we try just one more time?"

"You're the man," I said, and we were trolling back to the wreck. Ronnie had a bait ready to go as I passed over the wreck, and he dropped the bait to the bottom. As he was bringing it up, the rod bent over, and Timmy was hooked up again. After a thirty-minute battle, a bigger warsaw floated behind the boat. It took all three of us to pull the 325-pound grouper over the transom of the *Sea Boots*.

As we ran home toward Pier 5, Timmy changed back into the three-piece suit with spats, and Ronnie measured all three groupers, the two dolphin, and the big sail. At the dock Timmy asked about mounting the sailfish and the largest grouper. I just happened to know its exact length. I told Timmy the forty-inch bull dolphin was an exceptional catch also, so he had that mounted too. Of course he paid in cash and gave Ronnie and me a hundred-dollar bill each. This was unheard of in 1970.

I could not let Timmy just walk back to his hotel after how good he had been to Ronnie and me, so I said, "Let me drive you to your hotel." Timmy climbed into my beat-up Chevy El Camino, and we were off! I did not know exactly where the Sir John's Knight Beat Hotel and Club was, so Timmy told me where to turn. I made a bunch of lefts and rights in the dark side of town, and then Timmy said, "Quick, turn left here."

After bouncing over the curb in some strangely shaped parking lot, I came to a stop where Timmy was pointing. The car was instantly surrounded by a bunch of black guys who were bigger than NFL players. I immediately regretted volunteering to give Timmy a ride to this hotel. Both of the doors on my El Camino were jerked open by the NFL team, and I prayed. The next thing I heard was, "Timmy, how ya doing, bro?"

CHAPTER 11

Pier 5, Miami, Florida, March 9, 1971 The Giant White Marlin

Four sailfish weighing 61, 63, 74 and 77 pounds and one big white marlin weighing 137 pounds with Bill Harrison. Caught on the charter boat Sea Boots with captain Bill Harrison and mate Steve Tellam. Pier 5 Miami, Florida March 9, 1971

A YOUNG FISHERMAN'S DREAM COME TRUE

I was running the *Sea Boots* out of Pier 5. Steve Tellam was mating that day. We had five clients sent to me by a big-name Miami law firm. The law firm gave me about six trips a year that always had great people who were fun to take fishing. The firm wanted their clients to leave early in the morning and be back at the dock around one in the afternoon. I got paid for a full day, and the lawyers got to conduct business all afternoon.

Two yellow taxis pulled up just before seven in the morning, and we were off. On the way out of Government Cut, I got to talk to several of the guys about their fishing experience. It was the first time for all but one. The one who had fished before had gone out on a friend's boat in the Palm Beach area and caught and mounted a sailfish two years earlier. He was very satisfied with his beautiful mounted sailfish and thought the four others should also catch and mount sailfish.

This was good news for me, because we had been catching sailfish every day, and the wind was northeast at fifteen miles an hour. This was a great wind direction for flying a fishing kite with live baits for sailfish. Kite fishing with live bait usually produces larger sailfish than trolling dead baits. During the 1970s there were no size limits, and most of our sailfish were killed and mounted.

Pier 5 was the most famous dock on the East Coast. It was a true tourist destination, and hundreds of people came down in the afternoon to see the variety and volume of fish the charter boats brought in daily. Some of the people were tourists while others stopped by to purchase fresh fish for their families. There was fresh fish caught every day, like amberjack, dolphin, kingfish, tilefish, groupers, snappers, cobia, wahoos, barracuda, and mackerel. In Miami, if you could catch it, there would be someone who wanted to buy it.

Once I reached the deep water, I had to run the *Sea Boots* at a slow speed down south to the middle of Key Biscayne, where I found a great blue-water edge in 120 feet. It took thirty-five minutes to get from our dock to the deep water directly off the middle of Key Biscayne. I put the fishing kite up from the flying bridge, and Steve had a small bonito ready to go. We used lots of small bonitos called feather bonitos, since we caught them on a chain of trolling feathers. Sometimes we would catch eight or ten baby bonitos at a time. I always jumped down from the bridge ladder to help the mate unhook these small fish because barracuda, kingfish, and sometimes a sailfish would grab the last bonito on the chain.

My fishing method back then was easy. I fished one kite with two live bonitos from the flying bridge chairs on flimsy rods with red 4/0 Penn Senator reels filled with thirty-pound test monofilament line. When fishing for sailfish, I liked to fish the short riggers in the cockpit with live bonitos, mullet, or blue runner.

The mate then dropped one wire line rod down on the coral bottom out of each of the two chairs that were closest to the back of the boat, called the transom. As we fished the two live bonitos out of the fishing kite for sails, we also caught a few dolphin and kingfish. The rod and reels filled with wire line that we fished out of the back two chairs would catch mutton snappers and a few groupers. Every bottom fish, snapper, or grouper we caught would help the crew financially, since the party seldom took any fish, and we had a great market waiting for us at the dock when we backed in.

The species of groupers caught off Miami were black, gag, red, and scamp in the shallow water and snowy, warsaw, kitty mitchell (speckled hind), yellow edge, and mystic in the deep water. It was common to bring in four or five different kinds of groupers in one day. Mutton and vermillion snappers made up almost all the snappers

A YOUNG FISHERMAN'S DREAM COME TRUE

we caught off Miami. A true red snapper caught off Miami was very rare. I used light wire on the bottom baits back then and frequently caught nurse sharks, blacktip sharks, and a few small bull sharks. I even caught some big stingrays while bottom fishing.

Sailfishing started off wild and crazy. We caught a seventy-plus-pound sail right away and put it in the boat. The next was a big sailfish that jumped so many times it died, and Jim, the angler, wound the dead fish to the boat. When Steve laid it alongside the first sail, it was almost as big. Once Jim caught his sailfish, he went down to the cockpit, and Steve put him to work catching mutton snappers on the wire line rods.

The snappers were biting good that day, but the groupers were not. We had seven mutton snappers by ten o'clock. The next angler missed a sailfish. There were many more sails to come. The sailfish were tailing with the northeast wind. I would see them on top of the water tailing down the face of the waves like surfboard riders. Every big wave had a group of sailfish gliding down it, with the tops of their tails out of the water.

As the sailfish kept tailing down sea, I continued to put the live bonitos in front of the tailing sails. By 11:00 a.m., we had four big sails in the boat to be mounted. Bart was the only person who had not caught a sailfish that day. Since he had already caught one off Palm Beach, he had been a true gentleman and had given up his place to catch a sailfish. He watched and waited till all his friends had caught their first sailfish. He then had all the rods to himself. It was finally his turn to catch a sailfish.

The long kite bait suddenly went crazy trying to escape something that had a lot of light-blue color showing deep in the water. Sailfish show black and are usually slow feeders, but this fish had lots of florescent blue and was making fast slashing movements at the small

89

bonito. Bart wound the slack out of the kite line, and a huge white marlin jumped toward the sky.

Bart yelled, "I want to mount it." The marlin jumped several more times and swam down sea as I backed the *Sea Boots* behind it. After about a mile of slow backing, the white marlin was becoming exhausted. Steve had the long-handle gaff and was patiently waiting to make a good gaff shot. He was one of those classic Southern boys that never wore a shirt and had a glowing South Beach sun tan. He was also one of the best with a gaff I had ever seen—he never missed!

After we did a little more backing, the white marlin made a huge mistake and turned to the east. The dying fish then slowly rolled and made a partial backflip, allowing the hook to come out of its mouth. The white marlin was vertical in the water when I backed up; Steve jumped over and gaffed it in the tail.

The marlin tried to swim down sea with Steve dragging behind. Once I backed the boat close, Steve yelled, "Help, I can't hold on." Being young and dumb, I put the boat in neutral, grabbed a short-handle gaff, and leaped over the side of the cockpit. I gaffed the marlin in the high shoulder muscle and wrapped my fingers around its long nose.

Steve and I looked at each other and started laughing, since the five charter clients were up in the flying bridge taking pictures of the captain and the mate wrestling a huge white marlin in the blue Gulf Stream water. In my mind I could only fast-forward and see Buddy Carey, the owner of the *Sea Boots*, firing me. The best paying job of my life was gone!

The marlin and Steve had given up, so I swam both back to the boat. I had the strength to climb in the cockpit, and I pulled the white marlin in headfirst. Even though the charter party was laughing hard, we somehow managed to pull Steve in the boat. I headed the boat for Government Cut and let Steve steer while I showered and changed clothes below. After docking we laid out the four sails and the one white marlin. My friends from the law firm drove up and laughed at the unbelievable story.

The president of the taxidermy company called me that night and said, "The sails weighed sixty-one, sixty-three, seventy-four, and seventy-seven pounds. By the way, the white marlin weighed one hundred and thirty-seven pounds." This was the largest white marlin I had ever caught.

Steve and I sold the twelve mutton snappers, the four dolphin, and the nurse shark before Buddy Carey backed into his slip later that day. About a month went by before Buddy walked down early one morning and said, "I heard the strangest story…"

CHAPTER 12

PIER 5, MIAMI, FLORIDA, MARCH 12, 1971 CATCHING A 496-POUND JEWFISH

496 pound jewfish caught on the Sea Boots. Captain Bill Harrison and mate Johnny Feathers. Pier 5 Miami, Florida March 12, 1971

It was Saturday, and I was running Buddy Carey's second charter boat, the *Sea Boots*, out of Pier 5. Johnny Feathers was mating that day. His real name was Johnny McGivney. He had walked up behind the *Sea Boots* at six thirty one morning wearing a girl's hat he had stolen from a prostitute in the Overton area of Miami. The hat had a huge peacock feather lodged in its red headband. Buddy shouted to Johnny, who was standing on the upper dock, "Look, there's Johnny Feathers." The name stuck till he died of an overdose of heroin at age forty-two.

Randy McCowan was a good customer who booked me several times a year. That day he was living up to a promise he had made to his two sons—something about getting good grades during the first half of the school year at Palmetto High School in the South Miami area of Dade County. I took the scenic route and ran down Biscayne Bay and out by the Cape Florida Light House. I started trolling just west of Fowey Rocks Light House in the shallow water. Fowey Rocks Light House was built on a shallow reef less than three miles southeast of Cape Florida in 1878. The reef inside Fowey (the west side of the 110-feet-tall lighthouse) was full of life, with schools of ballyhoo, blue runner, and other baitfish all winter and spring.

Johnny put out two electric 12/0 Penn Senator reels filled with Monel wire that were pinned through the gimbals of the chairs located in the back of the boat, nearest the fish box. Buddy Carey had adapted an electric motor to the handle side of each reel. We started trolling a feather and a bait for groupers on the two wire lines. This bait consisted of a three-and-a-half-ounce jap feather with two 3407 Mustad hooks and a carefully tapered mullet strip.

Johnny put two ballyhoo on the long outrigger rods that I fished up with me on the flying bridge from the long rigger chairs. The 9/0 Penn Senator reels were filled with eighty-pound test monofilament line and were drilled and pinned to the long rigger chairs. Randy stayed up talking with me while his two sons, Scott and Tom, caught fish on the two electric reels. Randy had also included two of his sons' friends, Jake and Robbie.

The cero mackerel were biting so fast, I did not even slow the boat down. They were only one or two pounds, with an occasional six-pound fish. The four boys alternated winding in the 9/0 reels as the ceros ate the small white feathers I fished from the short outrigger rods. We caught five black groupers on the electric reels before I turned the *Sea Boots* east to head for the deeper water, to catch some vermillion snappers for Randy's wife. She liked these small, bright-red snappers to fry whole for dinner.

Tommy Curray, who owned Tommy's Boat Yard, had asked me to do something with a dilapidated sailboat that had been rotting in the back of his boatyard for six years. The owner had died, and the family could not be found. I covered the hull with tar then put heavy plastic over the sticky black mess. I then nailed stripes of lath over the plastic to keep it together. On a rainy September day, I had a truck fill the hull with two tons of concrete.

Tommy put the forty-foot sailboat in the water late that afternoon, and I picked it up at ten that night and slowly towed it to a spot three miles south of Fowey Rocks Light. It sank like a rock to the bottom in a little less than two hundred feet of water, and the vermillion snappers started to school around the sailboat wreck within a month.

This wreck sure paid for itself, because I caught so many vermillion snappers, gag groupers, red groupers, black groupers, and mutton snappers and a dozen jewfish over the next twenty years. I helped Tommy and Bo Curray out by removing and sinking a total of five abandon boats over the years that provided me with so many bottom fish, I sold behind my boat at my retail fish market.

Johnny Feathers put a six-hook rig on each electric reel and baited them with small pieces of cero mackerel. The vermillion snappers were there and waiting for the baits. Scott, Tom, Jake, and Robbie took turns pushing the button on the electric reel as the vermillion snappers were pulled to the surface. After they caught about fifty, I started to troll south to the next spot. We caught a doubleheader of big dolphin on our way south.

Johnny put two different rigs on the wire line rods and dropped both of these electric reels on the second spot, which was a little deeper and seldom had vermillion snappers in it. He baited each rod with a live pinfish. One rod bent over immediately, and moments later the other electric had a bite. Each boy caught a fifteen-pound gag grouper. Johnny dropped two more pinfish, and we caught another gag. Nothing ate the other live pinfish. For some unknown reason, this wreck never had as many fish around it as the other four I had sunk in similar depths.

Time to move to another wreck. All these wrecks were small sailboats I had towed out at night and sunk in a range of 160 to 200 feet of water.

The next wreck was in 175 feet and had lots of baby amberjack around it. The boys took turns catching these five- or six-pound jack. Johnny would drop a live pinfish to the bottom and bring the bait up twenty feet, and the rod would bend over with an amberjack. After about twenty-five jacks, the rod slammed over as Jake was catching a small jack. A shark had eaten the back half of the amberjack. Once the boys heard the word *shark*, they wanted to catch it.

Johnny needed time to make a shark rig, so I trolled offshore and found a log with two dolphin swimming around it. We caught both. As I returned to the wreck, Johnny had the jack that had been chewed in half ready to drop to the bottom. Robbie had never caught a shark, so he was the designated angler. Once the bait was on the bottom, all four boys watched the tip of the wire line rod. Finally it bounced a few times, and I put the boat in gear. The rod bent over, and we had a shark on and pulling line off the reel. Robbie caught his first bull shark, and all the boys helped pull the seven-foot fish into the boat.

I trolled south toward the next wreck in about the same depth of water and asked Johnny to rig two reverse ballyhoo to drop to the bottom on it. These were great baits for mutton snappers. This wreck produced lots of muttons for some reason. He dropped both wire lines to the bottom and caught two muttons, about eight pounds each. I trolled back to the wreck, and Johnny again dropped reverse ballyhoo to the bottom on both electric reels, and the boys pushed the buttons as the rod tips bent over. They caught two more muttons.

I had about fifteen minutes before I needed to start trolling home, so we dropped again, and one of the muttons was eaten by something big on the way up. The ten-pound mutton snapper was totally scaled, which meant the big fish was not a shark.

I asked Randy if he wanted to try to catch whatever had swallowed the mutton snapper. He asked the four boys, and all four yelled yes. Johnny rigged the scaled snapper on some heavy leader wire with a big hook. The four boys took a vote to decide who would be in the fighting chair if a fish ate the bait, and Scott jumped in the chair. I trolled back to the wreck, Johnny dropped the snapper to the bottom, and we all waited.

Finally the rod started to move, so I put the boat in gear, and Scott pushed the button. The wire line rod bent over with authority. We had hooked something big! Johnny had the boys stand on both sides of the wire line rod and lift till the rod was as high as they could reach. Scott would push the button on the way down. This is called pumping. The boys would gain twenty feet of wire line, and the fish would pull nineteen feet back off the reel.

Randy was sitting on the bridge with me, loving this tug-of-war between the four boys and the unknown monster fish as he drank his Budweiser. This was a real battle for twenty minutes, until the four boys started to win. A huge jewfish finally floated up behind the *Sea*

Boots. It took a lot of tugging and pulling from everyone to get the 496-pound jewfish in the boat.

I pointed the *Sea Boots* toward Miami and trolled in the northbound Gulf Stream to gain an additional couple of knots of speed. The Gulf Stream is like a huge escalator that carries everything north. March is a good month for big dolphin, and we found several pairs before Randy wanted to run for the dock. Pier 5 on a Saturday would have hundreds of people wanting to see what the charter boats caught and brought in to the dock.

Once docked Randy wanted only to hang and weigh the jewfish. I have caught a lot of jewfish off Miami, but this 496 pounder was a whopper. All the tourists wanted to take pictures of themselves and the fish. I told Johnny to fill some buckets with thirty or forty of the vermilions, and I started scaling and gutting as fast as I could. After I'd scaled and gutted about twenty of the snappers and taken the gills out, Randy said, "That's it." I shook everyone's hand, and I thought they were off.

In the car I could see the boys pleading with their dad, but I had no idea what was going on. Soon the four boys and Randy opened the car doors and walked back to the boat laughing.

Randy said, "Write up that fish for the taxidermist. We're going to mount it and put it on the wall behind the pool table." I knew he had been drinking lots of Budweiser, but I had no idea he'd drank that many!

CHAPTER 13

PIER 5, MIAMI, FLORIDA, SEPTEMBER 19, 1971 FISHING WITH BOB AND ROLAN

It was Sunday. I was running Buddy Carey's second boat, the *Sea Boots*, out of Pier 5. I had two of my favorite Texas clients, Bob Watkins and Rolan Braman, fishing with me that day. I'd met Rolan two years earlier when a limo pulled up in the Pier 5 parking lot, and out jumped a guy wearing a cowboy hat and shouting, "I want to go deep-sea fishing and catch some big fish!"

Since it was September, the worst month of the year for booking charters, I was open. I said, "You got the right boat."

Rolan waved his arm at the limo and said, "Come on, honey," and out jumped two gorgeous blondes.

September in South Florida has either great weather or ugly and gloomy weather. It's our rainiest month of the year and the month with the greatest chance of a hurricane forming and passing close by some part of South Florida. This day was beautiful, with a light north wind and a one-foot sea in the Gulf Stream. Fishing was usually good in September. There usually is a great variety available from shallow-water fish and deep-water bottom fish.

Like always, Rolan and his friend, Bob, arrived early in a limo. And of course out jumped two cute Texas gals. On the way out of

Government Cut, the four rode up in the bridge, with me talking about the cruise ships we were passing that docked at Dodge Island. Miami has a huge cruise ship industry, with thousands of passengers departing and arriving every Sunday. The cruise ships dock on the north side of Dodge Island, and the cargo and container ships dock on the south side of the island.

Mating for me that day was Johnny "Machine Gun" Gavin. He got his name from his habit of talking too fast and too much. He was a very good mate and was always well prepared for every kind of fishing. With all the people in the bridge, he had everything to himself in the rigging area of the cockpit and had all the hooks sharpened, wire leaders made, and knots tied for every kind of fishing that day.

We started with two long outrigger rods up in the bridge chairs, two short outrigger rods in the short rigger chairs in the cockpit, and two electric reels trolling out of the back two chairs. We called these back two chairs the wire line chairs, since we (the boats that fished out of Pier 5) always trolled wire lines.

The color change was in twenty fathoms (120 feet) that day, with the green water on the inside (west) and the blue water on the east side. These conditions occurred the majority of days off Miami and usually gave us great fishing. Once we started fishing, Rolan and Bob stayed up in the flying bridge with me, sitting in the two long rigger chairs. Edie and Debbie, Rolan's Texan friends, went down to the cockpit and sat in the two wire line chairs.

September was a great month for trolling off Miami. That day the bonitos were biting like wild dogs. The electric reels were perfect for the two girls. All they did was push the buttons, and the bonitos and kingfish were wound to the boat. If they had to crank all the fish in on conventional reels, they might have broken a nail! The bonitos were biting so fast, we caught two every time. Debbie and Edie were loving the nonstop action.

After we caught twenty bonitos, Machine Gun put out six hundred feet of wire line on Debbie's electric reel. The rod bent after a few minutes, and Debbie pushed the button for a while, bringing in the six hundred feet of wire line. She caught a small kingfish, called a snake since it was so small and skinny it looked like a snake. Edie caught another bonito while Debbie wound in the snake kingfish.

Once we were trolling again, Debbie had another strike and pushed the button on the electric reel. At that same moment, the left long outrigger bait popped out of the pin, and Rolan hooked a nice dolphin. That time of the year, dolphin usually swam in pairs. Like magic, Bob's right long outrigger bait popped out of the outrigger pin, and he had hooked another fish, which ended up being a thirty-pound bull dolphin. Debbie was catching a kingfish while Edie was catching a bonito, and Rolan and Bob each had nice dolphin on and jumping, all at the same time. Machine Gun was good; he put all the fish in the fish box and had new baits out in moments.

By then we had a mixed catch of about thirty-five fish in the box, and Rolan wanted each of the girls to catch something really big. I had Machine Gun rig one of the smaller bonitos with a 12/0 hook and some heavy leader wire. There was a small wreck in about 180 feet of water close by. It was usually good for a snapper or two and a few groupers. Jewfish or goliath groupers liked this spot for some reason, and I usually caught three or four a year while fishing for them with large baits. While I moved offshore to find this spot, the two girls finally had time to change into their small colorful bikinis.

Machine Gun put the bonito on Debbie's electric rod and reel and dropped the bait to the bottom. After ten or twenty seconds, the rod started to bounce. I put one engine in gear, and Machine Gun told Debbie to push the button. The rod bent over, and Debbie had hooked something big. With line pulling off the reel on a heavy drag setting, I knew it must have been a shark or jewfish. At that time the renaming of jewfish to goliath grouper had not taken place.

Machine Gun lifted the forward part of the rod, and Debbie pushed the button as he lowered the rod to the transom. This procedure is called pumping. It let Debbie gain two or three feet of line each time he lifted and lowered the wire line rod. The base of the rod, called the butt, had a quarter-inch pin that went through the gimbal of the chair and rod butt, making it impossible for the rod to fly out of the chair.

I kept the boat headed into the current, and Debbie and Machine Gun started to gain some line. All the big groupers we caught from deep water started to float as they got close to the surface. It wasn't long till we saw a big yellow and black grouper float up behind the boat. It was a 150-pound jewfish. They always look larger than they are because the pressure near the bottom is much greater than at the surface. This pressure causes groupers, Cubera snappers, and jewfish to have their stomachs pushed out of their mouths and their eyes bulge out of their heads. After we loaded the 150-pound fish in the boat, we dropped another big bait with no success. We did catch four mutton snappers from ten to fifteen pounds off that spot before we started trolling again.

Rolan wanted Edie to catch something big, so I moved to the east to try one of my secret spots in more than 350 feet of water. September is a great month for warsaw grouper fishing off Miami. We caught a few schoolie dolphin (two or three pounders) while I lined up on a good area of rough bottom where we sometimes caught warsaw groupers, snowy groupers, and kitty mitchell groupers. Machine Gun put a rigged ten-pound bonito on Edie's electric reel and sent the bait down to the bottom when I slowed the boat. Conditions were good, with a slow north current and clear blue water. He hit the bottom and brought the bait up twenty feet, and we waited.

It was not long till the tip of the wire line rod started bouncing. I put one engine in gear while Machine Gun had Edie push the button, and the rod bent over, with line screaming off the reel. I liked a very heavy drag for warsaw grouper fishing—that way they rarely got back in the wreck.

While Rolan and Bob were cheering for Edie, both of the long outrigger ballyhoo baits snapped out of the pins, with large dolphin jumping. Both guys caught their dolphin while Edie was still tussling with the big warsaw grouper. After gaffing and putting both big dolphin into the fish box, Machine Gun went back to lifting the rod, and Edie pushed the button as he lowered the rod. It was not long till a 250-pound brown and white warsaw floated up behind the boat.

Since both of the gals had caught something big, I trolled west to the edge of the Gulf Stream and turned north toward downtown Miami, knowing the kingfish would still keep biting. About a mile before the Sea Buoy, I saw a sailfish behind the bonito strip fished on the left short outrigger rod and gave Machine Gun a shout. He dropped back the bait and hooked the sail. It went ballistic and jumped and tumbled out of the water. Both the girls had their bikini tops untied and were half asleep sun bathing. Bob saw the sailfish jump and called down to Edie to get in the short outrigger chair and catch the fish. As she excitedly leaped out of the wire line chair, her bikini top fell to the deck.

Sometimes we raised two or three sailfish at a time, and that day was no different. I saw another sail behind the right long outrigger bait and quietly moved to the rod and watched the sail eat the small ballyhoo. With only one engine in gear and the boat idling ahead, dropping back and hooking the sailfish was easy. Rolan saw the sail jump and called Debbie up to the bridge rod to catch the fish. Halfway up the bridge ladder, her untied bikini top fell off. That did not slow her down in the least. This was my kind of day! We had two sailfish on and jumping and two beautiful topless gals screaming and laughing. Machine Gun put the two sailfish in the boat, and Rolan pointed toward the dock.

We backed in a little earlier than normal that day, but Rolan still paid well, with a big tip. Most important, we kept all the fish to sell. Machine Gun and I walked Rolan, Bob, and the girls, who were now nicely dressed in shorts, blouses, and high heels, to the waiting limo. Debbie and Edie gave me kisses and Debbie said, "I want to do this again." As the limo drove away, I thought about the day—two sailfish, a big warsaw, a jewfish, four snappers, thirty mixed-size dolphin, forty kingfish, and dozens of big bonitos all caught in less than six hours. I bet the girls would like to do this again. So would I!

CHAPTER 14

Pier 5, Miami, Florida, October 16, 1971 Captain Red Hagen Mates on the *Sea Boots*

Red Hagen helping to pull a jewfish onboard the Sea Boots. Captain Bill Harrison and Mate Red Hagen. Pier 5 Miami, Florida October 16, 1971

It was Saturday, and Red Hagen was mating for me. I was running Buddy Carey's second boat, the *Sea Boots*. Red worked for Alan Fogg, running his boat, the *I-NU-IT-TOO*, and had the weekends off if Alan was not using the boat. Red had mated for Buddy in the early 1950s, so

A YOUNG FISHERMAN'S DREAM COME TRUE

it was easy for him to work the cockpit of this *Sea Boots*, since it was set up like the Norseman-built boat he had spent five years working on.

For several years Paul Hendry, his best friend Lester, and a few friends would drive over from the west coast of Florida and go fishing with me. They all owned big ranches and starred fence lines (whatever that means). I considered them the perfect charter party, since they would take only one mutton snapper each and leave the rest for the crew to sell. Bottom fishing during October usually produced lots of mutton snappers ranging in size from eight to fifteen pounds. It was easy to give the party five or six muttons and keep the majority of other fish to sell.

Paul's favorite kind of fishing day started by trolling wire lines on the shallow reefs as we headed toward Beacon A. At that time, in 1971, Beacon A was a floating buoy the same size as the Sea Buoy off Miami's Government Cut. The coast guard would anchor Beacon A in different depths, since it broke loose in the winter during rough weather.

There was no loran or GPS back then, so the coast guard looked at Triumph Reef and guessed where to drop a giant piece of concrete used to anchor the buoy. That was where Beacon A would stay till another big blow took it away by breaking the huge chain that held the buoy to the block of concrete. One year it was in sixty feet of water, and twelve months later the coast guard anchored it in one hundred feet of water.

I ran down Biscayne Bay early that morning and went out by Cape Florida Light House. I cut all the markers short (to the west), since I knew the water well. Once I reached thirty feet of water and was over the reef, I slowed the *Sea Boots* to trolling speed, and Red put out the electric wire line rods. These were two 12/0 black Penn Senator reels with twelve-volt electric motors that Buddy had adapted to the handle sides of the fishing reels.

We used long leaders with a feather and bait to troll for groupers. The feather weighed three and a half ounces and had a lead head with white chicken feathers. The bait was a mullet strip. I took twenty or thirty whole mullet each morning and cut them for reef trolling. Putting the mullet on its side, I started the knife at the mullet's lips and cut the head in half, going over the backbone and down to the tail. With my razor-sharp knife, I split the tail. One more cut to remove part of the loose skin in the stomach area and the strip was a perfect trolling bait to catch groupers.

Once we got to Long Reef, a mile and a half below Beacon A, we had six black groupers, three barracuda, five bar jack, and a bunch of cero mackerel in the fish box. I then headed offshore while Red got the electric reels ready to drop to the bottom to catch mutton snappers. I had seven different land ranges that always produced great catches of mutton snappers off the Long Reef area.

Paul was ready with a large mug of rum in one hand and a cigarette in the other. He liked sitting in one of the back chairs so he could fish one of the electric wire line rods. He would push the button with one hand and hold his mug of rum in the other while always keeping a cigarette in his mouth.

The Fathometer showed a large cloud of fish over the rock formation in 160 feet of water. The Fathometers we use today are so much better, with all the colors to help identify fish, wrecks, and bottom structures. When I slowed the boat and gave Red a nod, he dropped the left wire line down to the bottom with a special-cut bonito belly strip. Once Red reached the bottom, he immediately moved to the other wire line rod, placed the two-pound lead weight in the water, and dropped the rig to the bottom with another tasty bonito strip.

Just before Red got to the bottom with the second rig, Paul pushed the button, and his rod bent over with a fish. Moments later Lester was hooked up to a fish also. Both fish were mutton snappers, and Red had them in the fish box and was rigging two new bonito strips. I again lined up on the land range, and in less than one minute the wire lines were down to the bottom and fishing. Two more strikes and two more mutton snappers in the fish box, both in the ten- to fifteen-pound range.

The Gulf Stream flows north off Miami and the upper Keys most days, and that day it was going in that direction slowly, at just under two knots. I lined up on the ranges, and Red sent the baits to the bottom and brought each up ten feet. The rods bent over with fish, and Paul and Lester were whooping and hollering as their rum sloshed out of their mugs. As I lined up on the land ranges, Red came up the bridge ladder and told me one of the muttons was partially scaled. This meant a big grouper or jewfish had been drawn to the commotion of us catching mutton snappers. I slowed, and Red dropped both electric rigs to the bottom and brought them up ten feet.

Paul knew what to look for and pushed the button when the rod tip of his outfit started to show action. Lester did the same. As I watched the fish being wound to the boat, Paul's rod bent over double—something big had eaten his fish. I had Red use wire leaders on all our snapper baits so the fish would not be lost to sharks. Catching a half-eaten snapper was still worth money at our dock. Red lifted the snapper Paul had caught and showed me the completely scaled fish. Since this was the second snapper to be grabbed by a big grouper or jewfish, I was going solve the problem.

Red ran the boat in a big circle while I got out one of the barracudas we had caught trolling over the reef on our way to Beacon A earlier. The smallest barracuda in the fish box was two feet long, and I cut the backbone out, making it easier for the bait to fold up in a big black grouper's or jewfish's mouth. I put a 12/0 Mustad double-strength hook in the bait and fifteen feet of #15 leader wire to the drop weight before I went up the bridge ladder to take the wheel. Red went down and set a heavy drag on the 12/0 reel.

When I lined up this time, Red dropped only the barracuda bait on Paul's electric reel. It wasn't long before Paul shouted with his Southern drawl, "He's lickin' it," meaning the barracuda was being eaten. I put the boat in gear, and Paul pushed the button. The wire line rod bent over the transom with so much drag, Paul could not lift it off the back of the boat. Charlie, one of Paul's friends, walked back to help Paul catch the fish—meaning he took over drinking Paul's mug of rum and started smoking Paul's cigarette while Paul struggled to lift the rod.

The tussle went on for about fifteen minutes before Paul, huffing and puffing, started to gain some of the wire line. Charlie reminded Paul, "If you didn't drink so much rum and smoke so many cigarettes, you could wind that critter right to the boat." Paul was not in good shape, and we all were not sure for a while who was going to win. Paul finally did win, and a big jewfish floated up behind the boat. It was a nice one, just over three hundred pounds.

Time to move to the next spot and try dropping some live bait. Charlie and Lester wanted to catch something big, so I had Red rig a live pigfish on each electric reel with heavy leader wire. In the fall this particular wreck frequently had Cubera snappers living around it. Red dropped the first rig for Charlie and brought it up off the bottom ten feet. He then dropped Lester's live pigfish and positioned it just above the wreck. Once both rod tips were bouncing, I put the boat in gear, and Charlie and Lester pushed the buttons on their wire line outfits. The electric motors whined, and the rods bent over with big fish. The electric motors were strong enough only to wind in the slack line. They were not able to winch up fish from the bottom.

Watching the violent shaking of both of the rods from my captain's chair on the bridge, I thought Charlie and Lester might each be fighting a Cubera snapper. It wasn't long till Lester's dark-orange fish floated to the surface. Red gaffed the forty-pound Cubera snapper in the lower jaw and lifted it over the transom and into the fish box. Charlie was having a much more difficult time with his fish. Paul continually reminded Charlie, "Hell, if I were catchin' that varmint, it'd already be in the box." Once it had floated and Red had gaffed the snapper in the lower jaw, Lester and Charlie had to help Red put the eighty-seven-pound snapper in the fish box.

We dropped some more smaller live pigfish and caught only four or five twenty-to thirty-pound amberjack. Paul did not like catching amberjack, so we went back to the reef and started to troll our way back to Miami. We caught a variety of fish all the way past Fowey Rocks Light House, with the bulk being black groupers. We did have one nice thirty-pound kingfish right before we wound all the lines in and ran for Pier 5.

Red and I cut one mutton snapper for each person. The party jumped in Paul's station wagon, waved their mugs of rum, and started driving home at three fifteen to avoid the Miami rush hour traffic. Three hours and two bottles of rum later, they were in Paul's Fort Myers driveway.

CHAPTER 15

PIER 5, MIAMI, FLORIDA, NOVEMBER 6, 1971 FAT FREDY WORKS THE COCKPIT

250 pound warsaw grouper onboard the Sea Boots. Captain Bill Harrison and mate Fredy Harvey. Pier 5 Miami, Florida November 6, 1971

It was Saturday, and Fredy Harvey was mating for me on Buddy Carey's second boat, the *Sea Boots*. Danny Worthington had chartered me for a full day of fishing off Miami. A yellow cab pulled up at 6:30 a.m., and out jumped Danny with his girlfriend, Maria. Danny introduced himself and Maria to me and told me this was their first deep-sea fishing trip ever. I helped both get aboard the boat and introduced them to Fredy, who had brought a thermos filled with black coffee from the

Park Lee Restaurant across the street that was owned by our friend Sweet Relish. He poured both Danny and Maria mugs of java.

Within a few minutes, a black limo pulled up carrying Bentley Montemour. He wore a snow-white suit highlighted by an orange ascot, and two gorgeous gals in stiletto heels and skin-tight dresses accompanied him. All three stumbled to the boat. Fredy and I welcomed them aboard, and we were off. Pier 5 was located at the base of Fifth Street at the west end of Government Cut. As we went out of Government Cut, Bentley shared his knowledge about the port, the rum-running days of Miami, and all the gangsters who lived somewhere around South Beach. I smiled and nodded at his vast knowledge, but I knew he was full of sh**.

Once we reached 120 feet of water, the ocean turned deep blue, and I slowed the boat. Fredy put out two electric wire line rods for Bentley's two girls, Natalie and Coran. Maria, up on the flying bridge with me, did not want to fish. The wire lines had twelve-volt motors on the handle sides of the reels and were fished from the chairs closest to the fish box in the back of the cockpit.

Fredy threw two rigged bonito strips over the side for me to let out from the two flying bridge rods. I had two fishing chairs in the bridge that I fished the long outrigger rods from. I free spooled the line out to the mark and passed the mark to Fredy. He put each mark in the long pin of the two outriggers and pulled them to the top of the outriggers.

Fredy snapped two rigged ballyhoo on the short rigger rods that were pinned to the short rigger chairs in the cockpit and let them out to the marks before running them up the outrigger. The bonitos and kingfish were biting fast and furious for Natalie and Coran, who were sitting in the wire line chairs. They pushed the buttons on the electric reels, and the fish kept on coming to the boat.

It did not take long for the two girls to figure out that sitting sidesaddle in a fishing chair while wearing skin-tight dresses was not the way to enjoy a beautiful fall day of fishing. Luckily I had a couple of pairs of jogging shorts in the storage locker, and both girls changed out of their sexy, tight dresses and into the jogging shorts. They both declined the T-shirts I offered them by saying they wanted to get suntans. Maria had brought a small flowered bikini and changed also.

The electric reels were catching kingfish every few minutes, and the bonito strips trolling from the flying bridge rods were producing big bonitos just as fast. Nothing was eating the ballyhoo fished from the short outriggers. Bentley was up with me, sitting on the bridge bench seat, watching but not wanting to wind in any fish. Danny was jumping from left outrigger to right outrigger rod, catching big bonitos every two minutes.

Bentley suffered through one full hour of great fishing before he went down the bridge ladder and disappeared into the bathroom. For the next twenty minutes, everyone listened to the sound of seasickness. Bentley eventually emerged from the bathroom and was whiter than his suit. He passed out on the engine box cushion.

By noon the *Sea Boots* had reached Fowey Rocks Light. I had counted forty-some kingfish and more than thirty bonitos that had gone in the fish box. I turned the boat and headed offshore to try bottom fishing on some of my secret wrecks in three hundred to four hundred feet of water. November sometimes has some good warsaw grouper fishing off Miami.

Fredy, nicknamed Dock Box, was a Pier 5 captain who ran several charter boats out of the old wooden dock and knew the value of selling fish. He was a great bottom fisherman and loved to catch snowy, mystic, and warsaw groupers. I had him rig a six-pound bonito with a 12/0 hook and fifteen feet of heavy piano wire and snap the bonito and lead weight to one of the electric reels.

A YOUNG FISHERMAN'S DREAM COME TRUE

Natalie wanted to be the first to try to catch a big grouper. As we trolled down the 120-foot color change catching kings and bonitos, she squealed with excitement every time her rod had a strike. Once I passed over the first deep-water wreck and positioned the boat to drop the bait, I couldn't get Fredy to look up at me. He was too busy staring at Natalie's big, beautiful bare breasts.

Fredy finally pitched the six-pound bonito over the stern and carefully lowered the two-pound bank weight to the water. Down to the bottom went Natalie's rig. She was sitting in the wire line chair and cheering like a Dallas Cowboys cheerleader while she waited for a grouper to bite. Fredy looked up at me with a cigarette hanging out of the side of his mouth and said, "Go." He was quite a bit older than I was and had caught hundreds of big warsaw groupers, so I didn't question him. I put both of the *Sea Boots*'s engines in gear.

Natalie pushed the button, and the wire line rod bent over the transom. She squealed as the wire line raced off the Penn Senator 12/0 reel with a very heavy drag. Once the excitement slowed, Fredy got the routine down, with him lifting the front of the wire line rod up and Natalie pushing the button on the way down. This put a couple of feet of wire back on the reel each time Fredy raised and lowered the rod. The grouper would pull ten or so feet off the reel, and Natalie would gain fifteen or so back. I kept the boat in gear so the grouper would not get back in the wreck. It was not long till a two-hundred-pound warsaw grouper floated to the surface behind the boat.

Coran was the next angler. Fredy had a bait ready to go when I passed the boat over the wreck. I gave him a wave, and Coran's bonito was going down to the bottom. Fredy and I had an easy routine for bottom fishing that our customers liked. Once a big fish was hooked and the rod was bent over the transom, Fredy would wait for the fish to calm down; he then started lifting the forward part of the rod, and the angler pushed the button as he lowered the rod down. Natalie danced around the cockpit and cheered Coran as she fought the big fish. It was not long till a 125-pound warsaw grouper floated up behind the boat.

Freddy dropped another bonito bait to the bottom as Natalie jumped back in the chair and hooked a real tugger. She knew what to do now and pushed the button every time Fredy lowered the wire line rod. This fish was a real fighter, and Natalie's thumb was starting to hurt when the warsaw grouper finally floated. It was a nice-size grouper, well over two hundred pounds. Maybe two hundred and fifty pounds.

Before we could load the fish into the boat, a school of big dolphin ate the four outrigger baits, and we had two squealing topless girls, four jumping dolphin, and a floating two-hundred-plus-pound grouper behind the *Sea Boots* at the same time. Fredy gaffed the four dolphin and swung them into the fish box, and I came down from the bridge to help him pull the grouper over the stern of the boat. Luckily Danny gave us a hand. The grouper was larger than I'd thought.

As I lined up on my land ranges, Coran sat down in the wire line chair. The routine was the same. Fredy dropped a bonito to the bottom and brought it up twenty feet. Something big ate the bait, and Coran and Natalie started squealing as the wire line rod bent over the transom, with line pulling off the reel. Once the fish slowed down, Fredy started to lift the front of the wire line rod while Coran pushed the button on the way down. After a few minutes, a small warsaw floated to the surface. This one looked to be less than one hundred pounds.

Coran got another chance, since her last grouper had been so small. I lined up the boat and passed over the wreck at trolling speed. Once we were far enough past the wreck, Fredy dropped a bonito to the bottom. Coran was sitting in the fighting chair, and Natalie was sitting on the transom, with one leg overboard and one leg inside the boat, watching the tip of the wire line rod.

A YOUNG FISHERMAN'S DREAM COME TRUE

Once the rod started to bounce, Natalie squealed, and I knew a fish had eaten the bait. I put the boat in gear, and Coran pushed the button. She was again hooked up to something big. Fredy started lifting the front of the rod, and Coran pushed the button. It wasn't long till both girls squealed as a warsaw floated up behind the boat. Another puppy—about one hundred pounds.

Danny had had enough of watching the two girls catch groupers, so we went back and trolled toward the blue-water edge. After we caught some more kings and bonitos, we were attacked by a school of baby sailfish. November is the prime month for catching very small sailfish off of Miami.

That day we had a sail behind every bait. I hooked two on the small bonito strips that were attached to the bridge rods, but Fredy could not hook the small sailfish on the larger ballyhoo. He gave up and pitched a bonito strip over the back of the boat that was snapped on a small rod with a red 4/0 Penn Senator reel and immediately had a bite. Natalie climbed the bridge ladder and started catching the sail on the right long outrigger line, and Danny started winding in the sail on the left long outrigger rod.

Fredy was trying to buckle the rod belt around Coran as she was fighting the small sailfish. He was unsuccessful, because her large bare breasts were bouncing around as she cranked the fishing reel. Finally Coran stopped jumping up and down, and Fredy got the rod belt buckled so she could catch her fish. Fredy put all three sailfish in the fish box, and Danny said, "Take us home." Bentley was still passed out on the engine box cushion.

As we entered Government Cut that afternoon, we passed close by a departing cruise ship. The two topless girls danced around the cockpit and waved to the hundreds of cheering passengers. About five minutes from docking at the Pier 5 marina, Danny came up the bridge ladder and paid me. He then took care of Freddy very well.

Unfortunately I reminded Natalie and Coran that I needed my jogging shorts back. They then changed back into their tight cocktail dresses. After the *Sea Boots* was docked, the girls woke Bentley, who looked worse than death. Once the cabs arrived, Fredy and I got a couple of quick kisses from Natalie and Coran. The two cabs drove down Fifth Street, and I never head from any of the five again.

CHAPTER 16

BIMINI, BAHAMAS, MAY 8, 1972 THE FIRST BLUEFIN TUNA OF THE YEAR

526 pound Bluefin tuna. Angler Joe Lopez's first Bluefin tuna caught on the Jingo with captain Bill Harrison and mates Copperhead Rolle and Laughing Sam. Blue Water Marina Bimini. May 8, 1972

It was Monday, and I was running Joe Lopez's Merritt, called *Jingo*, with two Bahamian mates named Copperhead Rolle and Laughing Sam Lavarity out of the Blue Water Marina on North

Bimini. I frequently fished Joe Lopez on a freelance basis for tournaments in many different locations throughout the Bahamas. I had flown in on a seaplane owned by Chalks International Airlines out of Miami, with Barkey Garnsey and Billy Black, who were mating for captain Billy Baum on Dick Shubot's boat the *Bobby Bell*.

Joe had bought the thirty-seven-foot Merritt from a famous lady angler named Dorothea Lincoln Dean. The boat had a great history of catching tuna. Joe had owned a thirty-six-foot Prowler-built boat named *Banjoe*, which he'd fished in many different places, but he had always dreamed about catching a bluefin tuna in the Bahamas. That was why he'd bought the *Jingo*, which was specially designed for catching tuna in the Bahamas. The two Seamaster gas engines were great for bluefin tuna fishing, since the small propellers threw very little white water behind the boat when we were baiting schools of tuna, and the gas engines gave an instant response when fighting these big fish.

Copperhead Rolle's two brothers were also fishermen. Manny owned a charter boat in Bimini named *Golden Bill* and at one time weighed the largest marlin ever caught in the Bahamas at Weech's Dock. Shoestring, his older brother, ran a forty-one-foot Hatteras for the Landwier family, who owned a beautiful home on Porgy Bay that faced the shallow-water side of Bimini. Copperhead and I had worked together on many boats.

Laughing Sam was a living legend on the island of Bimini. He had worked for all the greats who fished out of the island, including Ernest Hemingway and Michael Lerner. Unfortunately he was at the end of his fishing career, and the cheap price of rum on the island had taken its toll on him.

He had gotten his name from the cheerful attitude he always had at the dock and while fishing. Sam's first wife had died, and he'd then married a much younger Bahamian lady from Nassau, named Maybelline. She had a reputation for severely punishing the young Bimini kids who took money out of Laughing Sam's pockets when he would stumble home drunk from fishing a long day.

The bluefin tuna migration started late that year because of the lack of wind out of the south. In order to fish tuna in the Bimini-Cat Cay area, the wind must blow out of the southeast to the southwest. This gets the seas and waves rolling north. The bluefin tuna get a push from the northbound waves the same way a surfboard rider does, except the tuna swim below the surface of the water. The northbound tuna get this energy-saving push as they head for their summer feeding grounds off the New England coast.

The spring of 1972 brought one of those crazy weather phenomena where the wind did not blow at all. In the Bahamas we had day after day of no wind and calm seas. The Bimini and Cat Cay tuna boats went out in the morning and turned around and returned to the dock. Bluefin tuna fishing in the Bahamas is a sight fishery. Without wind from the south area of the compass, only a rare school of pushers would be seen. These tunas would push small waves ahead of their heads on calm days.

That Monday we departed with high spirits for our first day of looking. Tuna fishing involves two crew members to ride the tuna tower all day, looking for the schools of tunas that are swimming in a northerly direction. Copperhead rode the tower with me as we ran south to Gun Cay Lighthouse, and then I slowed the boat down to about ten knots. The Cat Cay tuna boats were all on the edge of Tuna Alley, gently rocking in the calm seas, since there was no wind blowing.

After a half hour of watching all the Cat Cay boats return to the dock, Joe asked me to come down from the tower to have a powwow on what to do. I recommended a place ten miles south where I always caught cero mackerel around the time of the full moon. Joe said, "Great," and we were off. While the boat ran south, Copperhead and Laughing Sam made rigs of small Jap trolling feathers on wire leaders. Cero mackerel have sharp teeth and will bite through everything but wire.

We arrived to find perfect conditions, so I stayed in the tuna tower to look for pushing tunas while running the boat through the area where I had caught cero mackerel before. Copper put out a feather tied to a 4/0 Penn Senator reel mounted on a small rod and instantly had a strike from a cero mackerel. Laughing Sam put out a spinning rod with the same bait and hooked another cero. Joe did the same with another spinning reel and hooked up. The mackerel were everywhere that flat, calm day.

The guys in the cockpit had caught at least forty cero mackerel, which weighed from one to ten pounds, when I looked inshore and saw a group of small waves that was characteristic of tuna pushing their way north in the shallow water of the Great Bahama Bank. Since the tuna rod was in the fighting chair and the leader wire and split-tail mullet were snapped on and ready to fish, I shouted down to the guys to get ready to bait a school of pushers.

I ran the *Jingo* a quarter mile north and waited for what I hoped to be a school of pushing tunas swimming their way north in the calm sea. The tuna gods were on my side, and six bluefin appeared like ghosts swimming just below the surface of the shallow water. Copperhead threw the mullet to the left of the cockpit while Joe let the 130-pound test Dacron out to the short mark. Sam stood behind the fighting chair, steering it to make the unlimited rod point toward the bait.

The group in the cockpit had to have total trust in me, since there was no way they could see anything that would make them feel that a school of tuna were swimming toward the bait. I was looking off to the side when that magic moment happened, and all three in the cockpit yelled at the same time. I looked behind the boat and saw a giant explosion as one of the tuna inhaled the split-tail mullet.

I immediately turned the boat to keep the fish from heading offshore, where it would dive deep in the Gulf Stream water. Luckily this tuna was easy to turn back toward the east, where it sprinted on top of the shallow water. The tuna swam as fast as it could, throwing a mass of white water behind its powerful tail, with us in the *Jingo* close behind.

Sam was steering the fighting chair while Joe cranked the reel and Copper pointed at the fleeing tuna from the starboard corner of the cockpit. This high-speed chase was great for us; the tuna would eventually tire because it could not keep swimming at this fast speed.

As I chased the tuna bow first from the tower of the *Jingo*, the powerful fish kept swimming much farther than I thought possible. The bluefin tuna abruptly gave up in ten feet of water in the middle of a huge white-sand area. Copperhead wired the fish while Laughing Sam gaffed it in the right shoulder, and I came down from the tower and put a meat hook in the lower jaw of the exhausted fish. Joe opened the tuna door, and all four of us pulled the fish into the cockpit of the thirty-seven-foot *Jingo*. Victory was ours!

Since this was the first bluefin tuna of the 1972 season, we ran for the dock to weigh it. This would be the first time I had ever caught the first tuna of the year. On the way north to Bimini, I saw the *Bobby Bell* trolling, with Barkey Garnsey and Billy Black in the cockpit making tuna baits while Bill Baum looked for tunas on this flat, calm day. I made sure to run very close to them so I could point down at the tuna in the cockpit, in case they did not see the flag.

On our way into Bimini Harbor, Laughing Sam saw his son, Sherman, and told him to go get his stepmother to see the weigh-in of the fish. Joe always liked staying at the Blue Water Marina, since it was small and quiet compared to the larger Bimini Big Game Club. It took about thirty minutes to find the owners of the two sailboats that were rafted in front of the dock with the gallows and scales, which allowed Sherman to round up Maybelline and as many neighbors as possible.

The dockmaster of the Blue Water Marina, Frank Hensey, waved me over to the finger pier while we waited for the owners of the sailboats. He told me to go to the Bimini Big Game Club and weigh in our tuna. The crew that weighed in the first bluefin of the season at the Big Game Club would get a hundred-dollar bill from the manager, Bill Garcia. That was big money back then, so off we went.

The crowd of mostly Bahamians migrated north two blocks to the club while we backed up to the gallows and scales. The bluefin weighed 526 pounds, and Bill was there to make sure the Bimini Big Game Club got credit for the first tuna of the season. Bill encouraged everyone in the crowd of onlookers to take lots of pictures of him shaking my hand in front of the sign that said "Bimini Big Game Club." He then handed me the hundred-dollar bill and was off to the club office about as fast as Laughing Sam guzzled his first rum and Coke.

Shirley, who was Maybelline's neighbor and was tending bar at the Big Game Club, heard we were leaving and ran out to be photographed with Laughing Sam's fish. She was a sexy Bahamian lady who enjoyed posing with American boat owners next to their catches.

A YOUNG FISHERMAN'S DREAM COME TRUE

Being best friends with Maybelline, she invited her in for a free drink or two. By the time Maybelline and her two friends departed the Big Game Club bar and headed for the Blue Water dock, they were already celebrating.

After about fifty people posed for pictures with the big tuna, we loaded it in the cockpit of the *Jingo* and idled back to the Blue Water Marina to unload the fish and cut it up for the eager Bahamians, who love to eat these big fish. Sam had his second rum and Coke on the short ride back to the dock and was pouring another as we put the dock lines on the boat.

By the time the tuna was cut up and given away, I had lost count of how many rum and Cokes Sam had consumed, and so had he. Since I had only a bunch of twenty-dollar bills, I gave Copperhead two and Laughing Sam two. I ended up with the short end of the stick, but I was still happy for this special day in my life—catching the first bluefin of the season.

Maybelline and her friends arrived at the dock to find Sam sitting on the tuna's severed head, with a rum drink in one hand and big cigar in the other. The tuna head made a perfect chair. He had just stood up and wrapped his arms around Maybelline, saying how much he loved her, when Bill Garcia stomped up and started screaming about me deceiving him by weighing our tuna at the Big Game Club and not paying for dockage at their marina.

He then demanded the hundred-dollar bill back! I looked over at Laughing Sam, who was stumbling up the dock with Maybelline's arms around him for support, and I told Bill I had just put the money in Sam's left pocket and to reach in and take it back. When Maybelline saw Bill reach in Sam's left pocket and pull out some money, she gave him a roundhouse punch that would have sent Mike Tyson to the canvas. Bill staggered back, holding his right eye, and fell to the concrete dock, hitting the back of his head on the power pedestal, splitting the skin. This caused blood to flow.

The next day I heard that Bill Garcia had been hit over the head during a robbery, and he'd had to go to the Bimini medical clinic to have six stitches put in the back of his head. I never heard how he got the black eye of the century.

CHAPTER 17

Pier 5, Miami, Florida, April 16, 1973 The Mysterious Mr. Jones and Mr. Smith

362 pound warsaw grouper caught on the Sea Boots. Captain Bill Harrison and Mate Bobby. Pier 5 Miami, Florida April 16, 1973

It was Monday, four days before Good Friday, and I was running the *Sea Boots*, with Bobby mating and "Mr. Jones" and "Mr. Smith" as my charters. They owned several check cashing stores and jewelry shops, and all of us at the dock knew these were not their real names. They always arrived early in the morning in a black limo, accompanied by several gorgeous gals. They were a charter boat captain's dream. They paid on the spot in cash and always left a big cash tip without ever taking a single fish.

The week before Good Friday was our best fish-selling week of the year: everyone wanted fresh fish for the holidays, and the amberjack schooled over all the wrecks off Miami, so catching a boatload to sell was easy. Amberjack love to eat live pinfish, which moved into the marina area each winter and spring to eat the scraps we threw in the water. With fifteen charter boats all cleaning fish and throwing ribs and backbones in the water every day, the pinfish could feast.

Every afternoon a group of kids showed up to catch pinfish for ten cents each. All I did was give them a five-gallon bucket and a heap of cheap spinning rods. For five or ten dollars, I could have my live-bait well filled with enough live pinfish to catch a thousand dollars' worth of amberjack.

The fastest and easiest way to catch a lot of amberjack was to use two electric reels that I fished from the back two chairs in the cockpit, near the fish box. Buddy Carey, the owner of both *Sea Boots*, had adapted an electric motor to the handle side of a 12/0 Penn Senator reel. The reel was filled with 120-pound test Monel or stainless steel wire and was mounted on a solid glass rod with case-hardened guides, so the wire line would not wear through the loops on the guides. A big swivel tip with a large roller was used at the end of the rod.

Glamour girls love to fish with the electric reels because they can sit in the sun and get tanned while pushing the buttons on the reels without ever breaking any of their manicured nails. I didn't think the girls who rode along that day worked with animals at the local humane society, but their names were Kitty and Bunny.

As soon as I slowed the boat to trolling speed, Bobby had the ballyhoo out and up to the long outrigger tips. He did the same with the short outrigger rods. I fished the long baits up in the two long rigger chairs on the flying bridge. If there was no one riding up with me, I could hook fish and leave the rod in the chair gimbal till someone climbed the bridge ladder to catch the fish.

The bottom of the rod, called the butt, was drilled to match a similar hole in the chair gimbal. I then put a stainless steel pin through both so the rod could not fly overboard when the fish was pulling line off the reel. I used 9/0 Penn Senators filled with pink eighty-pound test monofilament line for all my fishing outfits.

Bobby went to work on setting up the drop rigs for fishing live pinfish baits for amberjack. I liked to take a metal clothes hanger and put a two-pound bank weight at one end and then make a loop at the other end. I then made a small circle with the piece of the hanger that went over the wooden clothes rod. Then I passed the leader wire through the small circle and snapped it to the top loop of the clothes hanger. I also snapped the fishing line that went to the fishing reel to the top loop. This cheap rig never tangled.

I was trolling in a southerly direction about a quarter mile from the first wreck that I wanted to fish when Bobby said, "Left long." I had been staring at the screen of the Fathometer and did not see the thirty-five-pound bull dolphin chasing our long outrigger ballyhoo. Once I hooked him, I left the rod in the gimbal of the chair and slowed the boat down. The bull dolphin's girlfriend started swimming toward the right long ballyhoo and soon was hooked and jumping also.

Since Bobby had worked with me for a long time, he knew to send the two bikini-clad lovelies up to catch the dolphin. Bunny was a squealer and squealed till her dolphin was gaffed and in the fish box. Kitty could not believe how beautiful these gold, green, and blue fish were. When she had her fish close to the boat, I told her to go down, lean over the side of the boat, and see the beautiful colors more closely. I also told Bobby to hold on to her waist so she would not fall overboard. Yes, Bobby and I had worked together for quite a while.

There were only two dolphin I could see, so I continued trolling south till I passed over the wreck. Bobby pitched the pinfish behind the boat and let the line out till it reached the bottom. He then pushed the button on the electric reel and brought the bait up thirty feet. Bobby put Kitty in the chair, and I put the boat in gear as the rod bent over, with an amberjack pulling wire off the electric reel.

Bobby put another pinfish on the other electric reel and threw it behind the boat, letting it out till the two-pound bank weight hit the bottom. It too had an instant strike. Bunny left the bridge to catch the amberjack. Mr. Smith and Mr. Jones climbed the bridge ladder and started laughing at the girls in the wire line chairs, who were squealing and laughing like ten-year-olds as they pushed the buttons on the electric reels.

Bobby gaffed both amberjack and put them in the fish box while I moved the boat back in position to drop two more live pinfish on the electric reels again. When the first bait was almost to the bottom, a fish ate the live pinfish, and Bobby pushed the button, hooking the amberjack. Kitty was a veteran by then and knew what to do with the fish. Bobby dropped the second wire line to the bottom, and Bunny studied the roller tip, waiting for it to bounce. Sure enough, she asked Bobby if that was a bite, and he told her, "Push the button." She did just what Bobby said and then yelled, "Fish on."

A YOUNG FISHERMAN'S DREAM COME TRUE

After catching five doubleheaders in a row, we were attacked by a school of large dolphin. Mr. Jones, sitting in the right long bridge chair, was the first to have a bull dolphin eat his ballyhoo. Next was the right short, which Bobby hooked; then he moved Kitty into the short rigger chair to turn the handle. Next was the left short ballyhoo, which Bobby hooked, and he moved the ever giggling Bunny into the chair. Finally I saw another female, or cow, dolphin swim over and eat Mr. Smith's left long ballyhoo. All the dolphin were between twenty and thirty-five pounds.

I asked Mr. Jones, who always handed me the cash and was a man of very few words, if he wanted to catch some more amberjack, and he just gave me a thumbs-up.

Bobby was the best charter boat mate I ever had. He knew by the way I ran the boat that we would be fishing for amberjack for quite a while, without me saying a word. The more jack we caught, the more money we both made.

I slowed the boat, and he sent Kitty's bait to the bottom and brought it up thirty feet. He then told her, "Push the button when the rod tip bounces." Before he had Bunny's bait to the bottom, Kitty had a big jack on and fighting. With the bait in position, Bunny concentrated on watching the rod tip. All of us in the flying bridge heard Bunny squealing, "Bobby, Bobby, Bobby." All he said was, "Hit the button."

When the wrecks had that many amberjack around them, I used heavy leader wire and a 10/0 3412-C hook—a double-strength hook that would never straighten out. I wanted to catch as many fish as possible in the shortest amount of time.

The two girls were now almost as good as a regular charter boat mate. They knew exactly when the rod tip bounced enough times to push the button and when to stop the reel as the clothes hanger rig almost reached the rod tip.

As we were fighting our tenth or eleventh doubleheader of amberjack, Mr. Jones's outrigger bait popped out of the clip, and the spool clicker started to make noise as the unknown fish slowly pulled line off the reel. Bobby simply shrugged his shoulders when I looked down at him asking if he saw the fish.

Both girls were still fighting fish on their electric reels as the boat moved slowly south, with only one engine in gear. Frequently while we were bottom fishing, we caught small blacktip sharks on the ballyhoo that acted exactly like this by pulling off line slowly and not jumping, so I did not pay much attention to the line being pulled off the reel.

After Bobby gaffed both amberjack and put them in the fish box, I maneuvered the boat so Mr. Jones could gain line on the fish he was fighting. It stayed deep, but after ten minutes Mr. Jones was gaining line. Bobby, who was always ready for every situation, had his cotton gloves on and the long-handle gaff out in case he needed it.

Sitting in the helm chair, I saw Bobby gaff the fish and pull it over the starboard covering board and into the cockpit. When I looked down, I was surprised to see a seventy-pound blue marlin lying motionless on the deck. Kitty immediately went over and touched the fluorescent blues and silvers on the fish's fins and body.

Mr. Smith asked the two girls if they wanted to catch some more amberjack, and both said yes. Back we went till we had more than forty amberjack in the boat. Mr. Jones pointed toward downtown Miami, and I turned the *Sea Boots* in a northerly direction and headed toward the Miami Sea Buoy.

Reaching a great color change in about twenty fathoms (120 feet), I turned and trolled north for about ten minutes, then I saw a sailfish behind the right short outrigger. I called down to Bobby, who hooked it on the first shot. He got Kitty in the chair, and she was a great angler. The right long ballyhoo popped out of the outrigger pin, and I asked Mr. Jones if he saw the fish as I dropped back the bait. He indicated no with his hand, so I pushed the drag lever up and wound the slack out of the line. As the boat moved forward, the rod bent over with a second sailfish jumping.

Mr. Jones looked at me and pointed to Bunny, so I called down to her. She had no idea what was happening. She climbed the bridge ladder, and Mr. Jones pointed to the chair with the rod bent over and the line being pulled off the reel. She jumped into the chair like a star.

Once she realized a sailfish was on her line, it was like Christmas morning. She squealed and screamed till Bobby had the fish in the boat. With both sailfish in, Mr. Smith said, "I think it's time to go home." We ran for the marina and got to the dock a little earlier than the rest of the charter boats.

After we were tied up and the girls had changed out of their bikinis, the black limo pulled up. Bunny wanted to lay all the fish out so everyone could see what she had caught. I looked at Mr. Jones. He pointed toward his limo. I told Bunny, "Next time."

She knew what was happening. She gave me a big kiss and said, "This was my first time fishing."

Bobby climbed out of the cockpit just in time to have Bunny and Kitty both hug and kiss him over and over. As the limo drove away, I said to him, "Wow, I didn't get that!"—referring to being kissed by both girls at the same time.

Bobby smiled and said, "I bet you didn't get Kitty's phone number either" as he held up a piece of paper.

I said, "No, but I did get Bunny's." And I held up the piece of paper she had pushed into my pocket!

CHAPTER 18

BIMINI, BAHAMAS, APRIL 14, 1975 THE FIRST BLUEFIN OF THE SEASON

703 pound Bluefin tuna and angler Yohannes Hekimian. Caught onboard the Miltown II with captain Bill Harrison and mate Steve Tellam. Bimini Big Game Club April 14, 1975

I was fishing out of the Bimini Big Game Club on the forty-five-foot Hatteras *Miltown II*, with Yohannes Hekimian as the angler, and Steve Tellam was the mate. A late-season cold front had almost arrived, so the wind had swung clockwise to the south at twenty knots. Luckily I had brought along my bluefin tuna outfit, which consisted of a 12/0 Fin-Nor reel filled with 130-pound test Dacron line and an unlimited rod built by Biscayne Rod Company. I also had some split-tail mullet for tuna baits in the freezer.

Even though I had grown up fishing out of Bimini as a kid, I still enjoyed seeing the clear water around the docks that had everything from huge sharks to small tropical fish swimming together. That morning there were several big orange starfish under the boat on the white-sand bottom, with a dozen blue parrot fish swimming by. A group of bar jack had a massive school of glass minnows pushed against the side of the boat, turning the clear water to foam as they ate the minnows for breakfast.

As we were casting off the dock lines, a couple of the mates wished us good luck because we would be the only boat on the edge in Tuna Alley looking for bluefin tuna. Tuna Alley is an area of light-blue water that starts about one half mile north of Cat Cay and runs south for over ten miles, separating the deep-blue water from the reef area of the Great Bahama Bank.

The schools of bluefin tuna swim north in the Gulf Stream and sometimes come up in the shallow water of Tuna Alley and ride the northbound current over this strip of sand bottom that runs from 80 feet to about 120 feet in depth. Since these fish average from five hundred pounds to more than eight hundred pounds, seeing their dark bodies is easier over the light-colored area of Tuna Alley.

There was a huge snow-white sandbar that ran just to the west of Bimini that the boats had to cross when they departed the harbor to go fishing. On that particular day, this one-mile-long area had a big sea rolling over the bar, with lots of white water, which was a good sign for tuna fishermen. Any time there are big waves out of the south, the schools of bluefin will be on top of the water, enjoying the push they get from the northbound waves. The migrating tuna rarely eat as they head to their northern feeding grounds. April is usually too early to count on seeing schools of bluefin, but some fish get the biological urge to migrate a little earlier or later than the main group.

Once the boat was over the sandbar, the huge waves made me run the boat at a slow speed as we headed south to Tuna Alley. After traveling a couple of miles that way, I went up the tower leg to the top of the tuna tower and started looking.

Bluefin tuna fishing is simple. You head south until you see a school of northbound tuna, then you turn away from the school and run a ways north to get ahead of it. Then you slow the boat to about ten or so knots while the mate and angler put the bait out roughly two hundred feet. While keeping the boat ahead of the school, you drive back and forth, presenting the bait to most of the fish in the school. Sometimes you get a strike on the first school, and other times you might bait fish for days without getting the big bite.

All the way down the edge to Gun Cay Lighthouse, the conditions were great. Incoming tide, clear water, and lots of big northbound waves. Even though it was early in the year, I was positive we would see tuna. About a half mile down Tuna Alley, I saw the first school of twelve tuna riding a big wave north straight ahead of the boat.

Even though it had been ten months since I had baited a school of tuna, everything went perfect—except getting a strike from a tuna. After making five or six passes with a perfectly rigged split-tailed mullet while headed north in the Gulf Stream, I gave up and started looking for another school of northbound tuna.

It took over an hour to find another school. Just inside of Tuna Alley, a group of twenty fish came swimming down a series of big waves. I circled offshore and ran ahead of the school as Steve threw the split-tailed mullet behind the boat, so Yohannes could let it out to the short mark on the Dacron line.

As I turned the boat and made the second pass ahead of the school, I saw a huge shower of white water where the mullet used to be. Both Yohannes and Steve yelled; the battle was on. Being off shore of the fish was good for the rundown, since tuna usually try to head offshore in the shallow water. It was fishing at its finest when we had a seven-hundred-pound tuna up in thirty feet of clear water swimming over a white-sand bottom.

The bluefin was headed toward Cat Cay at fifteen knots, with the *Miltown II* racing behind, bow first. When the tuna finally slowed, it was in less than thirty feet of water and over the whitest sand in the area. Yohannes was good at putting huge amounts of pressure on big marlin or tuna, and that day he was at the top of his game!

Once the fish tired, it turned on its side. Yohannes went into kill mode. He was up in the air, growling and leaning back in the fishing harness, with sweat pouring off his back, holding the spool of the 12/0 Fin-Nor reel so no line could leave the reel. Since the tuna was on its side, the shine coming off its seven-hundred-pound body was a Kodak moment. I called a captain friend of mine who was reef fishing just west of me to come over, since his boss was a great photographer, and this was a very rare thing to see. The captain ran over, and he and the owner of the boat took pictures from the top of the tuna tower while everyone else took pictures from the flying bridge.

With the tuna swimming on its side thirty to forty feet from the back of my boat, we could maneuver close for spectacular action

A YOUNG FISHERMAN'S DREAM COME TRUE

shots of this big, beautiful fish. On this charter I had only one mate, so wiring, gaffing, and landing this big tuna was going to be a challenge. The tuna started to tire and make big circles, called pinwheels, which was good because the fish would be very predictable as it gave up. Preparing to land this fish, Steve threw a pair of wet cotton gloves up to the bridge along with a pair of wire cutters for his safety. I'd had mates pulled overboard by large fish before.

The other boat pulled up alongside to watch and photograph the last of the show, since the tired tuna was now doing smaller and smaller pinwheels, with its head inches from breaking the water's surface. I told Steve to grab the leader wire as the tuna circled up, and I would go down the ladder and gaff the fish as Steve held its head out of the water.

All went as planned. I gaffed the seven-hundred-pound tuna under the right pectoral fin, and Steve and I both held its head out of the water. We were so lucky that nothing went wrong, because the other boat was alongside taking pictures with four different cameras. Yohannes climbed out of the chair and held the gaff while I put a tail rope around the bluefin's tail and tied it to the stern cleat. This meant we owned the tuna, so Yohannes jumped onto the fighting chair, flexed his massive biceps, and gave a victory yell for the cameras. The Ethiopian giant had again conquered the beast!

After lots of cheering from the other boat, they turned toward Cat Cay and ran for the dock. We now needed to get this enormous fish in the boat. Steve and I had done this before, with a little teamwork and the help of the windlass on the bow of the *Miltown II*. Steve went forward to the bow and got the one-inch-thick nylon anchor line while I put a meat hook in the tuna's mouth. Once I attached the anchor line to the meat hook, Steve activated the windlass, which was normally used to pull the boat's anchor.

I stood off to the side of the tuna's head with a heavy rope tied to the meat hook while Steve retrieved two feet of anchor line at a time. Each time he activated the windlass, I would pull the tuna's head sideways in the tuna door till it started to slide into the boat. It was like a gigantic bar of soap scooting across the cockpit floor. Yohannes tied the tuna's tail to the stern cleat, and I tied the head to the base of the fighting chair while Steve returned to the cockpit and shut the tuna door. We were off to the Bimini Big Game Club to weigh in the first bluefin tuna of the year.

I called the dockmaster of the club on the radio and had him notify the Bimini commissioner, since he liked to verify the weights of big fish weighed in at the club. The commissioner enjoyed posing for the cameras with the fish, and then he would hold out his hand for the customary thank-you tip.

The bluefin tuna weighed 703 pounds—far from my biggest, but it was special for all of us to catch the first of the year. At that time the Bimini Big Game Club gave $100 to the captain who weighed in the first tuna, so I was off to the Big Game Club office.

CHAPTER 19

St. Thomas, US Virgin Islands, July 1975 Harry Tellam's Greatest Day

Harry Tellam had booked me for two days of marlin fishing in St. Thomas. He lived on the island of Key Biscayne, Florida, and loved to fish. His son, Steve, had fished with me on the *Sea Boots* out of Pier 5 as a freelance mate for several years. Harry had produced three sons who all started off as fishermen and then moved on to other jobs.

Harry was a longtime champion of releasing sailfish off Miami and always had a dozen or more in the annual Metropolitan Miami Fishing Tournament, which was run by the *Miami Herald*, a landmark newspaper. The tournament ran from December 1 till the end of April. Harry deserved a lot of credit for his fishing accomplishments, since he frequently fished alone on his boat, the *Branch Office*. I think it was a thirty-five-foot Bertram.

Since Harry was sleeping on my charter boat, the *Miltown II*, to save hotel costs, he got to meet my two good friends who were also staying on their boat, which was docked at the Lagoon Fishing Center. This was the old marlin dock that was built long before American Yacht Harbor was completed. It was located in the Red Hook area of St. Thomas. Ralph Christiansen Jr. and Roy Camero had planned a long weekend of marlin fishing on Roy's forty-five-foot Hatteras, which was tied up next to my charter boat.

I had some fresh fillets of yellowfin tuna and wahoo I had caught the previous day, so Harry, our grill master, invited Roy and Ralph over. It was my job to make a big salad. As their contribution to the dinner, Ralph and Roy supplied several bottles of Bacardi rum.

Harry had never fished St. Thomas, so Roy and Ralph told some stories about the four or five years the three of us had fished the North Drop together. As I headed for my bunk, I knew the rum was getting the best of the factual part of the fish stories. I did not remember Roy and Ralph catching nearly that many blues or the blue marlin weighing as much as they were swearing to. Right before I pulled the cockpit door closed, I heard Roy say, "Harry, that eight-hundred-pound blue marlin jumped thirty times, right, Ralph?"

At six o'clock the next morning, everyone was ready to go fishing except Ralph and Roy. One engine on Roy's forty-five-foot Hatteras would not start. They came over and talked to me about possibly sharing the cost of the charter and then fishing with Harry. I told Harry both of these guys were great anglers, and he could learn a lot from watching, talking with, and catching marlin with them. They all agreed to share the cost of the boat.

One huge problem had to be solved. Ralph and Roy had never released a marlin in their lives. Ralph's father had started him off at age fourteen with a 229-pound marlin he killed, put in the boat, and weighed. Ralph had killed every blue marlin since then and truly believed he would continue this practice for the rest of his life. Roy had also killed every fish of his career.

We finally got Jerry Black, the owner of Lagoon Fishing Center; Ronnie Hamlin; and Nelson Applegate to witness Ralph shaking hands with all the above and saying, "I will release a blue marlin if I catch one today." If this happened, it would be the first released blue of his long career, which ended with well over six hundred documented blue marlin caught and released by him.

Once we reached the North Drop and the mate got the baits out, Ralph and Roy came up to the flying bridge to talk about our past, with all the great fishing and the beautiful ladies of the night. Ralph was laughing at Harry as we looked down into the cockpit and watched him adjust the footrest, the gimbal, and then the back of the chair. Harry even took his fishing gloves and put them in a bucket of salt water then laid them out on the seat of the fighting chair for quick access.

As we shared exaggerated stories of times gone by, Harry was yelling, "Fish on!" How embarrassing for us veteran marlin fishermen to look down and see a new entry in the marlin fishing circle sitting in a perfectly adjusted fighting chair with the harness correctly snapped on the reel and wearing fishing gloves on both hands. Worse still for me, the reel had more than half of the fishing line pulled off the spool.

The first marlin of the day was over three hundred pounds. Harry had brought a bunch of tags from the National Marine Fisheries Service center, since it was a short bicycle ride away from where he lived on the island of Key Biscayne. He insisted on tagging the blue himself and made sure I photographed him with the tag stick. The picture was used on the ICCAT brochure for the following year. International Commission for the Conservation of Atlantic Tunas.

Ralph and Roy, with over two dozen marlin each, decided to stay in the cockpit for the time being. They were going strike by strike in a prearranged rotation system. This means if a marlin attacks your bait and you miss the fish, you give all the fishing rods up. The entire cockpit goes to the next angler in line till he has a marlin strike.

It wasn't long till I saw a nice blue on the left long outrigger bait and shouted to Roy, since it was his turn. He had three good shots at the blue and could not hook the fish. Silence in the cockpit. Twenty minutes later I saw another blue on the right long outrigger bait and called down to Ralph. Five good shots at the marlin, and he never bent the rod. Now it was after twelve noon, and we were one for three, which meant we'd had three chances to catch a marlin and were successful at catching only one fish. Worse still, the fish Roy and Ralph had missed were very hungry and kept coming back and coming back to bite the bait.

Harry, being a gentleman, relinquished his turn, since he had already released a blue. It was Roy's turn again. Right away he missed a marlin less than two hundred pounds. Ralph was sweating bullets by then; he got his turn moments later and missed. Harry again said to Roy, "Your turn." The right outrigger bait popped out of the pin, and Roy was hooked up with a blue that wouldn't make three hundred pounds, but it was close.

After lots of jumps the marlin turned down sea, and Roy had a short battle till we tagged and released the marlin. Then the pressure was on Ralph. I looked back and saw a five-hundred-plus-pound blue marlin behind the left outrigger bait and gave Ralph a call, warning him of the big fish. Ralph was one of the best anglers at hooking blues in the world. The rod bent over, and we all said, "Got him on" to ourselves. Ralph was in the chair with the fishing harness snapped on the reel, and the marlin was pulling line off the fishing reel. What a relief!

This fish jumped a couple of times and headed down sea like a rocket. Ralph knew what to do in the chair, and I knew what to do with the boat. I spun it around, and we were off at full speed, heading down sea. Roy was steering the chair and keeping the rod pointed at

A YOUNG FISHERMAN'S DREAM COME TRUE

the line while Harry was seeing what teamwork was all about. Ralph, Roy, and I had done this for years, so there was little to be said.

The fish stopped swimming west and went straight down a couple of hundred yards then stopped abruptly. Ralph stood up in the chair, locked his legs, and pinned the spool of the fishing reel with his fingers. He was the best marlin angler I had ever run a boat for.

Roy, Harry, and Steve, the mate, kept looking back and forth between Ralph and me. No one said a thing. Ralph leaned back farther and farther, and the rod finally started to rise. One crank soon turned into two. With a slowed down sea angle, the blue marlin kept rising.

Soon Steve took a wrap on the heavy leader wire, and about the time he had two good double wraps, Ralph screamed, "Get the gaff! Get the gaff!" I watched Harry take two steeps outboard, where he deliberately stood on the flying gaff handle with both feet. His arms were crossed, and he was not going to move. Ralph was Roy's best friend, so Roy had no idea what to do.

I left the steering wheel of the *Miltown II*, went down the bridge ladder, and grabbed the tag stick, which was propped up in the corner of the cockpit. I quickly tagged the marlin in the left shoulder, reached for the pliers on the mate's belt, then clipped the leader wire, and the fish was history. We all watched it quickly swim away with the red National Marine Fisheries Service tag in its shoulder. Ralph had officially released his first blue marlin! He and I would team up to release most of the next three hundred blue marlin he caught.

Everyone at the Lagoon Fishing Center had been alerted of our arrival. Jerry Black's cute nineteen-year-old blond daughter, Luanne, had the dockside bar set up, and the party started once Ralph and Roy stepped off the boat.

CHAPTER 20

ST. THOMAS, US VIRGIN ISLANDS, AUGUST 20, 1975 THE FOUR ANGLERS FROM THE GREAT STATE OF TEXAS

Bambe standing in the back of the Miltown II as we run for the dock of the Red Hook Marina in St. Thomas USVI. Captain Bill Harrison and mate Red. August 2, 1975

Bobby Gladney had arrived from Houston, Texas, the night before and was due at the marina at 9:00 a.m. He had chartered me out of Pier 5 in Miami several times and enjoyed catching everything that swam. Each time he chartered me, he brought along his "nurse," Bambi, so I thought she might join him during this trip to St. Thomas.

While fishing with me in Miami, he had mounted a twelve-foot hammerhead shark along with a 282-pound warsaw grouper, plus a few amberjack and barracuda. If we caught a blue marlin in the next two days, I hoped it would be a big one, because it was going on his office wall.

Stanley, the driver I used, arrived on time, and Bobby strutted out of Stanley's cab with his cowboy boots on his feet, his cowboy hat on his head, and Bambi on this arm. Every captain and mate who hadn't departed the marina ran over and helped us get away from the dock. With a dozen well wishes and good lucks, we were off.

It was a beautiful day. The shallow water of the Red Hook area was clear, and the mangroves that lined the edge of the harbor still had lots of birds sitting on the branches from the night before. In St. Thomas nothing gets up early in the morning—not even the roosters. I told myself, *This is a good sign!*

I slowed the boat down when we got to the North Drop and started trolling. I was using what Red, my mate, called our "charter boat tackle." This was two 12/0 Fin-Nor reels mounted on two unlimited rods filled with green two-hundred-pound test monofilament line.

I had Red use three turns of heavy leader wire on all the baits. #15 piano wire breaks at 360 pounds of pull and is sold in one-pound coils; three turns, after a bait is rigged, is five feet. Once the swivel hits the rod tip, the fish is five feet away. This is the perfect distance for a mate to successfully reach out and gaff a blue marlin, wahoo, or yellowfin tuna.

Bobby and Bambi had napped in the air-conditioned saloon on the way out and were now ready for a fun day of fishing on the famous North Drop. Bobby climbed in the fighting chair, and Bambi went up the ladder to ride with me in the flying bridge. She was always fun and cheerful and had a great figure. After she caught me up on their travels for the six or eight months since our last fishing trip, she finally said, "Do you notice anything different?"

As soon as she had stepped out of Stanley's cab, I had noticed she had been doing more than going to the gym, so I answered, "Yes." She smiled and turned away from me. She reached her hands behind her back, grabbed the strings on her red bikini, and gave them a pull. She spun around and asked, "What do you think?"

I could not take my eyes off of her big, fabulous breasts, but I did manage to say, "They are beautiful!" She then went into detail about going from a "firm C" to a double D. I had to apologize for staring.

Bambi smiled and said, "You can look at them all you want. That's why Bobby bought them for me."

Bobby asked me to put a smaller rod out so Bambi could catch something other than a marlin. This was great for my crew and me, since Daddy O's restaurant, across the street from the marina, would buy everything we caught. I told Red to steer the boat, and I went forward and got the wire line rod and reel. As bait I put out a #3½ Drone Spoon, and we were ready for a wahoo or yellowfin tuna.

There was very little bait showing on the Fathometer and only a few birds diving on bait schools. But soon luck was on our side, and Bambi was winding in a sixty-pound wahoo. I will never forget Red's eyes when he saw her come down the bridge ladder not wearing a bikini top to catch the fish.

A YOUNG FISHERMAN'S DREAM COME TRUE

Bobby missed our first chance at a blue, which was good because it was a small fish, less than three hundred pounds. Bambi soon added another wahoo that was a little larger than the first. A short troll down the drop and we had another bite from a blue. We missed him on the left outrigger bait; he moved over to the right outrigger bait, and the rod bent over on the first strike.

This marlin did everything I could have asked for. It did six spectacular jumps and then headed down sea, with its back out of the water and its tail throwing massive amounts of white spray in the air. After a one-mile run, it went down about two hundred yards and stopped. Red pushed the drag lever to fifty or sixty pounds. Bobby wasn't the best angler, but he had lots of body weight and knew how to use the one-to-one gear ratio on the Fin-Nor reel.

Bobby was running out of steam, so he pushed the drag lever to a full eighty pounds of drag, and ten minutes later the fish came up dead, with rigor mortis. Red and I slid it through the transom door without using a gaff. Bambi was bouncing around the cockpit, excitedly hugging everyone. When she went inside for a bottle of champagne, I asked Bobby if there was a chance I could take just one picture of Bambi and the marlin.

Bobby's answer was simple: "No. I would hate for that to jeopardize her job at the hospital." I always noticed that Bobby never took off his wedding ring.

When we got to the marina, Jerry Black had the forklift ready to hoist the marlin out of the cockpit, and we all went over to watch the weigh-in. The scales went to 466 pounds—a nice blue marlin anywhere. As Stanley's cab pulled into the parking lot, Bobby handed Bambi a handful of hundred-dollar bills and sent her off to buy a dozen bottles of champagne.

Once the cab was out of sight, Bobby told me to get my camera, and he quickly posed alone for the usual dead fish pictures. When Bambi returned with a dozen bottles of bubbly, everyone in the marina got a couple of glasses or more of champagne to toast Bobby's success.

While Ronnie Hamlin and Joe Lopez, the owner of the thirty-seven-foot Merritt *Prowess,* started sharing fish stories with Bobby and Bambi, Red and I took our two wahoos across the street to Daddy O's restaurant. We each walked out with a quick $100, which was big money in 1975.

When Red and I finished washing the boat, I called Stanley, and he recommended we call Harbor View Restaurant to make reservations for the three of us. However, Red was not allowed to go with us, since he was married, and his wife still thought the twelve hours a day he put in fishing was fun, not work.

After a great meal at the Harbor View, Stanley dropped Bobby and Bambi off at their hotel and then took me to the marina, which was still when I walked to my boat. I thanked my lucky stars for such a good day. I'd gotten to fish with some nice people, I'd mounted a blue marlin, and I'd sold two big wahoos.

The next morning Stanley dropped Bobby and Bambi off at 10:00 a.m. Their clothing was more subdued than the previous day. On the way out, they relaxed inside the boat in the cold air-conditioning. Once Red had the baits out and we were fishing, Bobby climbed in the fighting chair, and Bambi went up the ladder to the bridge.

She looked great in a fiery-hot pink and yellow bikini. She never wore makeup during the day because she was naturally pretty. I liked her on the bridge because she enjoyed me pointing out schools of bait and the big frigate birds that circled overhead. Once in a while, I would spot a white tropic bird, with its tail that was three times longer than its body. Most of all she enjoyed seeing a shark.

The first marlin strike was a small fish, maybe 225 pounds. Bobby missed it on the left outrigger several times, and then the marlin moved over to the right outrigger. Again Bobby missed it. The next blue marlin was a small, fast fish that Bobby missed for several bites. As we were now on a down sea troll, every one saw the next marlin come out of a wave and clear the water before it landed on the bait.

Since Bobby had promised Bambi a chance to catch a blue, he felt the pressure to hook it for her. Once he had missed hooking the marlin, Bambi went down the bridge ladder and started rubbing his shoulders. She told him it did not make any difference if she did not catch a marlin.

As Bambi rubbed his back, she thanked Bobby for the two beautiful wahoos she had caught the previous day. She reminded him how nice his 466-pound blue marlin was going to look in his office. After a couple of sweet kisses on his cheek, Bobby made the mistake of saying, "If you hook a blue marlin on your own and wind it to the boat, I will mount it for you."

She almost drowned him in a flurry of quick kisses and said, "You are the best!"

Any charter boat captain who'd been around would have known what was going to happen next. Bambi got in the fighting chair (unfortunately wearing her bikini top) and started gesturing behind the boat, saying, "Come on, Mr. Marlin, come to Mama." She called Bobby over and gave him a long kiss on the cheek while giggling as Red yelled, "That's him!" I did not see the strike or the fish, but the rod bowed over, and Bambi was hooked up to a blue marlin.

I came down from the bridge and snapped the fighting harness to the reel. Since I had left one engine in gear, the marlin stood Bambi up in the chair. She dug her well-manicured fingernails into my forearm and said, "Promise me that I am OK."

I answered, "I promise, but I have to drive the boat."

When I got to the bridge, I looked back and saw a nice-size blue marlin gagging on the mackerel, with blood pouring out of its mouth. This fish was hooked deep in the gills and was spouting massive amounts of blood. The marlin did a couple of halfway jumps and started swimming down sea.

Bambi was in great shape, since she danced a lot at night, and she listened carefully to whatever Red told her. I had the boat spun around and was following the marlin down sea, watching the huge amount of bright-red blood trailing behind the swimming fish.

I was also watching Bambi in the fighting chair at a right angle to me. She was listening to Red and doing everything right, with her legs locked and her body high in the air, using her entire body weight to tire the marlin. She was actually doing better than most veteran anglers. Red would instruct her, "Lean back, now lean forward and take two cranks." After a couple of minutes, she looked up at me and gave me a couple of cute waves. I knew she was having fun!

The marlin kept pumping huge amounts of blood out of its body with every beat of its tail. With the blood loss and the heavy drag Bambi had on the fish, it gave up and died quickly, without a fight. Red and I pulled the dead fish into the cockpit of our boat. Bambi jumped out of the chair and gave Bobby so many small kisses, he couldn't breathe. She then grabbed Red and squeezed him so hard, he blushed. This was funny, since he was a local St. Thomian with a dark complexion. She then grabbed me, knowing what I liked, pushed her new big, beautiful breasts against me, and gave me a quick kiss. Bobby said, "Take us home."

Jerry Black had the forklift pushed against the bulkhead of the marina, so I backed under the two forks while Red put the nylon loop over the end of one, and the marlin was quickly up and out of the boat. Once I docked the boat, Red and I were out like a shot. We got to see Jerry read the scales at 402 pounds. A great first blue marlin for such a fun lady!

Everyone but me got to take pictures of Bambi in the colorful bikini with her first blue marlin. Bobby made me stand with him well in the background, so we were never captured in the same picture with Bambi and her marlin. Bambi was so sweet, she never questioned why Bobby could not be in the same picture with her.

Bambi had Bobby give Stanley, our cab driver, a handful of hundred dollar bills and sent him off for a case of her favorite champagne. Once Stanley returned with the champagne, Bambi, now dressed in an expensive outfit, invited everyone in the marina to celebrate her first blue marlin.

The champagne flowed for an hour. Everyone was feeling the effects of a long day in the hot sun. Bambi staggered over and wrapped both her arms around my neck. She then gave me a big kiss on my right ear and said she wanted to do something very special to thank me for the fun day. To avoid trouble I called Stanley and put Bobby and Bambi in his cab. Jerry Black quickly ran over and had Bobby sign the two taxidermy agreements for mounting both blue marlins. I often wonder what Bambi did with the thirteen-foot blue marlin in her apartment.

CHAPTER 21

St. Thomas, US Virgin Islands, August 8, 1975 Jim Lambert's First Blue Marlin

287 pound blue marlin. Angler Jim Lambert's first blue of his long fishing career. Caught onboard the Miltown II with captain Bill Harrison and mate Scottie. St. Thomas USVI August 8, 1975

A YOUNG FISHERMAN'S DREAM COME TRUE

My charter party was Jim Lambert and friends. I had never meet Jim, but he was very excited to go marlin fishing the times we talked over the phone. He liked to fish, but he said, "I have never been big-game fishing before." His father-in-law was a fishing fanatic from Key Biscayne who had steered Jim my way. Whenever someone tells a first-time charter party, "This guy is the best, you must charter him," it's like the kiss of death. Either the wind blows hurricane force and rain pours from sunrise to sunset, or the fish don't bite.

The summer of 1975 in St. Thomas was very dry, with less wind than normal and no rain. That took care of two of the variables. Now we needed to have a blue marlin bite. We had a great average size for blue marlin during June, July, and the first week of August. I looked forward to meeting Jim the next morning and talking with him on the way out to the fishing area.

Jim rode out to the North Drop with me in the bridge. He was a fun guy with great stories. Above all he wanted his sixty-five-year-old dad to catch a blue marlin. Jim had already picked out a place in his father's house to put the mounted marlin. Since Jim had never caught a blue, he also wanted to mount his first marlin. I learned later his two business partners wanted to mount their first blue marlins if they could catch them.

As we arrived at the North Drop, the water turned a deep blue. This was a good sign, since we had suffered with lots of off-colored water that slowed down the marlin fishing in July.

Things happened fast! The first strike was an acrobatic blue marlin that jumped ten times. After the fish calmed down and went down sea, Scottie, the mate, pushed the heavy drag up on the 12/0 Fin-Nor reel. It was not long till the marlin started to tire and turn brown. The exhausted fish gave up easily at the side of the boat. Scottie put one gaff in it's shoulder that was not really needed but was the insurance policy for not losing a blue marlin that was to be mounted.

I called Jim up to the bridge and told him to keep his dad out in the cockpit, because things looked good for another bite. And I was right. Immediately the rod bent over, with the green two-hundred-pound test line running off the 12/0 Fin-Nor reel, and Jim's dad was nowhere to be found. He was using the bathroom. Jim's other partner climbed in the fighting chair and went to work on the marlin. Like the first marlin, it ran down sea, with us going bow first after it. After fifteen minutes it went down two hundred yards and stopped. The angler went to a heavy drag, and it killed the fish. We pulled the blue marlin through the transom door located on the starboard side of the back of the boat, and the marlin looked to be a little larger than the first one. That took care of the other partner.

I told Jim having two bites and catching both was somewhat common, but going three for three would be rare. His two partners were now inside, asleep in the air-conditioning, so only Jim and his father were in the cockpit. Jim's dad was asleep on the drink box in the shaded corner when a blue came completely out of the water and landed on the flopping mullet we were trolling.

Seeing the marlin attack the bait, Jim jumped in the chair and started fighting the fish. Halfway into the battle, Jim realized this marlin should have been for his dad. The fish was a jumper. It must have gone into the air fifteen times before it took off down sea. It swam a long way before going down about one hundred yards. Jim was the best angler of the group. He pumped the tired fish up, and Scottie made a great gaff shot. Jim helped us pull his marlin into the cockpit.

By then it was two o'clock, and we had caught three marlin out of three different bites. It did not take long to have another bite. A blue marlin was on and jumping. Once Jim's dad was in the chair, the rod straightened up. We had pulled the hook, and, worst of all, we watched the fish swim away.

For over one hour, Jim concentrated on watching the baits in silence. Everyone knew how badly he wanted his dad to catch a blue marlin. As I turned the boat down sea and headed toward the corner, we had another strike. Jim had five good shots at a very hungry marlin, and we did not even bend the rod on this fish. Jim climbed the bridge ladder and was visibly upset when he said, "What are we doing wrong?" I told him we had caught three out of the five marlin strikes, and this was a good average for any part of the world where there are blue marlin.

As Jim went down the bridge ladder, and I reminded him, "Keep your Dad in the fighting chair." We were not fishing for world records; Scottie could pass Jim's dad the rod and snap the harness to the reel. I had to remind Jim he was on a charter boat and was fishing for fun!

While Jim was sitting on the transom, looking forward and talking to his dad, the left long bait popped out of the outrigger pin, and the rod bent over. Scottie was inside making a sandwich, and I was looking forward to see where we were on the North Drop. Jim's scream could have awakened a dead man! He was so happy his dad was hooked up! I had no idea if Jim was religious or not, but I did see him look up to the sky and say, "Thank you."

I had the boat slowed down, with one engine idling forward. We all watched the line slowly leave the reel, with a good bend in the rod. I first asked Jim and then his dad if anyone had seen the strike. No one had. At that late hour in the afternoon, catching a wahoo or yellowfin tuna was common, so I felt our luck might have run out. I told Scottie to push the drag up to fifty pounds. The line started flying off the reel. That answered my question. It was a blue marlin. Wahoo and yellowfin tuna cannot pull line off a 12/0 Fin-Nor reel like that!

By then Jim's two business partners were out in the cockpit cheering Jim's dad on. Everyone was looking back behind the boat about one hundred yards, where the line entered the water. One of the guests tried changing our luck by pouring cups of rum and passing them around the cockpit.

It worked—the rod bounced a couple of times, and a five-hundred-pound blue marlin shot straight out of a wave and headed toward us at a speed faster than my forty-five-foot Hatteras could go. "Greyhounding" is what marlin fishermen call it when a marlin jumps several times parallel to the water at a high rate of speed. That was exactly what this blue did.

The fish passed very close by our starboard side and kept on jumping. The plastic cups filled with rum slipped out of everyone's hands, since no one onboard had ever seen a five-hundred-pound marlin head straight toward them in the cockpit. Jim's friends later told the crowd at the dock, "We could have touched the marlin when it went by." I never told them how hard it would be to touch a blue, and anyway, both of the guys were on their knees peeking over the covering board when the marlin flew by.

Several blues have jumped in the boat, so when this fish first started greyhounding toward us, I said, "Not again." Even though I had both throttles pushed all the way forward, a twelve-foot marlin can accelerate faster than any sporting fishing boat. This was good! Jim's dad was in good shape and now was excited and ready to wind. Jim got to steer the fighting chair for his dad and give him some instructions.

When the fish came by the boat, it gave Jim's dad lots of time to retrieve the free line till we came tight with the marlin again. With a 14/0 Mustad hook and #15 piano wire, which breaks at 360 pounds of pull on two-hundred-pound test monofilament line, I had no doubt he would catch the blue marlin he wanted for his house.

Once the fish stopped jumping, we chugged west for thirty minutes with the drag advanced to sixty or seventy pounds. Nothing kills a blue faster than really heavy drag as the fish tries to swim down sea. I was the only captain fishing St. Thomas that year with only one mate, so I used five feet of heavy leader wire on all my mullet and mackerel. When the swivel touched the rod tip, the blue marlin was an easy gaff shot away for a mate, especially a good one.

I watched this marlin turn brown as it swam just ahead of where I was driving the boat from in the flying bridge. I had the fish swimming at the perfect angle for me to see everything that was happening. I could look down and see the guys in the cockpit and look ahead and see the marlin swimming.

Jim came up and told me his dad was tiring, so I accelerated and closed the gap between the fish and the boat. When Scottie looked up, I gave a nod. He put the flying gaff over the shoulder of the marlin and pulled the nylon rope tight on the stern cleat. The marlin had nothing left. The heavy drag had taken every bit out of the fish. We pulled the marlin through the transom door and headed for the dock.

Jerry Black had the forklift ready. Ronnie Hamlin was waiting at the bar with a blackboard ready for taking bets. Each fish would have guesses made, and Ronnie had created some formula that he deliberately made complicated so that the combined weight of the four marlin would pay a percentage to the top three bets. He would then decide how and where the money would go. This allowed him to pocket a larger percentage than normal. Nelson and Gloria Applegate were laughing at the carnival atmosphere. Nelson's mate, Lincoln, even stayed around for the weigh-in. Sandy and Donna Bartram were there that summer with their captain, Bill "Bull" Wilderman and Bobby "the German" Iban. Sandy's boat was the *Tintanio*, a forty-six-foot custom-built Broadhurst design.

Jerry put the fork over the cockpit, and we lifted the first fish of the day out of the boat. Three hundred and five pounds. At sea I had told Jim this fish would probably make three hundred pounds. I'd made a lucky guess.

The next marlin to be lifted out and weighed belonged to Jim's partner. The weight was 347 pounds. I had not guessed at this fish when wed been at sea. The next marlin was Jim's. I'd said it would not make three hundred pounds. It did not—only 287—pounds, but this was a great blue marlin for the first of an intensive marlin fishing career that lasted just short of thirty-five years. Now Ronnie and Sandy Bartram were doing the addition, which would make the last marlin pay off to some crazy formula that now had a handicap division. I was so happy I did not have any money bet with those guys.

Jerry moved the forklift over the cockpit and lowered it so I could put the nylon loop that was attached to the fish's tail on the end of the fork. I looked up at Jerry and gave the OK, and up went the marlin. Jim's dad was so happy to see his fish lifted out of the cockpit, because it was the largest marlin by far.

Jim's dad walked to the scales to watch the weigh-in as Jerry's teenage daughter, Luanne, handed him a rum drink. Jerry read the scales at 597 pounds. I am not sure who was the happiest, Jim or his dad. Jerry's daughter gave him a kiss on the cheek, as did Donna Bertram. This was his first saltwater fish. He was such a happy man. After fishing with this man, I could see why Jim was so proud of his father!

They have both since sailed on.

CHAPTER 22

St. Thomas, US Virgin Islands, August 20, 1975 The Crazy Texans

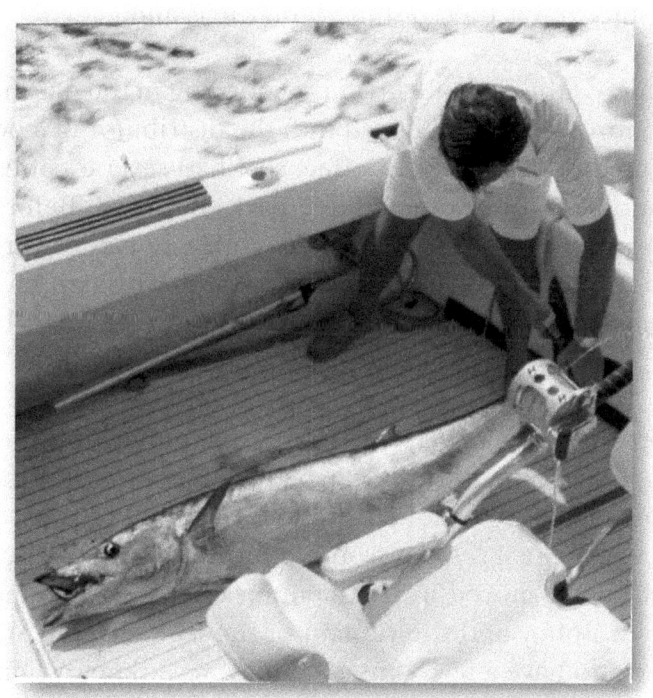

112 pound wahoo caught on the Miltown II. Captain Bill Harrison and mate Scottie. St. Thomas, USVI August 10, 1975

My Texas charters were always colorful and fun people. Mat Peacock and Dakota Perez chartered me out of downtown Miami's Pier 5 several times a year. When I told them I would be chartering out of St. Thomas for the summer, they both said, "Count me in!" Later they asked, "Where the hell is St. Thomas?"

Stanley, my St. Thomas driver, met them at the airport in Charlotte Amalie while I was fishing and took them to their condo. They arranged for Stanley to pick them up for dinner and to stay with them through the evening, going from bar to nightclub. I had recommended Harbor View Restaurant, so Stanley called ahead and made reservations. I had to dine with the charter party I'd been fishing with that day, since it was their last night on the island.

I was always the first one up in the morning in the marina and had a great routine. At Pier 5 I fished with the distributor of a popular all-in-one coffee pot called Mr. Coffee, so I had several coffeepots and a year's supply of preformed coffee packs onboard. Before daylight every morning, I would start brewing coffee in two or three coffeepots, and the marlin boat crews would wander over to my boat and pour themselves hot cups of coffee. I had just one rule—bring your own mug.

Bobby Eiben, a German, slept in the hammock on the east side of the Lagoon Fishing Center dock area. The owner of the marina, Jerry Black, had a small tan female mutt named Precious. Sometime during each night, Precious would jump up on top of Bobby as he slept and loudly snored in the hammock. This arrangement lasted all summer. Bobby and the captain of the *Tintanio*, Bill Wilderman, were known to have a few rums, so Bobby never knew when Precious decided to join him in slumber.

Most of the crews were gathered around my boat that early morning when Stanley pulled up in his cab with the Texans. Mat and Dakota

A YOUNG FISHERMAN'S DREAM COME TRUE

had two gorgeous gals with them, as always. It was easy to recognize Texans. All four wore cowboy hats, gaudy belt buckles, and cowboy boots. They stood out, since this was St. Thomas, where the dress code was sandals, shorts, and a blunt of marijuana. Stanley looked beat. He had driven them around to every nightclub and bar he could think of, and finally they'd ended up at a local bar in Frenchtown singing songs like "Home on the Range"—songs the local Frenchies had never heard or sung.

All the captains and mates loved seeing the cute cowgirls wearing their boots and short skirts. This day set a record; I had never had so many guys help untie the boat, push us off the dock, and wish us good luck. This was the first time the slowest boat in the fleet, the *Miltown II*, was the first boat to reach the North Drop.

During the one-hour-plus run to the Drop, Scottie, the mate, concentrated on sewing mackerel and mullet for our marlin baits. What I did not know was that Dakota had spun the air-conditioning thermostat so many times, he blew the breaker for the system. With no air-conditioning and two 8-71 GM diesels directly below the saloon floor, the boat heated up quickly.

Once I slowed the boat to trolling speed, I went down the bridge ladder to put a mackerel out in the left outrigger while Scottie put out a mullet in the right outrigger. After trolling several miles with no one in the cockpit, I asked Scottie to go inside the saloon and check on everyone. He came up to the bridge and said, "I looked through the bulkhead window, and I saw them all sleeping on the floor of the saloon."

It took about one hour before we had a marlin strike. The mullet was the first bait of choice. A small blue, about 215 pounds, was on and jumping. I was not concerned about not having an angler, since I was using two-hundred-pound test line and a 12/0 Fin-Nor reel. I told

Scottie, "See if anyone wants to catch a blue marlin." After checking inside he went to the back of the boat's cockpit, gave me a thumbs-up, and bent over laughing.

Laurie came stumbling out of the saloon door covered with sweat and wearing only snow-white thong panties. I had no idea all four had passed out on the way out with no air-conditioning. The inside of the boat must have been 110 degrees after two hours of running and trolling. All four had stripped to their underwear. Laurie crawled into the fighting chair and said, "What do I do?"

Since I was the captain, I went down to the cockpit and sent Scottie to the bridge to steer the boat. He did not know a clutch from a throttle or port from starboard. I thought this was a good time for him to learn. The first thing I did was ask Laurie to spread her legs, so I could put the rod in the chair gimbal. I then tried to snap the fighting harness to the lugs on the 12/0 Fin-Nor reel. This was one of the most difficult things to do when I had a blonde leaning forward with her very large bare breasts lying on top of the fishing reel.

I asked Laurie to lean back so I had enough distance to properly attach the reel. Even though her breasts were somewhat in the way, I managed to get the fishing harness properly adjusted and the rod ready to catch the marlin. Laurie and I laughed the entire time.

The marlin had long since stopped jumping and was dragging on the surface of the water some distance behind the boat. It took a while, but I carefully explained to Laurie how to put the reel in a one-to-one gear ratio. She was in great shape! She got that reel spinning like a pencil sharpener and wound the marlin to the boat like a pro.

Giving my full attention to Laurie, I was not ready to wire and tag this small blue. It took a while for me to find the gloves and tag stick. My earlier life as a charter boat mate came back quickly. I reached out and tagged the fish in the shoulder and had Laurie lean over the side of the boat so she could see her first blue marlin before I cut the leader wire and released it.

When she saw how beautiful the first fish she had ever caught was, she started to jump around the cockpit, spinning in circles and clapping her hands over her head. After I clipped the leader wire, I turned around just in time to have Laurie leap toward me, wrapping her arms around my neck and her beautiful long legs around my waist. I then got more kisses than I had received all summer on the island of St. Thomas.

Then Laurie told me how hot it was inside the saloon of the boat. I opened the door and went in to fix the breaker on the thermostat. I had to step over the three sleeping Texans to get to the control panel and solve the air-conditioning problem. I easily fixed it by throwing the breaker.

We were fishing again, and Laurie was sitting next to me on the flying bridge, telling me her life story, still wearing only white thong panties. We went a full hour before we had a marlin strike and missed it several times. After the mate put the baits back out and we were trolling again, Laurie started where she had left off and kept right on talking.

Finally we hooked a nice blue marlin. Scotty went inside the boat and woke Dakota. He came out blinking his bloodshot eyes and climbed in the fighting chair. He was wearing white boxer shorts with red hearts on them. The marlin jumped a few times, and Dakota started hooting and hollering. He then said something like, "This is more fun than riding a bull."

The marlin turned down sea, and we followed. Dakota advanced the drag a couple of times, and the marlin gave up. We pulled it through the door and positioned it out of the way on the side of the cockpit. Then Laurie went down to the cockpit to celebrate and jumped around and screamed while kissing Dakota.

Laurie banged on the saloon door and woke Mat and Bonny. They came out squinting their eyes and couldn't believe we had a blue marlin over four hundred pounds in the boat. Mat was wearing white boxer shorts with longhorn bull heads printed all over. Bonny was wearing only midnight-blue thong panties. Four adults walking around the cockpit in their underwear was a first for me.

When Bonny learned about Laurie's released blue, she pleaded with Mat to let her catch a fish, any kind of fish. I volunteered to put a wire line out to increase the chances of catching a wahoo, a tuna, or even a bonito. The wire line we fished was a 10/0 black sided Penn Senator reel mounted on a solid glass unbreakable rod with a swivel tip. The wire line was one-hundred-pound test Monel wire. Matt said, "Do it." Five minutes later we were trolling a wire line with a 3½ Drone Spoon bouncing three hundred or four hundred feet behind the boat for bait.

I headed the boat for the closest school of bait. The birds were diving, and the small skippies (skipjack tuna) were turning the water into a froth. Some kind of small Spanish sardines had been there for a month, and we got to see whale sharks feeding on the sardines on a regular basis. The wire line bent over with the clicker screaming, and a thirty-pound yellowfin tuna was on and tugging.

Once the tuna was in the fish box, I made another pass at the school of skippies with equal success. We put another small yellowfin in the boat. I lined up again, and we caught a nicer yellowfin tuna, about forty-five pounds. The owner of the restaurant up the hill from the marina had asked me for some wahoo, so I went back to the dropoff and looked for marlin or wahoo. Again the wire line had a strike, with a seventy-pound wahoo. During that summer I never caught a wahoo less than sixty pounds on the North Drop.

Bonny had caught three yellowfin tuna and a wahoo, so it was Laurie's turn. It was late in the day, and we needed to weigh Dakota's blue, so I turned toward the corner of the Drop and got ready to call it a day. With five minutes to go, the wire line went off with authority. The clicker on the reel sang, and Laurie screamed, "Its mine." She cranked the Penn Senator reel like a pro, still wearing only white thong panties.

Scottie needed help wiring and gaffing this wahoo, so I came down from the bridge. This was a nice fish, so I gaffed it in the head and had Scottie gaff it in the last third of its body. Wahoo have sharp teeth, so I moved everyone to the other side of the cockpit before we pulled the fish over the right side of the boat. I guessed it to weigh over one hundred pounds.

Now that the saloon had cooled off and we were on our way back to the dock, the Texan underwear group took turns showering and dressing. When we tied up the boat, I grabbed my camera and went to the scales. Dakota's blue marlin weighed 402 pounds, and I took lots of pictures with the pretty girls. Laurie's wahoo weighed 112 pounds, and Bonny's weighed 63 pounds. Dakota mounted his blue, and Mat would have to wait another day for his marlin. Daddy O's restaurant welcomed the three tuna and two wahoos. This was just another great day in my life.

Stanley picked us up, and we were off for an eight-thirty reservation at Harbor View Restaurant. Stanley had arranged for the piano bar to have our drinks ready, and Rudy, the piano player, was playing Laurie and Bonny's favorite old-time songs. Rudy reacted well to a folded hundred-bill the boss handed him. After dinner and a few more piña coladas, Laurie and Bonny were slow dancing with each other around the balcony to something from the movie *Casablanca*. Not long after, Stanley took the Texans back to their hotel. The departure time had changed from 6:00 a.m. to 10: a.m.

The next morning Stanley had everyone at the boat close to ten. We were the last boat to leave the dock. I set the air-conditioning thermostat as cold as I could while we were running. The Texans slept all the way to the drop, and we were trolling for a while before Laurie came up to the bridge. She was wearing a small blue bikini that matched her beautiful blue eyes. Immediately she picked up where she had left off telling me about her life. Her story was not as interesting as when she had been wearing only white thong panties.

We had a time schedule to keep, since our Texans were booked on a late flight out of Charlotte Amalie Airport. The bite did not happen till we were all the way out to the gun site. This is a visual lineup of land ranges we all used, since GPS had not been invented for boats at that time.

A blue marlin inhaled the small mullet I was fishing on the right outrigger, and the jumping started less than one hundred yards behind the transom. Matt finally had his blue marlin hooked and jumping. The marlin tired quickly on the heavy tackle, and Scottie gaffed it. Once we pulled the fish through the transom door, the two girls jumped and cheered. Both asked Dakota if they could fish the wire line for a while. Dakota and Mat were beat from the night before, so they said yes and went inside the air-conditioned saloon for a nap.

We had a ten-mile troll to the corner of the North drop. The wahoos cooperated and started to bite right away. The girls each caught three. Every fish was over sixty pounds. Once the boat reached the corner of the North Drop, which was the closest point to the marina, I tapped on the glass of the saloon door, and Mat gave me the sign to start running home. Two minutes later we were running to the marina. We needed to weigh Mat's blue marlin and write up the mounting information, plus everyone had to pack their suitcases for the flight home. It was nice to get in a little early.

The blue marlin weighed 316 pounds. It was a short, fat fish. We called Stanley and sadly said good-bye to the Texans—especially Laurie and Bonny. Having two gorgeous gals walk around the boat all day topless made fishing fun.

CHAPTER 23

ST. THOMAS, US VIRGIN ISLANDS, AUGUST 23, 1975 THE MIAMI GARDEN GROUP

It was Saturday, and the charter was Bob and Margie Mentelos's. They had flown in from Miami the previous afternoon along with Bob's sister, Carol. Bob and Margie owned Fantastic Gardens just south of Miami and were a great charter and fun friends who had fished a lot with me out of Pier 5. Several times, when I had finished a charter trip to Chub Cay in the Bahamas, they would fly in to fish one day and then ride home to Miami on the boat. We would dive some lobsters as we ran across the Grand Bahama Bank and anchor just before dark behind Gun Cay. Margie was a great cook and liked to make Lobster Diablo. This was a gourmet red-sauce-based meal with lots of garlic and chunks of lobster that she put over spaghetti.

The previous night we had gone to Harbor View, my favorite St. Thomas restaurant, for a spectacular dinner. Harbor View restaurant was high up the mountain, just behind the harbor in Charlotte Amalie, and gave the patrons a great view of the working harbor as a piano player sang some of the old songs of times gone by. After one of the best piña coladas on earth, the waiter nodded to us. We went inside the restaurant, where our table was ready, with salad and appetizers waiting.

Harbor View was famous worldwide for their desserts, which all the ladies swooned over. I have never enjoyed desserts; possibly it was because of my mother, who was a dental hygienist all her life. While she cleaned my teeth for one hour two times a year, she preached the evils of white sugar and sweets.

Bob, Margie, and Carol were staying in a nice condo close to the Lagoon Fishing Center in the Red Hook area called Cowpet Bay. Stanley picked them up at 9:00 a.m. and brought them to the marina so we could be moving at nine thirty. They enjoyed cups of coffee while we motored slowly out through the shallow water filled with mangroves and anchored sailboats.

The forty-five-foot *Miltown II* cruised at seventeen knots on a good day, so the twenty-plus-mile run gave my local mate, Ronnie, lots of time to rig mackerel, mullet, and ballyhoo. Every bait he put overboard had heavy leader wire because 1975 was a great year for big wahoo, which have sharp teeth. The conditions that day were the same as every day, with wind out of the east at fifteen miles per hour, and seas three feet tall. We had great visibility because there were only a few clouds and lots of sunlight. That was an exceptionally dry summer, so the clouds were few and far apart.

The fishing order was simple. Bob would get to catch the first blue marlin and Margie the second. If Carol wanted to catch a marlin and they were biting, she would get the next. Since I was chartering and had only one mate, I used a simple system. I fished two 12/0 Fin-Nor reels filled with green two-hundred-pound test monofilament line. The blue marlin in St. Thomas were very predictable and liked to jump a few times after they were hooked and then run down sea. We would get the angler in the chair and watch the marlin jump, and I would turn down sea and go bow first for about a mile, then turn the boat around once the marlin decided to go down.

At that time we went to fifty or sixty pounds of drag, just less than one third the breaking strength of the line, and let the fish pull for ten or fifteen minutes. Both the angler and marlin were tired by then, so we had a tired marlin swimming next to the boat that the angler could safely help tag, photograph, or gaff. I never liked those wild jumping fish that tore up the teak transoms or sides of the boat. My style was a slow, easy, and safe way that drew criticism from all the pros who ran the private boats that released blue marlin in less than two minutes.

After putting a mackerel in one outrigger and a mullet in the other, we waited all of ten minutes. With a typical St. Thomas strike, a four-hundred-pound blue attacked the mullet. Bob jumped into the fighting chair, and all of us watched the three minutes of spectacular acrobatics. Down sea went the marlin, with the old forty-five-foot Hatteras, *Milton II*, smoking behind. The heavy mono was easy to follow, and usually I could see the fish because its tail was out of the water. I liked to get a wave and a half behind the marlin, so the fish would have to pull line off the reel with a heavy drag as it went down the wave. Then we would get a push from the next wave, so the angler could easily regain the lost line with little effort.

After about one mile, we had the tired marlin alongside, and Bob tagged it while Margie and Carol took pictures. Back then we used National Marine Fisheries Service tags, so I quickly entered the weight on the card and left the info to be filled in at a later time. All captains have a fear of confusing tag cards at the end of the day and entering a fish's information and weight on the wrong card. A famous captain and good friend I knew never lived down the time he sent in a tag card for a tagged five-hundred-pound blue that was killed two years later and weighed in at 124 pounds. He had long since given up telling people they had caught and released two blues that day, a five-hundred pounder and a one-hundred pounder. Both were estimated weights on the confused tag cards.

After releasing Bob's blue, we were far to the west of the best fishing area, so I decided to point the bow into the big seas, put out the baits, and troll back to the North Drop. Once back on the edge, I turned left, and a 325-pound blue ate the mackerel and started to jump wildly. Margie was already in the chair sunning herself, so Ronnie snapped the harness to the lugs of the 12/0 Fin-Nor reel, and the battle started. Margie was a gorgeous redhead with an athletic figure. She always wore tight, sexy tops that had some extra buttons undone. That was why everyone on the dock of Pier 5 loved her!

The fish acted exactly like Bob's marlin but never went down. In just over forty minutes, Ronnie wired the tired marlin, and tired Margie tagged it. Once I brought my camera out, Margie started poising like nothing had happened. She loved the camera. I still treasure the many pictures I took of her on those beaches in the Bahamas when no one was around.

We trolled back to the edge of the North Drop and again had a bite. Carol was in the chair, and all one hundred pounds of her went to work on catching the first fish of her life, a three-hundred-pound blue marlin. This marlin followed the rules, and we were off toward the west at ten knots. Since Carol was very petite, her bikini-clad bottom never touched the seat of the chair.

The most important rule on my boat is simple: we were there to have fun! If the angler asked for help with catching a fish, the mate did it with a smile. Carol needed help and asked for it. Ronnie soon had the unlimited class rod resting on his shoulder. The marlin would pull line off of the reel as it swam down sea, and I would speed up a little when the fish bogged down as it swam up the back of the next wave. Carol would gain line until the marlin started down sea again, pulling the ultraheavy drag off of the reel. Soon Ronnie was assisting in the cranking also. Once the fish was alongside the boat, Ronnie wired the marlin, and Carol put a National Marine Fisheries Service tag in its shoulder. After a few pictures, we released the marlin, and it sprinted away in great shape. That was Carol's first fish ever.

As we returned to the drop-off, I saw a big school of small bonitos and skip jack. I asked Bob if we could catch some bait for the next day, and he agreed. He had fished with me many times out of Pier 5 where we'd caught and killed everything. I'd had a change in crew, so Ronnie was filling in for a while till my next mate flew in from Miami. When I brought the wire line rod and reel out, Ronnie was lost. Not only had he never seen a reel filled with Monel wire, he had never heard of trolling a wire line. I had a few rigged #3½ Drone Spoons ready, so I fired one out, and we were fishing.

With Bob now on the bridge and steering the boat, I told him to head toward the diving birds and splashing fish. I needed to show Ronnie how to fish a reel filled with wire line. It is a little difficult if you have never trolled with a wire line. I felt a little guilty for telling Bob I wanted to catch bait. The small yellowfin tuna had been there all summer, and I had been making a few bucks every day selling them and a couple wahoos to Daddy O's restaurant.

Once the wire line outfit was out and fishing, I asked Bob if he wanted me to steer the boat. He said no, since he was having fun driving through the diving birds. The bite happened, and, as I had hoped, it was a thirty-pound yellowfin tuna. Bob slowed the boat down and told Ronnie to wind him in. Ronnie had never had a charter tell him to catch a fish, so he jumped in the chair and loved it.

After catching a small yellowfin tuna and two skip jack, we caught another yellowfin tuna, about forty pounds. Bob had fished with me off of Miami, where we'd used a feather and a bait to catch wahoos in the deep water and black groupers trolling the reef, so this time he asked me to put out his favorite—a yellow feather and a bait. I said no, since I had caught too many blue marlin on the feather and bait rig and did not want to possibly lose all or part of my Monel wire.

Margie was in the cockpit looking at the yellowfins and skip jack. When Bob called Margie to the bridge ladder, I knew something was happening. Minutes later Margie had grabbed my hand and leaned forward, pushing her shoulders down and together, asking, "Could you please put out a feather and bait?" She had the most beautiful puppies, and I thought they might fall out of her unbuttoned shirt, so I said yes.

It wasn't long before I regretted my decision. A two-hundred-pound blue marlin had eaten the bait on the wire line and was jumping. Bob told Ronnie, "This one is yours." Margie steered the chair while Bob ran the boat, and I was the wire man. Much to my surprise, everything worked out perfectly, and we tagged and released the blue marlin. This was Ronnie's first blue marlin as an angler. Ronnie couldn't wait to tell his story to his dad, who owned a small charter boat in town.

Since it was getting late, Bob shouted from the bridge, "That's it for the day, folks" and pushed the throttles up, heading for what he thought should be Red Hook. After helping Ronnie clean up the cockpit for ten minutes, I went up to the bridge and saw we were heading for Puerto Rico and not St. Thomas. We had gone only a few miles out of our way, so a fun laugh was in order.

CHAPTER 24

PIER 5, MIAMI, FLORIDA, NOVEMBER 17, 1975 RONALD, THE STRETCH LIMO, AND THE THREE KIDS

Hammerhead shark and 160 pound jewfish caught on the Miltown II. Captain Bill Harrison and mate Tommy. Pier 5 Miami November 17, 1975

It was Monday, and an early cold front had just passed through Miami, giving us the most beautiful fall day imaginable. Two weeks earlier a black stretch limo had pulled up to the Pier 5 dock after most of the boats had returned, and a well-dressed man named Ronald asked several of the other captains where I docked. Ronald introduced himself and asked if I was available on November 17. When I said yes, he handed me an envelope and said, "I will be taking my three sons out fishing."

Trying to make small talk, I asked him, "Who recommended me?"

He turned around and said over his shoulder, "The boss." I watched him get in the back driver's side-door of the black stretch limo. I knew he was not telling the truth.

Dave Wolf, one of the older charter boat captains on the dock, walked over and asked about Ronald. Dave noticed he had not shaken my hand and asked about the envelope. I opened it and saw enough hundred-dollar bills to cover the charter in full, but no name, address, or phone number was included. Dave liked the stretch limo but thought Ronald was a phony.

Just before seven in the morning on November 17, the same stretch limo pulled up, and three well-dressed boys crawled out blinking their eyes. I recognized Ronald as he got out of the front seat door. He walked over to the upper dock and pointed to where the driver should place an expensive wicker basket filled with prepared food. The driver returned with a beautiful stainless steel cooler filled with drinks and imported bottled water. The three boys and Ronald were wearing sport jackets with gold buttons—odd for boys who looked to be thirteen or so going out fishing.

My mate, Tommy, helped me load the basket and expensive cooler on the boat and then turned to Ronald and stuck out his hand, saying, "My name is Tommy."

Before Tommy could finish, Ronald rudely interrupted by saying, "Tell the captain to get underway." Ronald then walked into the air-conditioned saloon without shaking Tommy's outstretched hand.

There was a light breeze out of the northwest, and the air had an Everglades smell that was characteristic of an offshore wind during late fall or winter in South Florida. Since it was such a pretty day, I chose to run the boat down Biscayne Bay and out by Cape Florida Light. One of the boys, who had reddish hair and freckles, came up to the bridge. I introduced myself and held out my hand. The kid shook it and politely said, "My name is Braxton." I asked about the other guys in the saloon and found out one was Winfield and the other was Ulysses. I thought, *We have the generals from the Confederate side of the Civil War fishing today.*

Braxton started asking some questions about the boat and what we might catch. I realized he was a nice kid, and it was going to be a fun day of fishing. About thirty minutes later, Winfield and Ulysses joined us on the bridge, and Braxton told them about catching sharks, amberjack, and groupers. Winfield was Braxton's older brother, and Ulysses was Winfield's best friend. I had the family figured out—or so I thought. I politely asked, "Is Ronald your father?"

Winfield glared at me and said, "That asshole is not our father, he works for our father." Luckily I had not been drinking coffee, because I would have spit it out all across the bridge.

The conversation about sharks continued, and all three boys talked about catching and taking home sharks. I shared my vast knowledge about mounting fish and what a great job the taxidermy company I represented did on perfectly preserving sharks. Pflueger Taxidermy was the largest in the world at that time, and I was very loyal to them. I even had a couple of large sharks mounted in my house, or so I said.

I called Tommy up to the bridge and told him about the possibility of mounting some sharks. His eyes got large as he saw dollar signs. I was hatching a plan to catch some barracuda for shark bait on the

A YOUNG FISHERMAN'S DREAM COME TRUE

shallow reefs before we moved to deeper water and tried fishing for them around some wrecks. Tommy had twenty ballyhoo rigged by the time I slowed the boat to try one of my favorite barracuda hot spots. Overboard went the ballyhoo, and the barracuda were waiting. The boys enjoyed this so much, I stayed till we had fifteen in the fish box, then I started trolling toward deeper water.

The plan was to catch some amberjack and groupers so we had something in the fish box and then try to catch a shark or two. Tommy would put Braxton in one fishing chair and Winfield in the other. The boys each would use a hand-cranked 10/0 Penn Senator fishing reel that was filled with Monel wire. I started by dropping a live pinfish to the bottom on each wire line rig, and immediately Braxton had an amberjack on and pulling. Winfield's rod bent over moments later, and we had a doubleheader.

While the two brothers were catching amberjack, both outrigger baits popped out of the long outrigger pins. Two nice dolphin were on and jumping. Ulysses grabbed the rod and started cranking. I called down to the boys, asking if Ronald would like to catch the other dolphin, since he was still inside the boat, enjoying the air conditioning. I heard a "hell no" from all three boys at the same time.

I let each boy catch four amberjack that averaged about thirty-five pounds per fish before I asked Tommy to rig a reverse ballyhoo on each wire line rod. This is a great bait for catching mutton snappers. After dropping both wire line baits to the bottom, Braxton immediately had a bite and hooked a fish while brother Winfield missed his nibble.

I went back to the wreck and dropped two more reverse ballyhoo for Winfield and Ulysses, and both caught mutton snappers. We tried again and caught a mutton on one rod and a scamp grouper on the other. All the boys were asking to catch something bigger, so I had

Tommy steer the boat in a big circle while I scaled a barracuda and cut the entire fillet off of each side. I was very good at cutting strips for groupers from all kinds of fish, especially barracuda.

I first scaled the 'cuda (a very messy job). Then I cut the two fillets from the backbone and trimmed each to a shape like a twelve- or fourteen-inch banana peel. The bait must be thin, so it slithers through the water. About the time I finished cutting and rigging the bait on heavy leader wire with a 12/0 hook, one of the outriggers popped out of the pin. It turned out to be a big bull dolphin. Tommy came down the bridge ladder and gaffed the fish while I went up the ladder and steered the boat back to the wreck.

The day was going well, with lots of nice fish and three happy kids. Once the boat passed over the wreck heading to the south, Tommy put the two-pound lead weight into the water and dropped the big barracuda strip to the bottom. He then moved over to the other wire line rig and did the same. Ulysses's rod tip started bouncing, so I put the boat in gear, and he started to wind the fishing reel. The wire line rod bent over with something big. Winfield brought his bait up so we could concentrate on catching whatever ate Ulysses's bait. After fifteen minutes of grunting, moaning, and groaning, Ulysses caught a 160-pound jewfish.

The boat was only two hundred yards from the wreck, so I quickly trolled back, and Tommy dropped the barracuda bait on Winfield's wire line rod to the bottom. We drifted past the wreck, and I was thinking about telling Tommy to wind the bait up when Winfield shouted, "Fish on." I put the boat in gear, and sure enough he was hooked up to a nice fish. I was hoping for a shark, but the rod was acting crazy, so I knew something was not right. It couldn't be a shark.

Twenty minutes later up came a two-hundred-pound brown stingray. Every two or so years, I caught one of these in the deep water while bottom fishing. They look like giant Portobello mushrooms, with long, skinny tails and pointed barbs used for defense. This is the same fish that killed the Steve Irwin, the Crocodile Hunter in Australia. We turned it loose.

The boys wanted to try to catch a shark, so I moved the boat to deeper water, and Tommy dropped a whole rigged barracuda to the bottom and put another rigged barracuda out of the outrigger near the surface. The top bait was on our shark rod with two-hundred-pound test monofilament line, and the bottom bait was on the standard 10/0 Penn reel filled with Monel wire. Winfield got the first bite and finally reeled in an eight-foot bull shark. This type had a huge head and very big teeth. It was the perfect shark!

So far our luck was beyond belief, and we set up again for shark fishing. The surface bait was the next to be eaten, and Ulysses was in the fighting chair, with the rod bent and the reel screaming. He was the best angler by far of the group and made quick work of a nine-foot hammerhead shark. It took all of us to pull the shark through the fish door in the back of the boat. The cockpit was filling up, with two sharks, a jewfish, two boxes of amberjack, and some snappers, dolphin and barracuda.

Again we set up to shark fish, with red-haired Braxton as the designated angler. It took a while for him to get a bite, but it was worth waiting for. A big shark ate the surface bait, and the fight was on. Braxton was the youngest of the boys and gave it everything he had. Soon he recruited Winfield to lift the rod while he used two hands to crank the reel. They soon needed Ulysses to lift the other side of the rod. This method is called pumping. While the older and stronger boys lifted the rod, Braxton wound the reel as they quickly lowered the rod.

I told Tommy to put on the wet cotton gloves and start pulling on the monofilament fishing line. What a sight. Tommy would lean over the stern, grab the line, and yell, "Pull" as Winfield, on one side of the rod, and Ulysses, on the other side, would lift. Braxton would then reel with two hands as they lowered the rod.

Soon Tommy yelled that he could see something very deep in the clear Gulf Stream water, so the group had renewed energy. The fish got closer and closer to the boat till we could see it was a big tiger shark. After Tommy put two large gaffs in the shark and we tied it to the side of the boat, everyone cheered—except Ronald, whom we had not seen all day.

We tried to pull the shark in the boat by ourselves, but it was impossible, so I sent Tommy to the bow to get the anchor rope. Once I tied the anchor rope to the shark's head, Tommy went to the bow and wrapped the line around the anchor windlass, which was extremely powerful. Tommy pushed the button to activate the windlass, which took two feet of anchor line at a time. He then waited for me to pull the shark's head sideways a little and repeated the process. Finally the tiger shark started sliding through the door. Once we got most of the shark in the boat, we all sat down and took a break.

Suddenly Ronald, who was sitting inside the air-conditioned saloon, beat on the glass panel facing the cockpit and pointed his finger at Tommy, motioning to him to come in. We then heard Ronald screaming at Tommy about getting to the dock. Tommy came out and told me the boat had to be at the dock at two thirty to meet the limo. I apologized to the boys, saying they had paid for an eight-hour day, so that was what I planned on giving them.

Winfield smiled at me and said, "Trust me, Dad's limo won't leave without us kids." I had a pretty good feeling Winfield was right!

Backing in the slip at Pier 5 was fun. The crowds loved seeing sharks. We pulled the hammerhead and bull sharks up on the dock easily, but we could not budge the big tiger shark. Some of the men in the crowd helped pull on the rope, but we were unsuccessful. One of the rednecks who came down to the dock to buy fish on a regular basis walked over to me and said, "Cappie, let me show you, fisher people, how we would do this on the farm."

He went across the parking lot and started his big red four-wheel-drive Ford pickup and backed up, jumping the curb. He was across the sidewalk and touching the upper dock in moments. He then pulled a Tarzan rope out of the truck bed and said, "Tie this to your fish." I tied the rope to the shark's tail, and the farmer put a loop on his trailer hitch. He revved his big red truck, and the fish customers started running. Once the truck was moving across the sidewalk, the thirteen-foot tiger shark slid out of the water and onto the dock like magic.

Tommy and I grabbed the measuring tape, measured the three sharks, and filled out the mount books as fast as possible. I had no idea if any of the fish would be mounted, but I wanted to be ready if this should happen. The boys were inside the boat changing and talking to Ronald, who had not left the air-conditioning all day. I recognized the limo driver when he walked up, followed closely by a mountain of a man. I apologized for being late. When they both smiled, I knew everything was OK.

Ronald was the first off the boat and was starting to dig through his briefcase when Winfield walked over to him and held out his hand, whispering something. The second time Winfield spoke, he loudly said, "I mean now!" This caught my attention, so I watched Winfield walk over to the redneck and shake his hand, saying, "Thank you, sir." He put something in the man's hand discretely. These boys had class!

Ronald then pulled out a checkbook in a shiny black leather case and said, "How much?"

I wasn't sure what he meant, so I said, "Which shark do you want to mount?"

Ronald looked me in the eye and said, "My time is very important. All of them."

I did the math for the three deposits and gave him the figure. As he was writing the check, Winfield asked me if I had measured the jewfish Ulysses had caught. Tommy heard that, leaped into the cockpit, and measured the jewfish in record time.

I gave Ronald the new amount, and he filled out the next check and handed it to me. As he jerked the mount slips out of my hand, I politely said I needed to fill out the names and addresses of the boys. Ronald again looked me in the eye and said, "That's why I have secretaries!"

I was happy to see him walk away until I heard Braxton ask Ronald if he had given the crew their tip. Ronald reluctantly reached into his pocket and handed him an envelope. Braxton brought it to me and sarcastically said, "Ronald sometimes has memory problems."

When they were getting in the limo, I remembered the expensive stainless steel cooler that was still in the cockpit and instantly felt guilty for taking a big tip and not saying something about the cooler. I ran to the limo and tapped on Ronald's driver's-side window. He rolled the window part way down as I said, "Ronald, that beautiful stainless steel cooler you brought—"

But before I could finish speaking, Ronald rolled the window up in my face. He then motioned to the driver to leave, and the limo rolled down the parking lot.

CHAPTER 25

Pier 5 Miami, Florida, December 1, 1975 Fishing the Russian

It was Monday, and I was running the *Miltown II*, which I leased from a Texan who lived in Houston. I docked the boat in the charter boat section of Miamarina in downtown Miami.

Scottie was mating that day, and his favorite charter party of all time was due to arrive at the dock in the late morning. His name was Vladimir Zalachenko, and he and several of his Russian friends owned several big strip clubs in North Miami. Vladimir worked all night, so he couldn't be at the dock at the crack of dawn like most charter parties.

His white limo pulled up at nine thirty, and Vladimir and two gorgeous strippers stepped out. He would bring two, three, or four gorgeous gals from his strip club with him each time he went fishing with us. Scottie and I would enjoy the scenery all day. Vladimir did not like driving in traffic, so we had to have the boat tied to the dock just before three each day he fished.

I went out of Government Cut slowly, so the girls could see the cruise ships that had not yet sailed, and they liked watching the small container ships that docked at the east end of Dodge Island unload their cargo. When I went by the Miami Beach coast guard station, a small boat ran out and stopped us, saying they needed to inspect the *Miltown II*. The rubber-sided boat had two young coasties who looked to be nineteen years old at the most. Their boat driving skills were nonexistent, so it took them three tries to get their small boat to our stern.

Vladimir, being Russian, hated anyone wearing a uniform. He explained this was a fishing trip, and we were heading out to sea, not smuggling anything back to the United States. This didn't work, so he whispered something to the two girls, and they walked over and stood about two feet from the young cadets, who were holding on to the stern of our boat. The two guys in uniform were wearing orange life jackets and standing in the tiny boat, looking up at these professional dancers and wondering how they were going to get onboard the boat to do their inspection.

Vladimir walked over and snapped his fingers. Both girls pulled their T-shirts off and leaned over the stern, putting their giant breasts inches from the boys' faces. Both boys both fell back into the rubber boat speechless and stared at each other before heading for the Miami Beach coast guard station at full speed. I liked the Russian way of solving problems.

When I got to 120 feet of water, there was a nice green-water meeting blue-water edge, with the blue Gulf Stream water slowly flowing north. Scottie put two electric reels filled with Monel wire in the back chairs and attached a #3½ Drone Spoon for bait to each rod. He then let out six hundred feet of wire line. The kingfish had been biting all of October, November, and December of 1975, with great catches of thirty or forty kings every day. They were small, averaging just three pounds.

Every day the schools of bottlenose dolphin, or porpoises, were waiting for the charter boats so they could steal the kingfish as they were being reeled to the boat. These mammals were smart; they grabbed kingfish by the middle of their bodies and quickly rolled sideways, snapping off the fishes' bodies from their heads. We would catch a dozen heads every day.

We fished all the way down Key Biscayne, catching kingfish and feeding the porpoises. The girls loved seeing these big mammals roll out of the water just behind the boat, with kingfish in their mouths. When we finally reached the southern tip of the island, I turned offshore to catch some amberjack for the fish customers who came by the dock every afternoon to buy fresh fish.

The small amberjack and Almaco jack showed up every year just before Christmas on several of the wrecks in 250 to 300 feet of water. This was a little early in December, but I had caught ten or twelve fifteen pounders several days earlier. Scottie rigged each electric reel with a two-pound lead bank weight and a wire leader. We used a 3412-C hook back then because the hook was double strength and never straightened out.

Scottie put the lead weights in the water, dropped both electric wire lines to the bottom for the girls, and told them to get ready to push the buttons that were mounted on the electric reels. Both rods bent over, and we caught one Almaco and one amberjack. We had a live-bait well full of pinfish, so we kept dropping live baits and catching fish. Both squealing girls had long since removed their bikinis so they could get total tans. They loved using the electric reels. Most of the Almaco jacks were ten or twelve pounds, and the amberjack averaged a little larger.

Seeing a frigate bird, or man-o'-war hawk, offshore of the boat chasing flying fish, I told Scottie to let two more ballyhoo out and put them in the short outriggers. Vladimir followed me to the tuna tower, and we both looked for some big dolphin as the birds dived on the flying fish the dolphin were chasing. Big dolphin are easy to spot because they turn bright blue, yellow, and green when they become aggressive and chase flying fish.

It did not take long to see a big bull dolphin jump out of the water and chase a flying fish that was airborne. I called down to the girls so they could watch the show, which ended with the big black man-o'-war bird stealing the flying fish from the hungry bull dolphin at the last moment. There were several large cow dolphin all chasing flying fish in the same area.

The big bull soon ate one of our long outrigger ballyhoos and hooked himself. One of the cow dolphin that was following him gobbled the other long ballyhoo and took off across the surface of the ocean. While the two hooked dolphin jumped behind the boat, two more cow dolphin saw the short outrigger baits and were on and jumping. We had four big dolphin on at one time.

Vladimir left the tuna tower and went down to the bridge and then the cockpit to show the redhead how to wind a reel with a handle instead of pushing the button on an electric reel. He sent the other up the bridge ladder to catch the big bull and cow dolphin that were on the long outrigger rods I fished from the flying bridge.

I had come down from the tower to help her with the conventional 9/0 Penn Senator reel. Neither of these gals had ever been fishing, so they screamed every time any of the big colorful dolphin would jump. We had one big dolphin on each of the bridge rods and one on each of the short rigger rods, so there was always a dolphin jumping into the air.

My gal did not make much progress because she stood up to point and scream every time she saw any of the jumping fish. Vladimir was a better teacher and had the redhead pumping and winding the rod and reel with natural skill. She caught her cow dolphin and switched chairs to catch the other fish.

I saw another big cow dolphin following the redhead's second fish, so I asked Scottie to put a rigged ballyhoo out on the short rigger rod that had just caught the fish. The fifth big dolphin swam up and attacked the ballyhoo, hooked itself, and started to jump. Scottie gaffed the next cow dolphin and put it in the fish box while the athletic redhead ran back to the other short rigger chair and started cranking. When she looked up and saw me laughing at what a good angler she had become, she gave me a thumbs-up and went right back to catching her fish.

Up on the flying bridge, my gal was still laughing and was now winding with both hands on the fishing reel handle. I guided the line for her and laughed almost as much as she did. The redhead in the cockpit took fishing very seriously and had her third big dolphin to the side of the boat quickly for Scottie to gaff.

Both of the big dolphin on the bridge rods were so tired, they just dragged behind the boat. The blonde finally had the big bull dolphin close enough for Scottie to gaff, and she switched chairs to wind in the next fish. Instead of lifting the rod and cranking the reel, she left the rod lying on the bridge railing and cranked the lifeless dolphin to the boat using both hands on the handle.

While I had maneuvered the boat as they'd fought the big dolphin, we had been carried quite a ways north with the Gulf Stream, so I started trolling toward downtown Miami and the Sea Buoy. This had been a very satisfying day for me. I had three happy people who got to see porpoises steal our kingfish and watch all the big colorful dolphin jump around the boat. It was also a beautiful, calm fall day with a clear blue sky.

Vladimir knew I was trolling toward home, so he went inside, laid down in the cool air-conditioning, and fell asleep in moments. After trolling for fifteen minutes, I looked back behind the right long outrigger bait and saw some light blue, and I knew it was a blue marlin getting ready to eat the ballyhoo. As it did so, I was already in position and dropping back. When I wound the slack out of the line, the blue marlin jumped.

I leaned over the bridge rail and asked the girls to wake Vladimir. He must have worked hard the previous night, because they could not wake him. When I asked the girls who wanted to catch this fish, they both climbed the bridge ladder screaming, "Me!"

The athletic redhead was the first in the chair, and she went to work. This fish was a jumper and did all the classic moves that make blue marlin so fun to catch. The crazy blonde squealed, ran in circles, and jumped up and down every time the marlin came out of the water. I think she did more jumping than the marlin did. Soon the blonde was cranking the reel with two hands while the redhead was pulling the eighty-pound test line in by hand.

I couldn't stop laughing. This was the first time I had two totally naked twenty-year-old girls catching a marlin on my boat together. It took about fifteen minutes to get the marlin close to the boat as the two girls took turns cranking the reel, pulling the line, and lifting the rod. The tired marlin had started to turn brown when Scottie gaffed it, and he asked for help lifting the fish over the side of the boat. I already knew where this fish was going, because I had a restaurant on Calle Ocho (Eighth Street in Miami) where the longtime owner, a Cuban gentleman, specialized in cooking all kinds of marlin.

Both girls came down the ladder and hugged and kissed me then asked if I would take their pictures with the marlin. After I used up all the film I had, I pointed the boat toward Miami and started to run for the dock at cruising speed. I made sure to run as close to the other charter boats as possible, letting the girls wave at the captains, mates, and charter parties.

When I slowed the boat down in Government Cut, I sent Scottie up to drive for the last ten or twelve minutes. Both gals were shiny all over with five layers of oily suntan lotion, so I handed each a bottle of shampoo and held the cockpit wash-down hose over their heads. By the time we docked, they were dried off and wearing cute outfits.

Our docking time was perfect, just before three in the afternoon. I went inside the saloon, and Vladimir paid me in cash and left a big tip along with all the fish. As he walked out of the saloon and into the cockpit, he saw the eighty-pound blue marlin and said, "What the hell is that?"

Both girls said together, "I caught it."

I walked the three to the waiting white limo and received many kisses and squeezes from the gals, who had been so much fun. Vladimir shook my hand and said, "Come up to the club and see them dance. It's on me."

CHAPTER 26

Bimini, Bahamas, May 21, 1976 Yohannes and the Record Bluefin Tuna

Bahamas record Bluefin tuna 919 pounds with angler Yohannes Hekimian. Captain Bill Harrison and mates Copperhead Rolle and Scottie Bimini Big Game Club May 21, 1976

A YOUNG FISHERMAN'S DREAM COME TRUE

Two Bluefin tuna weighing 919 and 762 pounds onboard the Miltown III. Captain Bill Harrison and mates Copperhead Rolle and Scottie. Bimini

While walking down the old wooden docks of the Bimini Big Game Club in the predawn hours, I could tell that the day's conditions were perfect for bluefin tuna fishing. It was Friday, and I was the captain of a thirty-seven foot diesel-powered Merritt named *Miltown III*. My Bahamian mate was Copperhead Rolle, and Scottie Taylor, my other mate, was from Miami. The angler onboard for the two-week charter was one of the most colorful fishermen I had ever encountered. His name was Yohannes Hekimian.

Yohannes had the most extraordinary past. He was born in Addis Ababa, Ethiopia, and during his illustrious career as a Special Forces officer he was noticed for exceptional strength, loyalty, and dedication. On account of that, he rose through the ranks to become the personal bodyguard for the historic figure King Haile Selassie. During those years Yohannes accompanied the king on safaris through Africa, hunting wild lions and elephants. He was the last line of defense between any manner of wild man or beast and the Ethiopian regent.

Yohannes's deformed fingers were his tools. Meaty palms and twisted fingers formed by so many broken bones, his and others', were met by bulky forearms and huge biceps. His shoulders were wide, and his oversize head was shaved bald, showing muscles on the back and a large friendly smile on the front.

Every year a dedicated group of men and a few women would assemble at Cat Cay and Bimini to fish the bluefin tuna migration that lasted roughly one month. Of this group Johannes, with his old-style European charm and great personality, was the best liked.

During the previous two weeks, bluefin tuna fishing had been very good, and, as I would later learn, it would stay great for another thirty days. We were on a good roll of our own. For the last three days, we had released one or more tuna each day averaging five hundred to seven hundred pounds. On this day conditions looked perfect. The current was flowing to the north with plenty of clean water, the skies were clear to partly cloudy, and, most important, the wind was blowing from the southeast.

So far that May we'd had south or southeast wind every day. The forecast was calling for the wind to drop off later in the day, but there was a low-pressure area on the way. This meant the wind would start right back up, blowing out of the southwest in a day or two. My crew and I were impatient to go fishing because we knew we had to be in early for some of our guests to make the last Chalk's seaplane flight out of Bimini in the afternoon.

Copperhead Rolle was my spotter, and Scottie Taylor worked the cockpit. I had great respect for Copperhead, as he and I had worked together since the mid-'60s. Copperhead was only five feet six (so he said) and was a native Bahamian. His black hair was burned a copper color by the brutal Bahamas sun. He had been a professional mate almost all of his forty-six years and had worked with me in the

A YOUNG FISHERMAN'S DREAM COME TRUE

Bahamas and St. Thomas. I liked having him fish with me because I knew I could always count on him and his good judgment. He was a true professional and absolutely one of the best in the cockpit.

Being born in Bimini, Copperhead and his family had an interesting history. On August 10, 1967, we helped his brother, Manny Rolle, unload a Bahamas ladies' record 723-pound blue marlin from his charter boat, *Gold Bill.* Manny would later open a grocery store across the street and a little south of the Big Game Club. It burned down twice in its twenty-five-year history. His other brother was also famous for running the *Bimini Babe* for the Landwer family. They had a beautiful home just north of Pogie Bay on the harbor side of Bimini. His name was Shoestring Rolle. Shoestring's gigantic hands could pick up a bowling ball without having to put his fingers in the holes. I made sure to stay good friends with Shoestring!

Copperhead and I had blue marlin fishing down perfect. Once the fish would get to the side of the boat, Copperhead would wire it, and I would run down from the bridge and gaff it. Together we would then drag the fish through the transom door and across the deck. Blue marlin fishing was fun, but the real challenge to Copperhead was tuna fishing. He liked the boat-to-boat competition and had good eyes for spotting the northbound schools of tuna. What I most liked about Copperhead was his willingness to ride the tower all day long.

The other mate who worked the cockpit was Scottie Taylor. As a teenager Scottie had worked for me when I fished out of Pier 5 in Miami. He had that youthful love of fishing and the desire to become better at it. He had a quick introduction to big-game fishing when he joined me on a trip to St. Thomas during the summer of 1974. He went from catching amberjack, groupers, and sailfish to suddenly wiring three-hundred- and four-hundred-pound blue marlin on a daily basis. Back in those days, many of our clients wanted to have their beautiful marlin mounted so they would be showpieces in their homes or on the walls in their offices. This meant Scottie, being the only mate, had to become a good wireman in a hurry. I give him credit for going to the really big-name mates in the St. Thomas marlin fleet and asking questions about wiring and gaffing blue marlin.

Having a body weight of 140 pounds, Scottie had a serious disadvantage when a wild five-hundred-pound blue was jumping at the side of the boat on the leader wire. As the days went by, he wired blue marlin after blue marlin and became better and better. He ended that summer with more than fifty blue marlin to his credit. Compared to many of today's wiremen, this is a lifetime achievement.

Yohannes's friends were flying back to Texas that afternoon, and he had promised them plenty of fresh tuna. I entered the restaurant of the Big Game Club and tried to explained to Rev. Pinder, the maître d', that we needed to have our breakfast and box lunches as soon as possible. We then had one of the good but notoriously slow breakfasts served to us at the club restaurant. After finishing our meal, we waited and waited and waited and waited for our box lunches.

This slowed our departure even more. Once we finally received our box lunches, we boarded the *Miltown III* and started out through the clear water of Bimini Harbor. The *Miltown III* had a hailing port of Houston, Texas, and was the first thirty-seven-foot Merritt to have small diesels installed. This meant it was the absolute slowest boat in the fleet, roaring seventeen knots wide open.

I chose to take the shortcut behind Turtle Rocks and Gun Cay in order to get us to Tuna Alley as soon as possible. Approaching Gun Cay Channel, I went to the tower while it was still calm, followed by Copperhead. Since our relationship spanned a large part of my life, I enjoyed Copper's company in the tower for the eight or ten hours we spent looking for tuna each day. I usually asked my mates to wear dark shirts when they rode the tower and to stay as low as possible, so

I could see over them when we were baiting schools of tuna. Copper was perfect in the tower; he was short, so I could easily see over him, and he was a native Bahamian, so the dark shirt was not necessary.

Ahead of me I could see five boats that were baiting schools of tuna, and already there was one boat that had hooked up and was offshore in the deep water, doing battle with a tuna. This day was just like the previous seven days had been, and the schools were marching up the edge of the Gulf Stream one after the other, all on their way north. As we ran south into the wind and current, we watched the five boats go by in the opposite direction, all leading their schools of tuna on their way north. After passing the last northbound boat, I slowed down, leaving a large gap of ocean before the next group of tuna boats that were fishing to the south. Like magic, a school of northbound tuna showed up right on schedule, and we had our turn to try our tricks.

Copperhead and I divided our viewing area in half. He got the shallow-water side to the east, and I took the deep water to the west. The shallows were anything from a depth of sixty feet to one hundred feet on the Great Bahama Bank. When the tuna were in shallow water, we could see them at a great distance, because their dark bodies stood out against the white sand. Even on the dark rocky patches of the shallows, the giant tuna definitely stood out from their surroundings.

Our first school was in the deep water to the west and looked to be about the same distance off the edge as the other five schools we had passed, except they had no escort boat to slow their rapid progress to the north.

Since the tuna boat was running to the south and the schools of tuna were swimming to the north, we had to take great care not to collide with the school and spook the front few fish, thus sending the entire group down and out of sight. Once a school of tuna was spotted, the boat had to turn away from the it and come around to get into a position where one bait would be dragged at a sharp angle ahead of the northbound school.

For our first school of the day, I came around on the east side of it and then ran north before slowing down to baiting speed. This is a standard operation for morning tuna fishing, since the sun is still on the east side of Tuna Alley, and the sun's rays help us to better see the fish to the west. Now we were in a perfect position, and Copperhead gave the signal to let the bait go. The signals are easy: one finger for a mullet, two for a mackerel, and a flat hand meant "try a flopper." A flopper is a big silver mullet weighing at least one and a half pounds that has had everything cut out of the inside of its body and is only one-half inch thick from the nose all the way down to the split tail. It flops on top of the water and is usually fished at the short mark on the Fin-Nor reel.

That day the wind was blowing just over fifteen knots, so we used six-ounce chin leads to make the baits swim vertically. The *Miltown III* was very quiet and threw an extremely small wake. This allowed us to bait the schools of tuna quite close under the right conditions. I fished the short mark at 150 feet and the long mark at 220 feet. I always started with the long mark at the tip of the rod. As the school was worked and the fish could be better controlled, we baited the tuna at the short mark. The hookup rate was higher at the short mark, and the strikes were definitely more spectacular!

Baiting the first school proved futile. We tried mullet, mackerel, floppers, and even an old squid that had been in the bait box so long we felt it was part of the crew. I always spent too much time with the first school of the day, hoping to start things off with the big bite. Reluctantly I gave up baiting this school, since several of the other boats we had passed earlier were now charging south along the edge, jeopardizing my desirable position.

A YOUNG FISHERMAN'S DREAM COME TRUE

Continually running south makes one think the boat will end up a hundred miles from home at the end of the day, but the geographic location changes north and south only over a twenty-mile area. The tuna boats are continually swapping positions due to the fact that one boat runs south at fifteen or twenty knots, then, finding a school of tuna, turns and baits the tuna as they head north for several miles. The Gulf Stream current usually flows at two, three and, sometimes four knots to the north. While baiting the northerly swimming schools of bluefins, the combination of the two north-moving objects accelerate their speed.

If a tuna boat is baiting an exceptionally large school of fish, the captain might stay with it for many miles. Getting the bait to every fish is difficult and takes a great deal of time. Once the captain gives up the school, he will again turn south and run till the next school is spotted.

We were baiting our third school without even having a looker—a bluefin that breaks out of the formation and follows the bait for the length of the school before returning to the northbound assembly of tuna. If the spotter shouts down to the cockpit crew that a looker is behind the bait, the excitement is increased with the anticipation of a tuna strike. The reality of tuna fishing is that the people in the cockpit almost always see the spectacular explosion of spray the violent strike causes, since they are at eye level with the bait and are watching as the line goes straight back behind the boat. The two men in the tower rarely see the strike, since they are keeping track of all the fish in the school.

Once the baiting is started, the spotter runs the cockpit crew, allowing the captain to devote his full attention to working the boat and the school of tuna. While baiting this school, Copperhead informed me another barracuda had chopped the bait in half. As we lined up a fourth time to make a pass on the school, Copper gave the signal, and the leaded mullet went over the side. When we were only two fish into the school, Yohannes's yell shook the boat. This sent Copperhead scurrying down the left tower leg into the cockpit while I brought the boat around to the deep-water side of the hooked bluefin. This tuna behaved exactly as I would expect and streaked across the surface as the *Miltown III* came chugging behind.

I saw the fish throwing water with its tail off the bow of the boat. Even though we were going forward wide open, the line on the reel was being rapidly dumped. Finally the tuna dived, and it was up to Yohannes to go to work. Since the tuna had gone down, I left the tower in favor of the bridge controls. Ten minutes later Yohannes looked up at me smiling, and I knew the tuna had finally stopped its dive to the deep water. Yohannes was about to switch and become the aggressor.

The 12/0 Fin-Nor spool on the reel never stayed still with Yohannes. It was either turning away as the tuna took line, or it was coming in as he would violently attack the fish and gain line inch by inch at any cost. He was known throughout the tuna fleet as a man who never sat in the chair and waited patiently. After Yohannes gained half of the four hundred yards of Dacron line back on the reel, the tuna abruptly rushed straight down, taking back another hundred yards. Yohannes stayed airborne in the fishing harness, with sixty pounds of drag on the tuna, till it stopped. At that exact moment, he went back to his wild attack with the drag on a full ninety pounds.

Having released every tuna we'd caught that week, we now planned to kill this one and put it in the boat. Yohannes's friends wanted some fresh tuna to take home that afternoon. I could see Copperhead wearing his wiring gloves and Scottie laying out the straight gaff and safety rope that went to the fixed gaff head. Rarely did a tuna take the straight gaff out of the mate's hands, but I insisted they use the added safety rope.

The mates would decide who would wire the first tuna of the day, and from then on they would alternate as we caught more fish. Since the tuna was going to be put in the boat, one of Yohannes's friends was steering the fighting chair to keep the rod pointing at the fishing line. The brutal Bahamian sun that beat down on Yohannes's muscled back caused the sweat to pour off his entire body as he pulled unmercifully on the tiring tuna. He had his own one-gallon water jug that hung from the chair and was never put on ice. Sometimes, in the harness, as he balanced high in the air, he would take a big gulp of warm water and then slosh a small amount over his bald head.

Finally the tuna started to pinwheel, and Yohannes went into kill mode. I knew there would be no joking or laughing until the tuna was up to the surface. Copperhead, wearing the wiring gloves, walked to the starboard corner of the transom and looked down into the blue water. He was a good wireman. Being short, he could keep his thighs under the covering boards and then pull with a straight back.

He saw the glimmer of a hooked tuna deep down in the clear water. It was swimming in large pinwheel turns that allowed Yohannes to gain line on the up side of the circle. As the bluefin turned and started on the down side of the pinwheel, Yohannes would hold the 12/0 Fin-Nor spool and rise high in the air, making me fear that he could break the two-hundred-pound test Dacron line.

Scottie held the gaff vertically, with its head pointing outboard. Copper looked deep into the clear water, then he turned toward me and said something, so I knew the snap on the leader wire was only a few yards away. Once Copperhead grabbed the wire, he would have complete control of the cockpit. Everyone, including the gaff man, would move out of his way. He would also determine when the tuna was ready to be gaffed. Once the wiring process started, these two professionals rarely spoke, even at critical times.

As Copper pulled the twenty feet of leader wire, Scottie moved to the starboard corner of the cockpit and held the gaff horizontal, with the point facing down. The gaff was directly over the upcoming tuna's head. I maneuvered the boat so Copper would not have to move from his locked-in position four feet ahead of the starboard corner. I could see the tuna getting closer and closer. Copper finally took a double wrap and pulled the tuna's head to the surface as Scottie gaffed it under the pectoral fin. I waited until Copper looked up and gave a nod, then I made one of my rare trips to the cockpit deck. My job was to put the meat hook through the tuna's lower jaw, which was easy since the tuna was now floating on its back. Once I took the strain off Copper, he released the wire and opened the tuna door. On a thirty-seven-foot Merritt, the tuna door is huge! All of us walked the fish aft and around the starboard corner. With one easy pull, the bluefin slid through the door and across the wet teak cockpit floor.

Pulling a bluefin tuna into a thirty-seven-foot Merritt is easy since the water level is just below the bottom of the door. As the three men went to the starboard side of the cockpit and pulled on the meat hook that was in the tuna's mouth, the waves helped wash the tuna into the boat. Once our tuna was in the boat, I shut the door and turned to Yohannes, making a guess that the tuna weighed seven hundred pounds before congratulating him with a handshake. Halfway up the tower leg, I looked down and saw Yohannes standing on the fighting chair seat, with his arms straight up in the sky and his fists clenched. I knew some sort of victory yell would follow.

On the way back to the edge of Tuna Alley, the two mates tied the tuna across the cockpit behind the fighting chair. There was still time to catch another tuna! In the forty minutes we had been involved with this one, the wind had dropped five knots, but the sea kept its perfect roll. The entire tuna fleet had changed position. Some had run to the south, some had hooked up, and others, baiting big schools of tuna, were halfway to Bimini.

The schools continued to show, and while baiting our next school of tuna we got the bite! Copperhead had seen a big school up shallow, and while we baited the fish I pushed them farther and farther into the shallows. After the bite I came around and broke the school up. A group of around ten tunas ran north over the sandy bottom, making it easy to follow our fish, since he was in the middle of this group.

As I followed, staying on the deep-water side of this group, the unthinkable happened. We were cut off by a lobster trap. Somewhere during the quarter mile we had run with the tuna, an underwater rope and submerged float had separated us from our second giant tuna of the day. This was a real letdown, since catching a tuna up shallow was so much fun for everyone onboard! Chasing a hooked tuna in the clear shallow makes everyone on the boat appreciate how fast these great fish are as they race over the white-sand bottom.

Yohannes's favorite rod and reel, which was a modified stump puller filled with two-hundred-pound Dacron line, was now out of commission, since the cutoff line caused the marks to be no longer usable. We broke out our standard tuna rod and reel—an unlimited rod with a 12/0 Fin-Nor reel filled with 130-pound test Dacron. We had only another hour to fish before turning north and heading home to Bimini.

Looking down from the tower at Yohannes as he adjusted the new rig, I knew a trip to the cockpit was necessary. I gave Copperhead the wheel and descended the right side tower leg to the bridge, then onto the cockpit deck. Knowing I could not tell Yohannes to be patient with his new lighter tackle, I chose simply to remind him that a little less drag might be appropriate. After a short talk and several reminders that this was far lighter than his familiar tackle, he reluctantly agreed to be patient and then reminded me I should be in the tower driving the boat and not down in the cockpit, where I did not belong.

The wind had dropped to less than ten knots, and the sea was down to a small heave. The next tuna school we spotted was not moving nearly as fast as the previous schools had. Not wanting to go into Bimini with just one flag for the day, we made two more unsuccessful passes on the school with a mullet. The last flopper we tried drew a looker, but it quickly gave up the chase and returned to the northbound formation, and the entire school then disappeared into the deep-blue water. We returned to the edge, where I slowed the boat to an idle, went to natural, and waited for the next formation of bluefins.

After a short lull, I saw the next school of tuna on their way north. It appeared to be a small school, maybe a dozen fish. After coming around on them, I found their northward speed surprisingly fast, since the wind had died out and the sea had dropped to a gentle roll. The tunas kept coming closer and were already in our wake when Copperhead gave the signal. Once the bait was out and the mark was at the tip of the rod, I heard some muttering coming from the other side of the tower. I looked back at the bait and realized the flopper was still being used from the previous school of tuna we had just finished baiting.

A flopper was Copperhead's least favorite bait, and toward the end of the day he would let me know by continually grumbling whenever we used one to bait a school of bluefins. Since we had caught many tuna together, I knew telling Copperhead of our success rate while using floppers as bait would automatically bring a response of how many strikes we had on mackerel, mullet, and any other kind of bait. At that point in the day, it did not bother me in the least to try a flopper first.

As I turned the boat back through the school, Yohannes's yell caught both of us standing in the tuna tower by surprise. Quickly looking back toward the bait, I saw a huge shower of white foaming water as tall as the top of our tuna tower. I learned later that two tuna had both lunged for the surface bait, and their colliding bodies had caused the huge eruption of spray. The angler and cockpit crew are always in the best position to enjoy these great surface strikes.

Headed offshore, the boat was at a good angle and a perfect position to come around on the fish, but the farther I turned the boat, the more southerly the tuna ran. At one point the bluefins went a full one hundred yards, throwing ten feet of white foaming water from its tail while running straight south. Since the sea had only a gentle roll and we were going to release this one, I stayed in the tower. The tuna finally stopped running across the surface and headed for the depths. Taking four or five hundred yards of line off of the reel, it finally stopped and held its position. Yohannes was rarely in a position where he was not gaining line or giving it back. But this was one of those rare times.

He balanced high in the air in his fishing harness and waited for what seemed like a very long time before letting his impatience show. I could tell he needed something to pull against. I came down from the tower to steer from the bridge controls, giving Yohannes someone to glare at as he waited for the battle to change. Finally the tuna turned, and Yohannes went to work pumping and winding. After getting back three hundred yards of line, the tuna again dived, going straight down for more than four hundred yards at a red-hot speed. Yohannes cursed me and my "light" 130-pound test tackle. Looking down from the bridge at the angler's mounting frustration, I knew better than to try to convince him that 130-pound test line was not considered light tackle.

The mood in the cockpit turned ugly as Yohannes's friends complained about the possibility of missing their afternoon Chalk's seaplane flight, and my two mates were sitting idly on the covering boards whispering to each other. Yohannes was not helping things either, since he was uttering strange words in the Ethiopian language, punctuated periodically with my name.

But soon things began to change. Yohannes was gaining line, and everyone was happy. Scottie leaped off of the covering board and put on the tuna gloves, which consisted of a thin leather lining with a wet outside cotton glove that had the last parts of the fingers removed.

As Copperhead steered the chair, Yohannes started to reel as fast as I had ever seen. We could soon see the bluefin, making huge pinwheels, deep in the clear water, which reflected the afternoon sun. This silver flash was a good sign. It meant we had a tired tuna coming up. I called down to Copper, and he in turn waved his pliers, acknowledging that he knew the tuna was to be released.

It took Yohannes an additional twenty minutes to get the fish to the boat. Once the wire was up, Scottie took a wrap and started to pull. The tuna then pinwheeled down, taking the wire out of Scottie's hands. Once it started to turn upward, Scottie got a double wrap and held on. I backed the boat inside the tuna's circle, so the tuna's head popped out of the water at the starboard corner of the transom. Scottie then took several more double wraps and moved forward. He pinned the big tuna to the side of the boat.

Copperhead immediately cut the wire that ran from the rod tip to the back of Scottie's gloves, leaving him holding only the last four feet of the leader wire that ran to the hook in the side of the tuna's mouth. Copper rushed to the transom corner to see the actual size of the tuna and watch it swim away once Scottie let go of the wire.

Trying to get my camera out of the bench seat, I didn't understand why they were calling for me. I again told Scottie to let go of the wire, but Copperhead shook his head no and frantically motioned for me to come down to the cockpit. Fearing that the tuna might die from exhaustion, I rushed down the side of the bridge and across the covering board. I placed one hand on Copper's shoulder to steady myself as I stood on the transom looking down at the tuna. Copperhead then told me he was sure this tuna was much larger than the 842 pounder we had caught the previous year.

As I ran to the bridge to get my camera, I told Scottie to let the wire go, but it was too late. Yohannes, overhearing what Copper had said, spun Copperhead around and pushed the straight gaff against Copper's chest as he shouted, "Gaff!" Copperhead's reactions were instantaneous. The exhausted tuna was on one end of the gaff, and both Copperhead and Yohannes were on the other end.

Once I put the meat hook in the tuna's mouth, we walked it around the corner and prepared to drag it through the door. We went through the same routine as always. We pulled on the tuna, and for the first time ever it stopped partway through the door. I had pulled tuna over eight hundred pounds through this door before and never had a problem. Again we pulled, and again we failed. This time Yohannes joined us, and after the old heave-ho, the tuna was still on the ocean side of the door.

The rest of the group joined us. After the third pull, the tuna was wedged tightly in the door. Luckily I had put a tail rope on it, which allowed me to work it back and forth while everyone pulled on the rope going to the meat hook. Finally the tuna came into the cockpit like a giant bar of soap and slid across the wet teak deck. I started to think Copperhead could have been right about the size of the fish.

We were almost to Bimini before I looked down at the cockpit to compare the two fish. The last bluefin was definitely larger than the first. I then felt that my guess of seven hundred pounds for the first tuna was probably too high and never thought any more about the weight. We arrived at the Bimini Big Game Club and tied the boat to the dock next to the scales. Don Smith, the dockmaster, cheerful as always, strolled over to help weigh the two tuna.

The first tuna was lifted out of the boat and then hung on the scales. A crowd gathered as Don called down the weight as 762 pounds. We all knew that the next one would be heavier. After lifting the second tuna out of the boat and up to the scales, Don was careful to weigh it before calling out, "Nine hundred and nineteen pounds!" This was the first giant bluefin tuna over nine hundred pounds to be caught in the Bahamas. It was also the heaviest game fish ever to be caught in the Bahamas at that time.

The commissioner soon arrived to verify the tuna's weight, and after he supervised the final weighing, it still stood at 919 pounds. Yohannes's friends stayed over for the big party at the Red Lion Restaurant, where Yohannes had booked the entire back room for a dinner celebration. Most of the tuna crowd attended, as did the Bimini commissioner for the Bahamas.

CHAPTER 27

BIMINI, BAHAMAS MAY 9, 1978 REVEREND PINDER AND OUR FISH

Chalks Seaplane over Bimini Harbor. Painting by Mike Hoffman Marine Artist

I was running the *Belama* out of the Bimini Big Game Club in Bimini, Bahamas. The *Belama* was a forty-three-foot Merritt owned by Newt Belcher, and my two mates were Mel and Mike. Since we were there for three weeks fishing the bluefin tuna migration, Newt had rented the upstairs of a house on the hill called Cirrhosis by the Sea. It had a balcony facing west and a snow-white beach below, so watching the beautiful sunset at the end of the day was a pleasure.

Fishing bluefin tuna off the Bimini-Cat Cay area is sight fishing that requires the wind to blow out of the southeast to southwest, making waves roll toward the north. The more wind the better, since the tuna like to get a free ride as they head north to their summer feeding grounds off the New England and Nova Scotia coasts. None of this had happened since May 1, with day after day of flat, calm seas and no wind.

The good part of this bad situation was the fact that Mel and Mike were tremendous free divers and spear fishermen. I would run the boat from the tower, putting both divers off on great reef areas, and then follow them as they shot all sorts of fish. After they shot the fish, Dee O'Conner, Newt's girlfriend at the time, would gaff the fish in the mouth and lift them into the boat. If it was a big grouper, she would open the tuna door in the transom and drag the fish through the door and into the cockpit.

We carried four big fish boxes loaded with ice, and once we filled everything we headed home to the Bimini Big Game Club dock to load the fish into a trailer hooked up to the back of Stanley Pinder's cab. He would sell the fish on a percentage basis and give me cash later that night. Mr. Pinder, as he liked to be called, was the maître d' at the club restaurant. He also tried to collect money from the boat owners as Reverend Stanley Pinder, to build some church that all us boat captains knew never existed and would never be built.

The *Belama* was fast, and Newt loved riding at cruising speed, so running fifty miles south to go diving was a daily ritual. I knew many great reefs between Riding Rocks and Orange Cay that were loaded with red groupers and Nassau groupers, with a few big black groupers also. I would drop both divers off up current of a ledge in thirty feet of water that ran for two hundred yards, and they would shoot fifteen or twenty groupers by the time we drifted to the end of the ledge, along with hogfish, margates, yellow jack, mutton snappers, and big cero mackerel.

I would gather up both divers and run a mile or so to another spot I knew and start all over again. Both mates would eat a couple of sandwiches and drink some Cokes as they rested for fifteen minutes between diving spots. There was no GPS back then, so knowing the area from past experience was the key to our success, since we were out of sight of land almost all the time.

May 9th was the kind of day both divers dreamed about, since the water was flowing in toward the Great Bahama Bank as it got closer to high tide. The incoming water was crystal clear, and there was not a breath of wind. This made the ocean like a mirror, so I could see the bottom perfectly while I drove the boat from the tuna tower.

As I drove into the current on our second ledge, I could see a lot of life all over the beautiful coral formation. Big parrot fish and angelfish were everywhere along with school after school of grunts, yellowtail, margates, and horse-eye jack. Both divers were sitting on the transom, eager to jump in the water as soon as I gave them the signal.

Once in the water, both mates came up with Nassau groupers or red groupers every dive. They were the perfect weight for selling—five to ten pounds each. Once in a while, they would dive down to a school of margates and shoot the biggest two. By the time they had drifted the entire length of the ledge, I saw a large fish that looked like a barracuda or kingfish. but from the tower it was hard to tell.

Once I pointed the big fish out, both divers started swimming slowly in its direction. I lost sight of the fish but had a good idea where it would be, so I circled with the boat to turn it toward the guys. Suddenly their fins went into overdrive, and both were headed in the same direction. I knew it had to be a big king fish.

I enjoyed watching the team work these guys used to get big fish. One would go down and shoot the fish and start it toward the surface while the second diver would dive down and take the fish out of the first diver's hands. The first diver would swim to the surface and get a lung full of needed air and dive down to grab the big fish if necessary. At the same time, both mates started waving me over, so I knew their plan had not gone as smoothly as they had hoped. Mike shouted up to me in the tower that he had made a good shot to the kingfish's head, and Mel had put a second spear through the gills, but the fish had swum away out of sight, bleeding badly.

I left them on the surface for a reference and started looking on the bottom of the clear water. Each sweep I made with the boat was an additional twenty yards farther from them. As luck had it, I found the dead king on the bottom and waved them over. The fish had managed to swim a good hundred yards before dying. Kingfish are easy to see because they lie on their sides when dead and reflect the midday sun.

Mike made the first dive. He grabbed one of the spears and started up toward the surface. Mel then made a dive, meeting Mike halfway up, and grabbed the speared fish. Mel finished the trip up to the surface. With so much blood in the water, I called to both mates to get out. Once I went to the cockpit, I heard the story of the kingfish. It was over fifty pounds and would be the biggest king they'd shot that summer.

It was one o'clock in the afternoon, so I turned the boat north and started running toward Bimini. I wanted to stop at an old Haitian sailboat that was on the bottom in fifty-two feet of water five miles north of where we were. I always rode the tower and looked for new spots, like coral heads of small wrecks I had never seen. With the perfect conditions, I easily found the old sailboat and did a couple of loops looking down from the tower at the surrounding bottom. Sure enough, I saw a big black grouper swimming toward the wreck.

Both the mates were well rested by then and were eager to kill some more fish to sell. Once in the clear water, Mel saw the big grouper first and went down and shot it in the head. The grouper went under the hull of the sailboat. Mike made the next dive and shot his spear in the area of the head, since it was a difficult shot. Newt handed both new spears, and they made several more dives but could not get a good shot at the grouper.

Since it was the top of the flood tide, the *Belama* sat over the wreck and did not drift inshore or offshore. I went down and talked to the divers about getting the fish out of the wreck. Mike thought he could put a gaff somewhere in the grouper's head area, so we decided to tie a quarter-inch white nylon rope to our tuna gaff and have Mike try to gaff the grouper.

Everything went as planned. Mike surfaced and told Newt and Dee to pull. The two tugged as hard as they could, with no results. I told them to wrap the nylon line around the stern cleat. Once this was done, I put the boat in gear, and the black grouper was out of the wreck and on the way up to the boat.

Once the big grouper was in the boat along with Mike and Mel, we started running toward Bimini. Again I rode the tower looking for anything to add to our mixed catch. During May and June, permit school to spawn on the edge of the Gulf Stream, so I always look for these beautiful fish. Sometimes a hundred or more will join in a great circle as the males emit milt and the females release their eggs. The schools can be seen from a good distance, since they look yellow or gold as they circle on the surface.

As I ran the boat north over miles of clear water, I finally saw a school of permit off Victory Rocks. Mike and Mel had been resting for almost an hour, so they were eager to get back in the water. The most successful way to kill the most permit is to pick out the fish that weigh ten to twenty pounds and have one diver shoot them through the head, then have the second diver go down and grab the spear shaft and swim the permit to the surface.

I had told Mike and Mel not to waste time shooting the really big permit but concentrate on the average fish, which are easier to kill, bring to the surface, and sell. The plan worked well; the divers brought permit to the side of the boat over and over. I went down from the tower, since the boat was drifting over the school of one or two hundred spawning fish. They killed about twenty-five permit before the school broke apart and swam away.

I headed the boat north for the twelve-mile run to Bimini while the mates cleaned the cockpit. All four boxes were full of fish along with the live-bait well, and we still had groupers and permit all over the deck.

The Reverend Stanley Pinder had a small army of young Bimini kids waiting for us as we docked at the Bimini Big Game Club. I tried to stay as low-key as possible with the amount of fish we were continually bringing to the dock. Mike would grab two groupers out of the box and pass them to Mel, who would lay only two fish at a time on the dock. Each kid would pick up the two groupers or snappers, run them up to Stanley's trailer, and return for more.

With the reverend's kids and a few more borrowed from the neighborhood, it did not take long to carry the fifty-five groupers, nineteen mutton snappers, twelve margates, twenty-two ceros, and twenty-five permit plus a few big black groupers and kingfish to the trailer. The big black grouper we had pulled out of the wreck with the boat weighed eighty-two pounds.

Mike grabbed a five-gallon bucket that had two fillet knives, a skinning knife, and a hatchet, and both mates ran for Stanley's waiting cab. Reverend Pinder gave his usual speech about the evils of alcohol to the onlookers who were amazed by the full trailer of fish. He jumped in his cab, and as he turned the corner heading for Porgy Bay, he smiled and handed Mike a bulging bag of Bimini's best, knowing that both Mike and Mel would roll and smoke a spliff before they arrived at the village where the three would sell the fish to the natives of Bimini.

Since the boys were making money selling fish, I was left to scrub out the fish boxes and wash and chamois the boat. I made sure my longtime friend, Don Smith, the dockmaster at the club, received two Nassau groupers every time we went diving. In return he always had two pushcarts filled with ice waiting for me to fill my fish boxes for the next day of diving.

About eight that night, both mates stumbled back to Cirrhosis by the Sea with bloodshot eyes and lots of cash. Mike had a bulging bag of Bimini's best, and Mel had a big smile. Shortie, a local Bimini girl with a special talent, had traded Mel her skills for a five-pound Nassau grouper.

CHAPTER 28

ST. THOMAS, US VIRGIN ISLANDS, AUGUST 18, 1978
DEE'S SIX BLUE MARLIN IN ONE DAY

It was a beautiful St. Thomas day. The wind was out of the east-southeast at fifteen knots, and the sea was perfect for marlin fishing. I was the captain of the forty-three-foot Merritt *Belama*, owned by Newt Belcher of Miami. We were docked at Lagoon Fishing Center in the Redhook area of St. Thomas. Mel was one mate, and Sam Leiser was the other. Newt was not fishing that day, so his girlfriend, Dee O'Conner, was the angler. She loved all kinds of billfishing. We were using 9/0 Fin-Nor fishing reels and heavy rods, which made it difficult for her at only 115 pounds. That year we were using one-hundred-pound test pink monofilament line.

Docked next to us was the *Xiphias*, run by Captain Bark Garnsey. That year Barkey decided the heaviest tackle to be used on the North Drop would be 9/0 reels and one-hundred-pound test line. This was done part in humor and possibly because I liked to have two 12/0 Fin-Nor reels filled with 130-pound test fishing line out at all times.

Being best friends, Barkey and Newt, the owner of my boat, shook hands, and the 12/0 Fin-Nor reels were retired. Bark was the self-appointed dockmaster and MC for the marlin fleet. He always found a way to keep all of us laughing from daylight to well after dark. His boat was great competition, since every day they were at the top of their game as far as numbers of marlin caught.

Dee, being the only one fishing that day on the *Belama*, did not take the pressure well. Mel and Dee did not get along. Her chain-smoking added to the friction in the cockpit. Sam Leiser got along with everyone, and he, being a smoker, was lighting cigarette after cigarette as he talked to Dee, who was doing the same.

She paced the teak deck constantly, making it difficult for the mates to do their job. At the time I did not know that Mel had selected the largest mackerel and kingfish we had in the dock freezer for the day's fishing. Mel and Sam had made a secret plan to troll these superlarge baits. They wanted to make it as difficult as possible for Dee to hook a marlin.

Dee was a member of the International Women's Fishing Association (IWFA) and continually talked about it to Sam and Mel. As Sam bent wire and sewed baits, Dee's words passed right by him, and he nodded and smiled. This did not work well with Mel. I could see him seething as he worked the cockpit, with Dee pacing close behind while reciting the bylaws of her fishing organization. Mel was good; he put out only perfect baits. Every hook was sharpened, and every bait swam or skipped like a real fish.

The first marlin of the day was a nice four-hundred-pound fish. After Dee missed the marlin four times, Mel wound in the bait as fast as possible. He proudly held up the empty hook for all to see and said with a smile, "Not very hungry, was he?" As the veins in Dee's neck stood out, the right outrigger bait popped out of the pin, since the fish had moved over to the other bait, and the blue marlin was on and jumping.

Dee struggled unsuccessfully to get the rod out of the holder, so "gentleman" Sam walked over, put his hand on her shoulder, and quietly said, "Remember, Dee, you back the drag off a little, then you grab the rod ahead of the reel." Sam's soothing voice reassured her, and she finally was in the chair and cranking. Mel stood behind her, where she could not see him, and hoped she would be pulled overboard and drown.

This fish jumped and jumped till it totally gave up, and Dee wound it to the boat. Mel wired the docile marlin, and Sam tagged it with a National Marine Fisheries Service tag. Dee insisted I photograph all of her blue marlin from the bridge, with her in the pictures. Something about documented proof for the IWFA for a blue marlin release to count.

Sam looked over at Mel as he held the fish close to the boat and said, "Mel, smile for Dee's picture." I tried not to laugh as I shot a few pictures.

I fished only two rods for Dee. It was so much easier on the crew. In spite of the friction in the cockpit, we had a great system worked out. Dee would be the only one to touch the tackle till the marlin was hooked or completely missed. If the marlin would destroy the bait and it was unfishable, Mel would grab the handle of the reel and wind the empty hook to the boat as quickly as possible while Sam would uncoil a new bait and toss it over the stern. Once Mel had the swivel to the tip, he unsnapped the used bait and passed the wire to Sam, who handed the new loop end of the fresh bait to Mel. Sam then coiled the old wire and hook while Mel free spooled the new bait out to the mark and ran it up the outrigger.

As the mates were doing this, Dee would have the other reel in free spool in case the marlin decided to move over to the other outrigger bait. The blue marlin of St. Thomas were some of the hungriest and most aggressive eaters I have ever seen.

Ten minutes after tagging and releasing our first blue, another marlin crashed the right outrigger. Dee had a couple of good shots at this fish but did not hook it. She moved over to the other rod as Mel reeled in the damaged bait. When the bait was halfway in, the marlin attacked Dee's second bait. Again she had several shots and did not hook the marlin. The mates had the other bait almost out when I saw the marlin behind the new bait. I told Dee to switch rods. Mel started cranking the damaged bait to the boat as Sam fired the new mackerel over the stern.

Mel had free spooled the third mackerel and almost had it in position when Dee missed the marlin again. I told her to switch rods. Up came the blue marlin again, as hot as ever. Dee missed it again. That time I saw the rod bump as Mel was letting the mackerel out. When he looked up smiling, I yelled to Dee, "Switch rods." If she knew Mel was dropping back to a marlin, the cockpit would have exploded.

I told her to push the drag up, so I could see the bait. She pushed the lever up and looked up at me, so I pretended to be a Hollywood actor when I said, "Look! He ate the bait when you were letting it out." Once she was in the chair, Mel let me know I was correct by raising his center finger high over Dee's head. Not a very exciting fight, but we tagged, photographed, and released the 350-pound blue.

It did not take much time before a big blue crashed the left outrigger. Since the fish did not come back right away, I turned the boat to make another pass at where I thought he would be, and the right rigger bait that was sinking in the middle of the turn came tight and popped out of the outrigger clip, bending the rod. Dee looked at Mel and said, "See? I hooked him myself." Mel showed his appreciation of her skill by again raising his center finger once her back was turned.

This blue took off down sea as fast as it could swim. I spun the forty-three-foot Merritt around and went bow first after it, and we soon caught up to the hot marlin. It ran for over two miles on the surface, swimming fast. It finally gave up, and we tagged, photographed, and released the nice 550-pound blue marlin. Dee was so happy, she jumped around the cockpit shouting, "I'm three for three!"

Sam said congratulations and shook her hand. He then said, "Mel, shake Dee's hand and congratulate her." Not a word was said as the cockpit turned to ice. Sam climbed partway up the bridge ladder and said with a big smile, "That made me feel so good."

I told the mates to take five, since we had a least a two-mile jog to get back in position on the North Drop. Mel used this time to find the biggest baits in the box. He wanted to end Dee's perfect average. Once I slowed the boat and turned, I saw Mel putting a small kingfish over the side of the boat to troll in the left outrigger. I could easily spot kingfish because they are much rounder than Spanish mackerel. Sam free spooled the reel to the mark, and Mel ran the pin up to the top of the outrigger. The next bait Mel had selected was a Spanish mackerel large enough to be gaffed. Again Sam free spooled the reel, and Mel ran the mark up the outrigger.

When Sam finally stepped out from under the overhang of the bridge, I asked him to come up to the bridge. He shook his head no. Now I knew he was in on the conspiracy. I had to slow down our trolling speed a little because the two baits were so large. I knew there was a problem when I could not see anyone in the cockpit. I leaned over the port side of the bridge and saw Dee sitting on the drink box as far outboard as was possible. I went to the other side of the bridge, leaned over, and saw both mates standing with arms crossed. I needed to fix this situation because fishing must be fun and enjoyed by all.

A YOUNG FISHERMAN'S DREAM COME TRUE

While I pondered how I would solve this problem, a huge blue, well over seven hundred pounds, pushed two thirds of its body out of the water and ate the kingfish. The rod bent over, and the fish was on. When I looked down at Mel, he had his hands on his head in disbelief; I turned and saw Sam laughing so hard he needed to hold on to the tower leg to keep from falling down. Nothing eases tension like a big fish.

This was a big blue, and it jumped, tumbled, and tail walked behind the boat. Ronnie Hamlin, who was running the *Gina K*, deliberately trolled by to see the acrobatic show this fish was putting on. Ronnie radioed Barkey and the *Banderlog*, saying what a performance this big fish was displaying. The marlin took off down sea, with us following bow first.

Once we caught up with the blue, it did not take much line because I had the *Belama* holding the same speed as the fish was going. All three in the cockpit watched the marlin's back and tail come out of the water every time it surfed down a wave. After a while Mel looked up at me and said, "Let me try him." I asked him if he had been smoking weed that day, and he said, "No, I mean it." I gave the call to Dee, since she was the angler and had been in the air for thirty minutes fighting the marlin.

When someone as small as Dee was in the fighting harness, the thirty pounds of drag we used on the 9/0 Fin-Nor reels lifted them up in the air. In her case she did not need to crank a lot, since both the boat and the fish were running down sea at the same speed. All she needed to do was keep the rod bent with as much pressure as she could put on the fish.

I could tell she was getting tired, so I told her to make the call. She said to Mel, "Go ahead." I told both mates to wear cutting pliers in case either had to cut the leader wire during an emergency. If Mel was lucky enough to get a wrap of leader wire, Sam was to cut the wire behind Mel's hands so he could dump the wire. This meant he could completely let go of the leader wire. If the mate touched the leader wire, the marlin counted as released for Dee's fishing club.

We were too far west for any of the other boats to see this if all went well. As I shortened the distance between the marlin and the boat, the fish showed no fear of us getting closer and closer. Mel was tall and a good wireman. The swivel was out of the water, and Dee was doing short cranks, inching the fish closer and closer. Mel had the wire and took a wrap. Soon he had a second wrap. Sam clipped the wire behind Mel's hands. Sam did a great job, since Mel was much taller than he was.

We now had another release for Dee, since the wire had been touched. Mel kept shortening the distance between the marlin and the boat. I had both of my hands wrapped around the port and starboard single-lever controls, since the boat was going ten or twelve knots next to the blue marlin. I'd had mates pulled overboard by marlin and did not want that to happen again.

All of us, as a team, were working so hard doing our jobs that we did not hear Dee screaming, "Tag him. Tag him!" Every time Mel got another wrap, Sam clipped off two more feet of leader wire. Sam, who was concentrating on Mel's safety, did not see Dee jump out of the fighting chair and grab the tag stick. She squeezed between Mel and Sam and stuck the tag into the marlin's left shoulder like a star. This was the first time she had ever tagged a marlin! Mel dumped the wire, and Dee looked up at me and asked, "How many pictures did you take?" She must have confused me with Houdini.

I called the mates to the bridge while we ran back to the North Drop and gave congratulations to both for the teamwork they had showed. I reminded both of them that we had one more hour to fish, and they would not put any more big baits out that day. Only small baits!

As we approached the one-hundred-fathom curve, I gave them the two-minute warning, and they both went down the bridge ladder muttering under their breath. When I had the boat in position, Mel waved a small rigged mackerel over his head, and I gave the thumbs-up. It was overboard and in the left outrigger pin, flopping behind the boat in moments. Sam waved another small mackerel from the other side of the cockpit. I gave a thumbs-up. Sam ran the bait out to the mark, and before he could run the bait halfway up the outrigger, Dee screamed, "Fish on!"

Dee was now five for five on hooking fish, and Sam, Mel, and I were in disbelief. This marlin put its head out of the water and started shaking back and forth. The mackerel was so far down the hatch (down the marlin's throat) that the hook would never pull. I told the mates to leave the other bait out, and I backed the *Belama* quickly to the choking and gagging marlin. Mel grabbed the leader wire, Sam tagged the fish, and Dee jumped out of the fighting chair to pose for the camera with the 350-pound blue marlin and both smiling mates. What a difference a couple of fish made.

I put the boat in gear and went down the bridge ladder to congratulate each member of our team. As the boat slowly moved forward, the line we had not wound in came tight, bending the rod. *Damn,* I thought, *I must have run over the line!* I was halfway up the bridge ladder, looking forward, when the screams started. We were hooked up to a marlin, and it was jumping. If we caught this blue, Dee would be the first lady to catch six blue marlin in one day as a member of the IWFA at that time.

This marlin jumped, swam down sea, and went two hundred yards straight down. Dee went to work and soon pumped the fish up so Mel could grab the leader wire. Sam tagged the fish, and I documented the catch of a two-hundred-pound blue marlin being released for the IWFA, with several photos showing the two mates, Dee, and the marlin. I said thanks to everyone for the teamwork it had taken for this to happen. Six blue marlin out of six strikes was a great achievement.

When we backed into our slip, Barkey had the party already fired off. Dee immediately called Newt, since he had just arrived at the rented condo in St. Thomas. Gloria Applegate, another member of the IWFA, was there to congratulate Dee. Gloria had caught more blue marlin than any lady in the world at that time.

As I poured Mel and Sam glasses of champagne, I thanked both for making this happen.

CHAPTER 29

ST. THOMAS, US VIRGIN ISLANDS, AUGUST 19, 1978 THE *BELAMA* CATCHES SEVEN BLUE MARLIN IN ONE DAY

One of seven blue marlin tagged and released on the 43 foot Merritt Belama. Captain Bill Harrison and mates Sam and Mel. St. Thomas USVI August 18, 1978

Newt and Dee were at the dock at 7:00 a.m. sharp. Dee had experienced some unbelievable marlin fishing the day before, going six for six on blue marlin. This meant we had raised six blues, had six blues eat our baits, hooked all six, and released every one of the blue marlin. Dee insisted on doing everything by the rules of her fishing organization, the IWFA.

On the way out to the North Drop, Sam Leiser and Mel, our mates, rigged mackerel and a few mullet. We were docked at the Lagoon Fishing Center in the Red Hook area of St. Thomas, which made it about a one-hour run to the area I liked to start fishing. We were going to start in the same spot, like we had the previous day, with one bait fished from each outrigger. The fishing tackle would be two 9/0 Fin-Nor reels with stiff rods made by Biscayne Rod Company of Miami. The line was one-hundred-pound test pink monofilament.

The plan was simple: Dee would take the first fish and hook, fight, release, and hopefully tag it. Then Newt would get the entire cockpit till he did the same. I liked to go fish for fish rather than strike for strike. Mel had his left outrigger bait out a little faster than Sam because Dee was following Sam around the cockpit bragging about not missing a single marlin the previous day. Sam looked up at me and smiled because he, being older, had more marlin fishing experience than anyone onboard and knew that Dee's good luck wouldn't last.

The conditions looked great on the North Drop, and fifteen minutes into fishing a hungry three-hundred-pound blue ate the left outrigger, which was a mackerel. Three good shots and Dee had nothing to show for her efforts. The marlin moved over to the right outrigger, and Dee again had a couple of good chances to hook the marlin. So much for her perfect average.

The mates had the system down perfect. Damaged baits were reeled in, and new baits were quickly free spooled out to the mark and run up the outrigger. The left outrigger went down again, and Dee took three or four shots at a small blue and missed each time. The marlin faded away. A new bait was put in position and was splashing behind the boat in moments. The cockpit was filled with smoke, since Dee was pacing the teak deck with a lit cigarette in each hand.

A YOUNG FISHERMAN'S DREAM COME TRUE

Everyone was waiting for it to happen, and it did. Dee had three good marlin shots on the left mackerel. The marlin moved over to the right outrigger and ate the bait. Dee missed every time and never bent the rod. The next blue was about 250 pounds and crashed the right bait, bending the rod in moments. Dee was in the chair like a champ and ready to do battle. After several jumps the marlin headed down sea, and I turned the boat and went bow first after him. Mel wired the marlin, Sam tagged him, and I photographed Dee, Mel, and Sam as they smiled for the camera. Again we had documented a blue marlin release for the IWFA.

Then it was Newt's turn. The first blue strike was a classic, with the marlin showing two thirds of its body out of the water on a down sea troll. Newt missed it several times, and the marlin faded back and disappeared. Again we were trolling, and a four-hundred-pound blue crashed the mullet. Newt hooked the fish on his second try. This marlin did lots of beautiful jumps, and the fish almost ended up in Barkey Garnsey's cockpit as the *Xiphias* trolled close by to see the show.

The marlin turned down sea, and I quickly went bow first after the tailing fish. It took over one mile for me to get the boat in position for Mel to grab the leader wire and Sam to tag the fish. We had released a four-hundred-pound blue marlin for Newt with a National Marine Fisheries Service tag in the marlin's shoulder. This blue marlin would be caught, killed, and reported to the National Marine Fisheries Service by a Cuban long-liner fishing out of Havana two years later. Unfortunately the marlin was not weighed when it was caught the second time.

It was Dee's turn. Another fast blue and a vicious strike with four misses. We got going again and this time had two beautiful mackerel out and flopping behind the boat. Sam shouted, "Nice fish." I did not see the strike, but I knew Sam was a great judge of the size of all kinds of fish. He had mated for Bill Staros when they caught and released 102 bluefin tuna off of Cat Cay in the Bahamas in just over one month.

Jojo DelGurcio was the angler and owner of a thirty-seven-foot Merritt called *No Problem*. Sam, George Staros, and Bill Staros fished the *No Problem* for bluefin tuna out of Cat Cay for years. Jojo used the *Ocean Motion*, a Hatteras yacht, to live on while they fished tuna for a month each year.

I asked Sam, "How big?"

He answered, "Fish got away." That was a classic statement from Sam. We all called them "Samisms."

For us on the *Belama*, marlin fishing was red-hot that day. The baits were out only a few minutes when another blue crashed the mullet, and Dee had it on. Moments later a 275-pound blue was jumping behind our boat. Ten minutes later the fish went down sea and dove deep. She was a good angler and knew how to use her body weight in the fighting chair. Once the fish had been pumped to the surface, Mel had the leader wire, Sam tagged the marlin, and I documented the catch, with Dee, Sam, and Mel smiling for the camera.

After releasing a blue marlin, Dee always ran inside the boat to write down all the information required for the IWFA, so each marlin counted as an official release. All of us onboard had to sign a form saying we had witnessed the catch of this fish by Dee O'Connor and that she had followed all the laws of the IWFA.

As Sam was putting the mark in the outrigger pin that had the splashing mackerel bait dragging behind the boat, a marlin was there to eat it. Newt missed the fish three times. Mel handed over a 9/0 Fin-Nor he was free spooling out of the right side of the fighting chair to Newt. Dee and Newt liked to leave the rods in the armrest of the fighting chair till a marlin was hooked. It was a great system with such aggressive fish.

Newt missed the next marlin several times. The crew had a new mackerel going out, and Newt took over free spooling the reel from Sam. The hungry marlin rolled up and made a sideways strike on the mackerel. Newt missed the fish, and it faded away. As Mel was free spooling a new mackerel out, a blue crashed the bait just feet behind the boat. Newt saw the fish and grabbed the reel then pushed the brake lever forward. The fish was gone.

We started trolling again. Since the blue marlin were biting so fast, Newt wanted a third bait put out in the short outrigger. Sam, who always smiled and agreed, put a mullet in the left short pin and ran it up the outrigger. The rod was fished from the rod holder in the covering board. Mel was sewing baits and bending leader wire as fast as he could, since it had been nonstop action once we'd put the baits out that morning.

Newt got his chance on the bait we fished on the left short outrigger when a hungry blue tried to eat the mullet. I shouted to Dee that I saw a blue behind the left long outrigger bait also. She reacted quickly and free spooled the bait after the marlin struck. Mel looked up at me and yelled that the right long bait was out of the outrigger. The bait popped out of the right outrigger pin without anyone seeing what had eaten the bait. I looked back and saw a small blue behind the right long bait.

Newt tried to hook his marlin while Dee did the same. We all looked at each other in disbelief. We had a triple-header and had missed all three marlin. Newt, Dee, and Sam all reeled in empty hooks while Mel grabbed three new baits.

The mates got a mullet in the left short, a mackerel in the left long, and a mullet in the right long outrigger as fast as I had ever seen. Dee was smoking like a locomotive. She had a cigarette in each hand and was doing laps around the fighting chair. Her size-four Top-Sider boat shoes were wearing a rut in the teak deck. Newt was chewing on the base of a big stinky cigar.

The left short mullet went down with a marlin strike, and Newt missed a two-hundred-pound blue. It moved to the mackerel on the left long outrigger, and this time Newt stuck him. Newt got in the fighting chair, and I saw a big boil of white water where the right long mullet had been. I called to Dee, and she hooked the marlin on her first try. Our bad luck had turned to good luck. Since Newt was in the fighting chair, I favored his fish and lined up the back of our boat with both marlin, one behind the other.

Newt's fish was seventy-five yards straight behind the boat, and Dee's fish was another fifty yards behind Newt's marlin. I liked to use this technique when catching doubleheaders. We backed to Newt's fish, and Mel got the leader wire while Sam tagged the marlin and clipped the leader wire. Dee's marlin had turned down sea, so I spun the boat toward the westbound fish. After some speed and a little zippie-do with the boat, Mel got the leader wire while Sam tagged and released the second blue marlin, after I documented the catch on film, with Dee grinning toward the camera lens. Dee ran inside the saloon and recorded the info.

I could see the atmosphere in the cockpit was improving, since no one was smoking. It was getting late, so I kept trolling toward the corner, giving us the shortest run home possible. We were five released marlin for seventeen marlin bites. With ten minutes to go, the mullet in the left short went down, and a blue attacked the bait three times. Newt missed it each time. The marlin then attacked the left long mackerel with a violent crashing strike. Newt had him on and was in the fighting chair.

Mel was getting his wiring gloves on while Sam was getting the tag stick ready. Dee, who was winding in the right long outrigger bait, looked up at me and said, "Something is wrong, I can't wind." I pushed both throttle levers forward, and the engines roared for three seconds as the boat jumped forward for fifty feet. Dee's rod was now bent over, with line screaming off the reel. We had hooked another doubleheader of blue marlin! All went well, and we tagged and released both.

We were running home after catching seven blue marlin out of nineteen strikes. In fishermen's language that is seven for nineteen. We had gone from bad luck to good luck to very good luck!

CHAPTER 30

PIER 5, MIAMI, FLORIDA, APRIL 1, 1980 VICKY'S GOOD FRIDAY AMBERJACK

It was Tuesday, and I was running my commercial fishing boat, the *Coconut*, out of Pier 5 in Miamarina. I had built this boat so I could be independent of everyone and could make money any day I wanted to work. All I had to do was get out of bed and drive to the dock, put ice in the fish hold, cast off the dock lines, and catch fish.

The *Coconut* was a thirty-four-foot Crusader with a Caterpillar diesel engine that pushed the boat and ran a hydraulic system that allowed me to run two bandits. A bandit is a commercial fishing reel that is self-standing, with a large narrow spool that is just over three feet around and holds over a thousand feet of wire line or monofilament line.

When I built the boat, I put an aft steering station with a clutch-throttle on top of a two-by-two-feet helm arrangement that was four feet tall and self-standing. This aft helm station was four and a half feet ahead of the transom. This way I could steer the boat and take the engine in and out of gear while I worked the two hydraulic bandits. I had a 1,200-pound fish box that rested on the helm station, which allowed me to catch fish, gaff them, and run the boat at the same time.

A YOUNG FISHERMAN'S DREAM COME TRUE

I had a helm and clutch-throttle station in the front right (starboard) side of the boat also. The VHF radio and Fathometer were both there. I had carefully thought this out so I could fish alone or with a crew. The way the boat was set up, it allowed me to troll for dolphin in the summer, fish deep-water tilefish in the fall, troll for grouper on the reefs in the winter, and fish amberjack in the spring. I also could tie the boat up and travel the world as a freelance captain.

Every year Good Friday was very special at our dock because of the tremendous amount of fish we sold for that holiday week. Amberjack made up the most volume because April was the best month to catch them, since they spawn over all the deep-water wrecks located off the Miami coast. The larger amberjack were all female and usually were filled with huge quantities of eggs.

I had a cute seventeen-year-old blonde named Vickie who sold fish for me on a percentage basis. It was a good job for her because she could sleep late and come to the dock after noon, set up shop, cut fish, and get a suntan. She liked to fillet amberjacks because they did not have sharp teeth or sharp spines and had a high yield of fillets.

It did not take her long to acquire a following of men who would buy fresh fish from her on their way home from work. We had a huge City of Miami parking lot directly behind the boat that had several hundred parking places. On weekends families would drive to Pier 5 to see all the fish the charter boats and commercial fishing boats caught. Some families bought fresh fish to take home. The tourists would pose with the sailfish and large sharks for treasured pictures to show when they returned to their hometowns. The young boys and girls loved sitting on the big sharks while being photographed. Working out of Pier 5 was a great life!

Vickie quickly learned that this hard work paid off well. She moved out of her mother's house and into a nice apartment just north of the boat. Her first apartment ever was located on the west side of Biscayne Bay, with a water view. She even bought a car, so she did not need to take the bus.

She bragged that many of the male fish customers gave her tips for cutting their fish. When I suggested she might try not wearing a bra and wearing a loose top, Vickie snapped at me, saying, "What kind of girl do you think I am?" A week later she tried wearing a lower-cut shirt and no bra, and the tips dramatically increased. As did the number of male fish customers.

That Tuesday, April 1, I departed the dock at five in the morning by myself, with over three hundred live pinfish and blue runner in my live-bait well. I went down Biscayne Bay and out by Cape Florida Light while it was still dark. At that time GPS had not been invented, so I needed sunlight to see the land ranges to fish the wrecks. I was near the first wreck I wanted to fish when the eastern sky started to turn red, then orange and finally yellow. I had thirty hundred-foot leaders of 120-pound test monofilament with 10/0 Mustad hooks coiled on plastic yo-yos ready to go for my backup rigs.

I dropped the first hydraulic bandit rig to the bottom long before the sun started to rise and had a bite from an amberjack. I threw the next live pinfish bait behind the boat and let the hydraulic reel lower it to the bottom as the right bandit was pulling the first amberjack to the surface. Hitting the bottom with the left bandit, another hungry fish instantly ate the live pinfish. I pushed the hydraulic valve down, and the amberjack was hooked and on its way to the surface.

As the bandit reels wound in the wire line, the four-pound weight had to be unsnapped when it reached the pulley at the end of the bandit arm. I would stop the bandit momentarily and unsnap the lead weight to the drop rig. Then the bandit would wind the hundred-foot mono leader to the boat so I could gaff the fish in the throat latch and lift it in the boat.

After I had six or eight amberjack on the deck, I would move them to the forward fish hold, which was below decks, and lay them on the ice. This went on for five hours, with a rare catch of a mutton snapper or a black grouper. Very seldom would I pull a hook or break the 120-pound test leader. Doubleheader after doubleheader came up and into the boat.

I kept a written score next to the forward helm because my big eight-foot-long dock fish storage box held only 120 amberjack. The amberjack averaged very large that day. By one o'clock in the afternoon, I had about one hundred amberjack, so I headed home at a fast troll to Miamarina. Vickie was waiting with dollar signs in her pretty blue eyes when I arrived.

I would lift five amberjack out of the fish hold and put them on the dock. Vickie would start washing out the stomach areas as soon as I gutted the jack and removed the egg sacs. She put the washed egg sacs, or roe, in a five-gallon bucket to sell later. Surprisingly, it took longer to clean, dress, and store an amberjack in the big fish box with ice than it did to catch one on a hydraulic bandit.

The big fish box started to fill with rows of fish and ice. As we stored the fish, the first amberjack faced east, and the next faced west and so on all the way across the box. Then we covered the row of amberjack with shaved ice.

When I was pulling the amberjack out of the fish hold, I would leave the very large ones till last. By ten o'clock at night, we had only about ten of the largest jack left to gut and ice. All ten of these big amberjack were females and weighed over eighty pounds each. I gutted all but two and iced the big fish in the front of the dock box. Vickie wanted me to weigh the largest two. Each weighed over one hundred pounds. By the time Vickie and I washed the dock and the boat, it was midnight, so I headed home.

When the alarm went off at four o'clock the next morning, I was so tired and sore from working an eighteen-hour day, I did not go fishing. I met Vicky at noon and started filleting the largest jack first. She sold the amberjack I cut into steaks while I filleted them till eight o'clock that night. Vickie sold almost all of the hundreds of pounds of amberjack I filleted, skinned, deboned, and staked to our loyal fish customers.

When the alarm went off at 4:00 a.m. on Wednesday, April 3, I was ready to go fishing. I arrived at the boat at 5:15 and put another four hundred pounds of ice in the fish box, and I was off. I planned on running south and trolling the reef for groupers with the wire line bandits. This was my favorite way of fishing. The shallow-water reef area that runs from Fowey Rocks Light on south to below Key West is a treasure of clear, beautiful reefs and coral heads. Black groupers, red groupers, gag groupers, and mutton snappers all loved to eat the feather and a bait I trolled on the wire line bandit hydraulic reels.

The wind was out of the northwest, and there was not one cloud in the blue sky. A cold front had gone by, making it cool and giving the clear reef all the colors that *National Geographic* magazine would dream of. The black groupers were biting that day. As I would let the hydrologic reels wind in the groupers, the cero mackerel would bite the white weathers I fished from the two 4/0 red-sided Penn Senator reels. I wanted to catch everything possible that day so Vickie could sell amberjack, barracuda, cero mackerel, bar jack, black groupers, red groupers, gag groupers, mutton snappers, and kingfish.

A YOUNG FISHERMAN'S DREAM COME TRUE

I returned to Pier 5 at dark and saw Vickie almost at her wits' end. The fish customers were lined up, demanding the amberjack she was trying to cut to keep up with the demand. I picked up my filleting knife and started filleting amberjack as fast as I could. By eleven o'clock that night, we had sold almost eighty of the amberjack I had caught two days earlier. Vickie begged me to catch some more the next day so she could sell fish all Good Friday.

Vickie and I unloaded the twenty-nine groupers, fifty cero mackerel, ten barracuda, five kingfish, and two muttons and a one-hundred-pound blacktip shark I had just caught. I also had two five-gallon buckets of bar jack, blue runner, needlefish, and a lizard fish.

I didn't gut anything but the blacktip shark, since Vickie sold the snappers and groupers whole and then filleted or staked them as the customers requested. Most the small cero mackerel were filleted after being weighed whole, and the kingfish were staked. Vickie always filleted the small sharks and sold the snow-white meat without ever saying what it was.

The next afternoon I backed into my slip with more than fifty amberjack and started cutting the few remaining from what I had caught several days earlier for the fish customers. When I finished the last of the one hundred plus amberjack I had caught on Tuesday, Vickie told the remaining customers we were out of fish. When everyone drove away, we started unloading amberjack after amberjack. We then gutted, washed, stacked, and iced each fish.

Vickie helped me wash the boat and put away the tackle. We then iced the fish hold in the boat and fed the pinfish in the live-bait wells. After locking the big fish box on the dock and locking all the storage lockers, we both looked at each other. It was midnight, and we were exhausted. Little blue-eyed Vickie had fish blood on her face and in her curly blond hair and was a mess. I had been up since 4:30 a.m. and looked no better, with fish blood on my face, arms, and chest.

Vickie stepped up on the eight-inch-tall wooden pallet she stood on to cut fish during the day. She looked at me with exhausted eyes, put her arms around my neck, and said, "Can I go home with you and shower?"

CHAPTER 31

PIER 5, MIAMI, FLORIDA, APRIL 13, 1981 JC DOBSON AND THE AMBERJACK

It was Monday, and I was fishing out of Miamarina on the *Coconut*. That year Good Friday fell on the seventeenth of April. During this holy week, the charter boats and commercial fishing boats would sell more fish off the dock than any other week of the year. The best-selling fish by far was amberjack.

Captain JC Dobson had no job at the time and wanted to make some money to pay his rent, so he asked if he could work on my commercial fishing boat for one day and help catch a load of amberjack to sell during the Good Friday week. I consulted Vickie, and she agreed. JC came down to the dock and caught live pinfish for three afternoons while Vickie sold fish at the dock. That was a good year for catching pinfish around our dock, so keeping the five live-bait wells that floated in my boat slip filled was easy. At that time of the year, I would fish for amberjack two days a week and then grouper the rest of the week. Amberjack were sold by the pound after they were filleted, skinned, and deboned. Grouper were sold whole and then cleaned and prepared to order.

JC and I departed the dock at four thirty on Monday morning, heading south down Biscayne Bay at ten knots in the cool darkness long before the sun thought about rising. We would fish two hydraulic bandits that ran off the hydraulic system driven by the caterpillar diesel engine. A bandit is a self-standing fishing reel with a hydraulic variable speed motor that turns a large spool made of high density fiberglass. I made my own special brake washers so the reels would be as smooth as the most expensive sport fishing reels on the market.

The system I refined on my commercial fishing boat was a work of art because I could start the bandit reel slowly, letting line out, and walk to the other reel and start letting the line out at any speed I wanted. Once the weight hit bottom, I wound the rig up ten turns, equaling thirty feet, and then walked several steps to the other bandit and did the same. I had a clutch, throttle, and steering wheel located four feet ahead of the stern of the boat.

Seeing the fiberglass arm with the big pulley mounted underneath the tip of the bandit bounce or bend over, I would initiate the hydraulic motor and hook the fish then slow the motor down so there was no way of breaking the 120-pound test leader or pulling the double-strength hook. If the fish ran, the break washers allowed the spool to slip while the hydraulic motor kept running. Once the fish stopped, the reel pulled the fish slowly up to the boat. I attached a four-pound weight with two long-line snaps that allowed me to unsnap the weight as the reel retrieved the line winding the hundred-foot leader onto the spool. All I had to do was gaff the fish.

With a hydraulic system, the electrical problems associated with electric reels are eliminated, and the overheating problem of catching thirty or forty big fish in a row does not exist. Hydraulic reels never overheat. The only problem is having a loose sleeve or open jacket get caught as the motor turns. The motor will not stop unless the oil entering the reel is shut off.

The first wreck I wanted to fish was just south of Fowey Rocks Light and was in a little over two hundred feet of water. I had caught sixty amberjack there the previous Saturday. On our way south, JC made up ten long leaders with 10/0 hooks all sharpened like razors. Most big amberjack swallow the baits. Once the fish was in the boat, I liked to cut the leader a foot or so in front of the amberjack's mouth to remind us to get the expensive hook out of the fish later. We would then retie a new hook on the rig, put a live pinfish on the hook, and send the rig to the bottom. After catching a dozen jack on one rig, a new leader was needed.

As I lined up on the wreck, the sun started to creep over the horizon. We both dropped our rigs at the same time and brought them up about thirty feet. Instantly we hooked a doubleheader. JC had never used a hydraulic bandit, so he needed a little coaching. The best part about fishing a hydraulic bandit is watching the reel do all the work. My fish was the first up, so I gaffed it in the throat area, making blood shoot up into the air. I pulled the fish over the transom and dragged it forward then got ready to drop again.

I tried to gaff the fish in the throat or gills so they bled profusely. The more blood the fish lost, the whiter the meat was when it was filleted and sold. As JC gaffed his amberjack, I put the boat in gear and moved the *Coconut* south to drop our baits again. That day the Gulf Stream was flowing north at a slow speed, so jack fishing was easy. We trolled a couple hundred yards into the current and dropped the live pinfish to the bottom.

Both hydraulic bandits instantly had amberjack on and pulling. This went on for about twenty jack before I hooked something small, and I quickly pulled it to the boat and gaffed the fish. A fifteen-pound mutton snapper had eaten my pinfish. JC pulled another forty-pound amberjack into the boat, and we were off trolling south. We dropped again and again, at least twenty times, catching doubleheader after doubleheader. We did not break a leader on a single jack, even though some of the fish were eighty pounds or more.

After catching about sixty amberjack, we started to brag about not losing a single fish to a shark—not one was even bitten by a shark. Even though the jack blood continued to pour out the scuppers in the back of the boat, not a single shark had come up behind the stern. Then, as I pulled my third mutton snapper up, I looked over and saw something big down in the blue Gulf Stream water. Really big! When JC's fifty-pound amberjack almost reached the surface of the water, a huge tiger shark slowly swam up behind the fish but did not try to eat it for lunch. As JC gaffed the jack, the thirteen- or fourteen-foot tiger shark rolled over and slowly disappeared back into the depths. JC looked at me and said, "That was a full-grown shark."

I started the *Coconut* trolling south while JC and I put new rigs on our bandits. The next drop went the same as every other. We reached bottom, brought the bait up thirty feet, and hooked a doubleheader. Since the blood was flowing out the back of the boat, both of us kept looking for the huge shark. My fish always reached the back of the boat first because I had much more experience running hydraulic bandits. This time I could see the huge tiger shark following my amberjack. I gaffed the big jack, and again the shark slowly rolled over and went down far enough to see JC's amberjack. He then followed JC's fish up to the boat but did not get close enough to bight the jack.

I trolled south, and we both dropped again. My jack came up first, with the huge tiger shark swimming five feet behind. It again rolled over so we could see its beautiful stripes and snow-white stomach then disappeared down deep, only to find JC's fish and start to follow it to the surface. Even though I would troll back two hundred yards, the tiger shark would find us and follow our jack to the surface.

JC and I had agreed to stop fishing when we caught just over one hundred amberjack. Since I kept score on the helm area with a pencil, I checked the score and saw we had just passed ninety. One hundred amberjack was about as many as we could handle, since we had to gut, wash, unload, and stack all of them in the big eight-foot fish box on the dock.

We'd had the entire fishing area to ourselves all day. Then a triple-engine outboard ran up next to us, with four members of a local fishing club glaring at JC and me. I smiled and politely said, "Fishing is good," to which I got no response. They all got their spinning tackle out, and I waited for them to drop their lines. Once all of them had gotten to the bottom, I put the *Coconut* in gear and trolled back to make another drop, leaving them fishing far behind the wreck.

Both JC and I were hooked up to amberjack when the other boat ran by us and turned only feet in front of my bow. One fisherman dropped his spinning rig and hooked an amberjack. I turned offshore and worked the *Coconut* around their drifting boat. About that time my fish was up, so I gaffed it as they watched. I told JC not to say anything about our big striped friend that followed up every one of our jack, including the one I had just caught.

The huge tiger shark turned down and saw JC's fish, as always slowly following it partway up to the surface. This time was different. The shark turned down and swam toward the outboard boat that was fighting the amberjack on light tackle. Since they were so close we could almost touch their boat, I said, "We have caught quite a few amberjack that would weigh over a hundred pounds." The four of them looked at each other, and their eyes got huge. Catching a hundred-pound amberjack would be a club record for them, so it was like winning the lottery.

JC suddenly knew what I was doing and muttered, "You bastard!" I drifted next to the other boat, watching a club member trying to catch an amberjack on his spinning outfit. He was making slow progress, with the amberjack inching its way toward the surface. As JC and

I expected, the rod bent over a little more, and the line started to leave the reel slowly.

I told the guys, "That one is over a hundred pounds. I guarantee that is a fact." I put our boat in gear, and we went back to catch a couple more doubleheaders before we headed home. We gutted and headed amberjack as the boat trolled toward home.

About three miles north, I saw the outboard drifting, with the angler battling his fish. I pulled up on the opposite side of the boat as the angler battled the mystery fish and asked if they had seen it yet. The captain, who now liked me, said, "Cappy, you were right. This amberjack must be over a hundred pounds."

I told all four, "Good luck on your club record" and put our boat in gear, heading north at trolling speed. JC and I agreed that the next time we saw that giant tiger shark, we would give it a big amberjack for getting rid of the outboard.

As I backed into the slip at Miamarina, I saw cute little Vickie waving me in and saying, "Faster, faster! I've been out of fish for two hours, and I have twenty customers waiting." I sent JC to help her cut amberjack, and I started stacking and icing our catch. I needed to keep a careful count, since both Vickie and JC were on shares, and I wanted a peaceful home front at the dock. We ended up catching 114 amberjack, five mutton snappers, and two black groupers. All the while the hydraulic bandits never complained or got tired.

CHAPTER 32

St. Thomas, US Virgin Islands, August 18, 1986 Ray Rosher and Monty Padilla

Ray Rosher tagging and releasing this 350 pound blue marlin for Monty Padilla from Mexico on Ralph Christiansen's boat Pescador. Captain Bill Harrison and mates Ray Rosher and Tito.

Ralph Christiansen and Monty Pidilla at Club Nautico de San Juan with Monty's two blue marlin 398 and 379 pounds. Caught on the Pescador. Captain Bill Harrison and mates Ray Rosher and Tito August 18, 1986

I was running the *Pescador* for Ralph Christiansen Jr. Ray Rosher and I had flown from Miami to Puerto Rico five days earlier and joined the boat at Club Nautico in downtown San Juan. We had to load the boat with two weeks of groceries and bait for a trip to St. Thomas to fish for blue marlin on the famous North Drop. Tito, Ralph's freelance mate, showed up two mornings later to ride to American Yacht Harbor in St. Thomas and help wash the boat.

Ralph's longtime fishing friend, Monty Padilla from Mexico City, would fly into Charlotte Amalie with Ralph to fish once we were set up and had the boat ready. This would be Monty's first time fishing on the Whiticar-built boat Ralph had recently purchased. I enjoyed marlin fishing and running the *Pescador* for Ralph because I knew all his crazy ways, since we had teamed up to fish St. Thomas starting in 1969. We had formed a bond that brought me back almost every year to captain his many boats for the three summer full moons of July, August, and September.

I was the only captain in the Caribbean who would get the boat moving before the sun would even show any color to the east and troll till it was so dark my mates could not see the marlin baits. When I ran the boat for Ralph, it was common for him to join Ray in the cockpit after we had the marlin baits out and had been trolling for over an hour. But sometimes his nighttime fun interfered with his fishing fun. Ray had several embarrassing times when we would hook a blue marlin, and he would run forward to Ralph's open cabin door to tell him about the jumping fish. Moments later my teenage mate would try to tell me, as I looked down from the flying bridge, why Ralph could not leave his cabin to catch the fish. All I had to do was see Ray's red face and his inability to explain exactly what Ralph's predicament was.

After facing this same situation so many times in the past, I kept a Hilton Hotel bath towel in the flying bridge with me. Once Ralph finished with the important things in life, he would rush out to the cockpit to catch the blue marlin that had finished jumping and was almost as exhausted as Ralph was. I would throw the towel down to him, and he would wrap it around his waist, making it easier on the crew. Ralph never figured out why all the marlin boats would troll close to us, and the crews would shout congratulations to Ralph when he had not yet caught and released the marlin. I got such satisfaction when I very professionally explained Ralph's situation over the radio for all the fleet to hear.

That week of blue marlin fishing on the North Drop was like a dream come true for Ray. Every night when we backed into our slip at American Yacht Harbor, the captains and mates came over to congratulate him. We were hot and the boat to beat for the rest of the marlin fleet. After fishing the North Drop for so many years with Roy and Ralph, I had the marlin bite figured out that year.

Ray went from hoping to catch one marlin in the Bahamas during each of his many trips to seeing five or ten blues every day off St. Thomas. We caught three, four, or five marlin every day that week. I was sorry Ray could not join us the next month, September 1986, because Bobby Jenkins and I caught and released thirty-nine blue marlin in six days of fishing before heading back to San Juan and flying home to Miami.

But back on August 18, the trip was over, and Monty Padilla wanted to ride back to San Juan on the *Pescador*. I asked Ralph if it was OK if we ran to the North Drop and fished for two hours before heading west to Club Nautico. Ralph was the greatest! He knew I was going to put a blue marlin or two in the boat, since I sold them in San Juan. This cash was put to good use. I could take my girlfriend out to a nice restaurant once I returned to Miami, since I had been gone for over two weeks.

Ray and I said good-bye to all of our friends on the dock and headed for the North Drop to marlin fish. I told Monty, Tito, and Ray we had two hours to fish. The boys had the baits out and fishing in moments. It did not take long for a very large blue to eat the mackerel that was fished on the right long outrigger. Monty was in the fighting chair and had full drag on the jumping fish. Suddenly the hook pulled. Ray wound the bait in and held up the hook. It had straightened out. This was a one in a thousand chance.

All was going great, and the *Pescador* was fishing again, with two mackerel flopping in our wake. A small blue attacked the left long outrigger, and Monty did not have the same luck as he had with the big blue earlier. He missed hooking the fish. We were off again, and a three-hundred-pound marlin crashed the right long outrigger. Monty

A YOUNG FISHERMAN'S DREAM COME TRUE

stuck him, and the battle was on. Tito steered the fighting chair while Ray put on the cotton wiring gloves. Ray would be the wire man, and Tito would be the gaff man. Everyone would help pull the marlin over the side of the boat if all went well.

After twenty minutes the marlin turned down sea, and I ran the *Pescador* up next to the fish as Ray grabbed the leader wire and Tito gaffed the tired marlin. I went down from the flying bridge, grabbed the blue marlin's nose, and started it up as Ray, Monty, and Tito pulled. The fish slid over the starboard covering board and into the cockpit of the *Pescador*. Monty jumped on top of the marlin and asked me to take lots of pictures. We were one out of three as of that point. This means we had three blue marlin strikes and had caught one fish.

Monty helped the boys get the baits out again, since we were down to less than thirty minutes of fishing time. Once I had the boat in a perfect position on the Drop, Ray yelled, and Monty hooked the marlin. I never saw it. Ray helped Monty get in the fighting chair, and we were back in action, with the rod bent double. Monty was the exact opposite of Ralph. He listened to everything Ray said. Monty watched the rod tip and the bend in the rod. He asked Ray about drag and the right amount of pressure to put on the spool of the reel. I could see they were a good team!

The marlin jumped a few last times and headed down sea. I put the *Pescador* in the perfect position for Ray to grab the leader wire, but the marlin started to dig. This is when a marlin is on its side and tries to turn its head down and pull against the person who is wiring it. I could see Ray's shoulders go up and down with the beating of the marlin's tail. A good mate can hold on only so long before giving up.

I took the port engine out of gear, and the boat slowed just enough for the fish to turn and stick its head out of the water. Tito placed the flying gaff over the marlin's right shoulder and pulled.

The exhausted fish shook and rolled over dead. Monty was out of the fighting chair and helping me with the nose of the three-hundred-pound marlin. The four of us pulled the fish over the covering board and into the *Pescador*'s cockpit. Monty was so happy! He sat on the fish and had me photograph him with both blue marlin.

I asked Ray if he wanted to troll the last five minutes, and he threw the mackerel over the transom without answering. As he ran the mackerel bait up to the right long outrigger, I saw a huge splash. A marlin had eaten the bait. Monty had the fish on and was in the fighting chair. The battle was on. This 350-pound fish put on a show. It jumped a dozen times and headed down sea.

I called Ray to the bridge and explained that Ralph had told me two blue marlin in the boat would be our limit. Once the 350-pound marlin was close, I told Monty, Tito, and Ray to get the tag pole ready with a National Marine Fisheries Service tag. Ray had the system down perfect. He would wire the 350-pound blue marlin, Tito would tag the fish, and Monty would get out of the fighting chair and move to the starboard side of the *Pescador* so I could photograph everyone releasing the tagged blue marlin.

Once this blue marlin was tagged and released, marlin fishing was over for me for the next two weeks. I headed the *Pescador* west toward San Juan while Monty and Tito collapsed in the air-conditioned saloon. Ray scrubbed the cockpit, coolers, and fish box for the next three hours. He finally came to the flying bridge as we rounded Morro Castle and headed toward Club Nautico.

This was before cell phones, so I called one of the boats tied up at Club Nautico on the radio when we were one hour away from the dock. I knew Ralph would like to be at the dock to congratulate Monty when we backed in our slip at the club. Sure enough, Ralph was standing on the dock with a group of his fellow fishermen. He was wearing a suit and had a drink in his hand.

We pulled both marlin out of the cockpit and onto the dock. The first blue weighed 379 pounds, and the second weighed 398 pounds. When I look back at the pictures, it's funny to see Ralph standing with Monty, wearing an expensive business suit. Ray, Tito, and I are all wearing shorts and T-shirts and are barefoot.

Ray and I chose to stay with fishing our entire lives so we would never need to wear suits to work. Several years later, when Ray and I had to accept some award, we both had to borrow sport jackets to go onstage. The awards committee let us wear our sandals.

CHAPTER 33

ST. THOMAS, US VIRGIN ISLANDS, SEPTEMBER 13, 1986
ROY'S BEST BLUE MARLIN DAY EVER!

One of eight blue marlin tagged and released off St. Thomas USVI on the Pescador. Captain Bill Harrison and mate Bobby Jenkins. September 13, 1986

Roy Camero would be the only angler that day on the fifty-six-foot Whiticar named *Pescador*. Roy's best friend and owner of the *Pescador*, Ralph Christiansen Jr., would be flying in later

A YOUNG FISHERMAN'S DREAM COME TRUE

that day. Bobby Jenkins was one mate, and Tito was the other. Roy wanted to fish all natural baits, so Bobby would rig mullet and mackerel all the way out to the fishing area. It was a typical St. Thomas day. The wind was east at eighteen to twenty knots, with a short sea forming on top of the North Drop.

We reached the corner, the area where I liked to start trolling for marlin, at eight fifteen in the morning and were the fourth boat to put our lines in the water. A big Hatteras named *Beast Master* was only two miles ahead and was the first boat on the edge. That day I fished two short outriggers with mullet and two long outriggers with mackerel for bait. The short rigger was run halfway up the outrigger, and the long rigger was run all the way up to the tip of the outrigger.

Roy would help by putting out the long outrigger bait and handing Tito the mark. Roy kept his hand on the spool of the 9/0 Fin-Nor reel while Tito put the mark in the pin and ran the line up to the top of the outrigger. Bobby put out the other long outrigger bait and ran the mark up by himself. He always let the mark go past the tip of the rod, leaving enough line out to reach the top of the outrigger while the reel was set at striking drag. Every day or two, we would get a surprise marlin strike while the mates were putting the baits out.

I had fished Roy on his honeymoon out of Bimini in the Bahamas in the mid-1960s. We had started a lifetime friendship on the first day of marlin fishing when Roy walked out of the cabin, looked up at me, and said, "What do you think?"

I looked at the baits and excitedly answered, "There's a blue marlin behind your bait."

As all true fishermen would do, Roy handed his bride, Carolla, his coffee cup and hooked the fish on the first shot. What a guy! He did catch the marlin. You would have to ask Roy the weight of his Bimini blue marlin, because I can't remember.

The following year I flew to Puerto Rico to fish the San Juan International Blue Marlin Tournament with Roy as one angler and Ralph Christiansen Jr. as the other. I would fish this tournament twenty more times with one or both of the above.

The *Pescador* was equipped with eight 9/0 Fin-Nor reels and matching rods. All reels were filled with one-hundred-pound test monofilament line. Ralph's father had passed down his collection of more than twenty Fin-Nor reels to his fisherman son. We would use only four outfits that day.

We started off by tagging and releasing a 275-pound blue marlin. Roy had him to the boat in fifteen minutes, and Tito had the wire. Bobby tagged the fish with a National Marine Fisheries Service tag. Tito loved to wire fish, and Bobby liked to tag and cut the leader wire on the marlin. Bobby was good at writing down the weights and times on the cards so there was never any confusion of information with the correct tag number and card.

Roy's next fish was a 325-pound blue. This one took a little more time, maybe twenty minutes, and we tagged the blue marlin and released it. Roy's luck ran out on the next bite. He had three or four shots on an average-size fish but never bent the rod. He hooked the next blue, but the hook pulled before he moved the rod to the fighting chair.

The next blue was about 250 pounds, and Roy had him to the boat quickly for a tagged and released fish. He missed the next blue. The next blue was nicer. About 475 pounds and was tagged and released. That made four blue marlin for Roy, and all of us were thinking the same thing: *two and a half hours of fishing time left.*

A YOUNG FISHERMAN'S DREAM COME TRUE

Bobby finally had to stop rigging baits and make some quick sandwiches for the starving crew. No one had time to eat, because Roy was trying to hook a blue on the left long outrigger bait while Tito was trying to hook another marlin on the right short bait. Bobby immediately saw the right long pop out of the outrigger pin, so he grabbed the reel and tried his luck. From what I could see from the bridge, everyone was doing things correctly.

Then came that dreaded moment when all of us realized no one had hooked a marlin. Roy was the first to see the empty plastic five-gallon pail, so he started kicking it. Then Tito joined in. Even Bobby had to give it a couple of kicks at the end. Three grown men kicking a plastic bucket around the cockpit did not bring back any of the missed blue marlin, but it did make them feel better.

With two of the four trolling baits out and flopping behind the boat, Roy hooked another blue. He quickly had the double line on the reel, and I turned the boat down sea. Up came the swivel. Tito wired the fish close enough for Bobby to tag it and cut the leader wire. This two-hundred-pound blue marlin made it five for the day. As the guys put out the baits again, Bobby thought he saw something behind his, so he called Roy over to take the reel he was dropping back. With nothing happening, Bobby called up to me, "Cappie, what do you see?"

I was looking forward, so it took a few moments for me to see the bait. I dropped to one knee and said, "Here he comes." A five-hundred-pound blue jumped three quarters of the way out of the water and crashed the mackerel bait. Roy was ready and hooked the fish on the first try. This fish jumped and jumped and jumped some more. By the time it turned down sea, it was so tired I simply ran up close enough for Tito to get the leader wire and pull the marlin close enough for Bobby to put a tag in its back. After Bobby snipped the leader wire, I watched him swim for 100 yards on top of the water down sea.

Now Roy had six blue marlin tagged and released. This was his personal best by far. We were ten minutes from the corner, and the *Beast Master* was running up behind us heading for the dock. They were docked next to us, and Russ Hinsley and friends were some of the nicest people I have ever meet.

When they got close alongside, Captain Dan called on the radio with congratulates for Roy and the crew of the *Pescador* for releasing six blues in one day. The three in the cockpit were standing on the port side waving, and I was standing on the port side of the bridge doing the same. The Fin-Nor reel Roy was leaning against started screaming with a 450-pound blue on and jumping.

When I slowed the boat down, I saw a second small blue marlin eat the right short bait and hook. It immediately shot into the air and jumped several more times next to the first fish. We now had a doubleheader jumping between the *Beast Master* and our boat. Roy jumped into the fighting chair to do battle with his marlin, and Tito fought his from the covering board rod holder.

When we backed into our slip next to the *Beast Master* with eight blue marlin flags flying, Ralph was on the dock with a big cigar in his mouth and two beautiful blondes, one under each arm. Denise Jenkins, Bobby's lovely wife, was one, and the other was the flavor of the day. Ralph was as proud of us as Roy was for catching seven blues in a single day.

Roy had accomplished a lifetime achievement by catching seven blue marlin in a single day, and Tito had a lifetime great for catching his first blue marlin ever. Ralph shook my hand and said, "Captain Dan came up to the bar and said we better walk out to the dock. When I ran by them, they had released six blues, and we watched them hook a doubleheader."

A YOUNG FISHERMAN'S DREAM COME TRUE

Ralph, Roy, and I would team up to release another couple hundred blue marlin.

Unfortunately Ralph has since sailed on.

CHAPTER 34

ST. THOMAS, US VIRGIN ISLANDS, SEPTEMBER 14, 1986
A GREAT BLUE MARLIN DAY ON THE PESCADOR

Nine blue marlin tagged and released in one day on the Pescador off St. Thomas by Ralph Christiansen and Roy Camero with captain Bill Harrison and mates Bobby Jenkins and Tito. September 14, 1986. Photo by Jimmy Loveland

It was Sunday, and I was running the *Pescador* with Bobby Jenkins mating. The wooden boat, owned by Ralph Christiansen Jr., was built in Stuart, Florida, by Whiticar Boat Works in 1965 and was the best marlin trolling boat I had ever fished as a captain. We had Roy Camero as our second angler and Marielle Brandon, the St. Thomas Fisheries biologist, and her friend, Mary-King, riding along. The previous day we had caught and released eight blue marlin out of twelve strikes. Marielle's job was to keep technical information and score of how many blue marlin we raised, hooked, tagged, and released. Mary-King was our cheerleader.

Bobby Jenkins and I had flown to Puerto Rico and run the boat to St. Thomas four days earlier. Bobby had mated for me out of Pier 5 in Miami, and we had fished together all through the Bahamas. Bobby had grown up working on charter boats and knew how to keep pace when fishing became really fast and hectic. Bobby was the best all-around mate who ever worked with me.

Our next mate was Tito, a local Puerto Rican who liked to catch marlin. Bobby would make all the mullet and mackerel baits, and Tito would keep the rods and reels fishing with good baits.

Ralph would fish the two rods on the left side of the cockpit, and Roy would have the two rods on the right. I fished a mackerel on both long outrigger rods and either a mullet or a lure on the short rigger rods. All four reels were 9/0 Fin-Nors filled with one-hundred-pound test monofilament line mounted on heavy rods made by Biscayne Rods of Miami. The hooks were either 11/0 or 12/0 Mustad double strength, with heavy leader wire that broke at 360 pounds rigged to every bait. Ralph or Roy would catch the blue marlin, then Tito would wire them; Bobby tagged and released them, and Marielle would record the tag number and information on a National Marine Fisheries Service tag card. The blond-haired, blue-eyed Mary-King would cheer.

The day was a little windy, but this was St. Thomas, and we were in the trade winds, so the wind blew hard almost every day. We were headed up sea on the North Drop at a fast troll when Ralph had the first bite of the day. With a mackerel for bait, he had three good shots at a hungry marlin and missed every bite. Marielle logged the info while Roy laughed. Two minutes later a blue crashed Roy's short rigger bait, and he missed it. The marlin faded back and ate the long outrigger bait. Roy was caught by surprise, and he missed two good shots before it swam away. Marielle and Mary-King giggled and logged the info.

Ralph complained to Bobby that the hooks weren't sharp enough, so Bobby handed him one. Ralph checked the point on his left thumb and drew blood. Marielle and Mary-King again giggled. While Ralph was studying the blood on his injured thumb, his left short bait disappeared inside an explosion of white water. A marlin had eaten the mullet, and the rod was bent, with line running off the reel.

Roy put the song "Tiny Winey" on the stereo, and we were off to catch our first marlin of the day. Tito wired the fish while Bobby tagged and released it by cutting the leader wire and Marielle logged all the info. Mary-King cheered. It was nice to have a plan come together.

Roy's right short bait was attacked while he was in the bathroom, and the lure did what most lures do best: it hooked the fish. The marlin jumped around for a while before the polished team went to work, and the marlin swam away with a tag in its shoulder. Everyone on the boat thought we had the system down to a science.

Ralph had a shot on the left short bait moments before Roy had a marlin grab the right short lure. They both missed their marlin, but I saw the same two marlin charge up behind the long outrigger mackerel. Both Ralph and Roy had several chances to hook the two marlin, but both fish slowly faded away.

Bobby handed Ralph a hook and said, "See if it's sharp enough." Marielle and Mary-King both giggled.

A YOUNG FISHERMAN'S DREAM COME TRUE

Bobby and Tito put the four baits out. Ralph had a strike two minutes later and hooked a marlin on the second try. Ralph was a great angler and knew how to use a heavy drag. He had a big cigar going when the double-line knot showed fifty feet behind the boat, and all of us watched as the fish got closer and closer. The double-line knot got to the tip of the rod, then to the reel, and when Tito was reaching for the swivel, the hook pulled. Five more feet and we would have had another released marlin.

The boat was as far out on the North Drop as I cared to troll, so I turned around and headed diagonally down sea. This was much more comfortable, and it was easier to see the marlin strikes when we were trolling down sea. Right away we had a doubleheader, and Roy stuck his marlin on the right long outrigger bait while Ralph missed his. I turned the boat around and circled Roy's fish. Ralph's marlin came up again on the right outrigger bait, but Ralph missed him. We then tagged and released Roy's second fish.

We had fished just over two hours and had nonstop great marlin action. Ralph had a shot on the left long mackerel and hooked him. This fish took off down sea, so I spun the boat and took off after him going bow first. After a one-mile run, the fish went down two hundred yards and stopped. Ralph went to work pumping the fish up to the boat, and we tagged and released it. Marielle logged the info. The mates put the baits out, and we were fishing our way back east to the North Drop.

As soon as the boat reached the drop-off, I turned right, and everyone saw the next blue marlin glide down a big wave and leap on Roy's long rigger mackerel. Both girls were squealing, and the line was running off the reel as Roy jumped in the fighting chair. This fish was the largest marlin of the day so far. It made three beautiful jumps, coming completely out of the water each time, and headed straight west. I went after him for a half mile while he swam on the surface. He then made a big semicircle and headed straight down for 350 yards. Roy pumped him up, and we tagged and released him in good shape.

Once all four baits were out, two marlin appeared behind the left short mullet, and another marlin grabbed the right short bait. Ralph and Roy tried their best but missed all the fish. Roy's marlin attacked the right long while Ralph's disappeared. Roy missed a couple of cheap shots on the mackerel. I circled back and could not find either blue, so I turned back down sea and started trolling again. Five minutes of trolling and I saw a marlin behind Ralph's long outrigger bait, and before I could yell, it crashed the mackerel. Ralph stuck him and jumped into the fighting chair.

This was a spectacular jumping fish that put on a show for the fleet of marlin boats. The marlin finally gave up and slowly swam on top of the water, making it easy to tag and release it as it swam down sea. Marielle logged the information while everyone rushed to get the baits back out, because marlin fishing was unbelievably good. Even Mary-King was helping to let baits out.

We had almost trolled our way to the corner where I would normally turn the boat back up sea when I heard shouting from the cockpit. A doubleheader of blue marlin had attacked the two long baits. Ralph and Roy did their best to hook both fish but missed each one.

Mary-King made the quickest lunch ever and brought the "bread and meat" out for everyone to eat. I had the boat in a corner and turned back up sea to again start our bumpy ride into a head sea. Roy shouted, "Got him on." He was in the fighting chair and doing battle for ten minutes before the marlin made its first spectacular jump and threw the hook.

I felt sorry for Bobby because he had been rigging and sewing baits all day and had not seen a single strike. Without him we could never

A YOUNG FISHERMAN'S DREAM COME TRUE

have kept the pace we had during this red-hot fishing day. Ralph had a fast marlin eat his left long outrigger bait. It jumped twice and was gone. As we were trolling up sea again, Ralph had a shot on the left short bait and hooked him. The marlin jumped six times and headed west down sea. I went after him, and we tagged and released the fish while Marielle recorded all the information.

We were running out of fishing time and were down to our last hour of trolling. I headed up sea for a short way, and Roy had a marlin strike on the right short. He hooked the marlin, and we were off again. The fish jumped a while and headed west, with us after it. Tito got the wire, and Bobby tagged and released another blue marlin. Marielle recorded the info, and Mary-King now let out the right long outrigger bait. She had been so helpful in the cockpit that day.

I turned the *Pescador* down sea, and we started to troll toward the corner on our last pass over the North Drop. Ralph had a shot on the left short and had the marlin on and jumping. Everyone was hoping to catch this fish, since it would set a record for the most blue marlin ever caught on the *Pescador* in a single day. The marlin jumped and headed west, surfing the waves down sea. I spun the boat around and headed bow first after the marlin. Once it made a long run, the fish went down a couple of hundred yards, and Ralph started pumping it to the surface.

It was getting late in the day, and everyone on our boat was thinking about sharks. All the boats in the fleet had lost marlin to sharks that summer but us. Ralph did a great job of pumping the marlin up to the surface so I could drive the *Pescador* close to it, allowing Tito and Bobby to wire, tag, and release the ninth blue marlin catch of the day. Marielle finished logging the information for the St. Thomas Fisheries Service while I ran the boat to American Yacht Harbor.

Once we reached the calm water, Ralph showered and put on his fanciest Hawaiian shirt while Roy mixed several of the standard St. Thomas drinks, rum and Coke. Jimmy Loveland, the mayor of the waterfront, had a mass of captains, mates, and well-wishers at the dock to greet the *Pescador*, which had nine blue marlin flags flying from the right outrigger. As we approached the dock, Ralph came up the bridge ladder to take the helm from me, so he would be driving the boat in all the pictures. I went down the bridge ladder to stand next to Bobby, who had made all this possible by keeping the beautiful baits available for all the anglers and crew.

I think Jimmy Loveland's story and pictures that went out to all the fishing magazines told a surprisingly good and accurate story from Jimmy's interviews of Ralph, Roy, Marielle, Mary-King, Tito, Bobby, and me, especially after fourteen empty Bacardi bottles and an unknown number of champagne and wine bottles were found behind the *Pescador* the next morning.

CHAPTER 35

THE GREAT BARRIER REEF, AUSTRALIA, NOVEMBER 5, 1986 RAUL'S THOUSAND-POUND BLACK MARLIN

1,025 pound black marlin weighed on the mother ship Manta Ray with angler Raul Gutierrez, captain Peter Bristow and mates Bill Harrison and Riley. Charter boat Avalon Great Barrier Reef, Australia November 5, 1986 Photo by Jim Rydell

It was Wednesday, and I was fishing on the Great Barrier Reef off Australia, mating for Captain Peter Bristow on his charter boat *Avalon*. We were using the *Manta Ray* as our mother ship. She was ninety feet long and twenty-five feet wide. The captain of the *Manta Ray* was Dirk, the engineer was Piet, the chef was Rachael, and the two stewardesses were Sadie and Nilly. My two anglers were Raul and Harry. They were both fishing clients of mine from Miami and the Bahamas.

On this trip to the Great Barrier Reef, Jim, a photographer friend of mine, and I gathered enough clients to require three fishing boats and crews to tie alongside of the ninety-foot *Manta Ray*, which most of us lived on. Jim did most of the work arranging plane tickets, hotel rooms, and sea planes and solving the usual problems associated with twelve people traveling form America to Australia.

This was a typical day on the reef for me. I would get up at five and get the *Avalon* ready to go fishing and then get some dive gear for Piet, Sadie, and Nilly. The four of us took the *Avalon* behind the main reef and would swim, dive, and exercise for just over one hour without Riley, who was Peter's full-time mate. Rachael, the chef, laid down the law to me that I was responsible for getting the game boat, as she called the *Avalon*, tied up alongside the mother ship and her "girls" back to work in the galley at eight thirty sharp.

Rachael and I became good friends because I was the only one onboard who took the time to go back in the galley after dinner and thank her for preparing the wonderful meals she worked so hard to create. Every night she cooked till after midnight to feed the boat crews and customers great gourmet creations. Each night she would select a different red and white wine she thought would go well with the dinners she prepared. This was interesting for those who wanted only their favorite wine every night. In chef school she had learned what wine went with a particular cut of steak or type of fish or bird. This forced some of my clients to try wines they had never heard about.

As Nilly, our blond-haired, blue-eyed twenty-year-old Australian stewardess, climbed onboard the *Avalon* to go diving, she looked more tired than usual. Each night she would help Rachael and Sadie clean the dishes off the table. Then Sadie would go aft to the back deck and start mixing and serving drinks while Nilly would help Rachael wash, dry, and put away the dishes. Nilly then had to go out on the back deck and help Sadie mix and serve drinks. Most of the anglers would retire at midnight, knowing they had to be at the dining room table at nine o'clock the next morning for breakfast.

Raul and Harry kept the party going. They would stay up for hours with the two blondes as the girls yawned and looked at the stars. Once the three game boats departed the mother ship in the morning, the girls started making the beds and cleaning the bathrooms. They still had to do the laundry and take the clean shirts, pants, etc., and put them in the different staterooms. Sometimes they got to sleep for an hour or so in the afternoon. They had to look their prettiest, with makeup on and smiling when the game boats docked at six thirty every night. They also had to have all the drinks poured and hot appetizers ready and on the bar so they could listen to the marlin stories of the day.

Each night both of these girls stayed very professional as the rum bottles emptied. The cutoff time was 3:00 a.m., and Raul stayed up till the last second. Several mornings Nilly would tell me to do something with "your octopus friend," who was sleeping on the floor of the back deck. Before we departed to go for our morning dive, I would go to the back deck and see Raul sleeping there. Sometimes I would find a full wine bucket, with a few ice cubes still floating in the water from the night before. Pouring the ice water on him did not wake him up, but it did make me feel good!

This was a great day, since we were behind Number Ten Ribbon Reef. This reef was beautiful and had been written about in every diving magazine around the word. All four of us got our exercise by diving and swimming in the clear reef water. Once I docked the *Avalon* alongside the mother ship, the two girls ran to the galley, and I headed toward my room to shower.

Rachael was known for her exceptionally good breakfasts, which Nilly and Sadie would have on the table at nine o'clock sharp. We usually had three kinds of homemade muffins, two big bowls of different flavored yogurt, bacon, sausage, coral trout fillets, and eggs served scrambled, fried, or soft-boiled. Three baskets of different toast were brought out at the last moment, so the toast was hot. Watermelon, kiwi, plums, and bananas were on the table. We all sat down except for Raul and Harry.

Just after nine forty-five the two other game boats departed for a fun day of fishing. Rachael had put two platters of prepared sandwiches onboard both boats. It was the crew's responsibility to put the drinks and beer onboard and ice everything. The *Avalon* could not leave because Raul, Harry, and Riley were nowhere to be found.

At eleven thirty Riley came stumbling out of the bow rope locker, where he had passed out the night before, and Harry showed up at noon. As Peter told me to throw the stern lines off on the *Avalon*, Nilly came running out on deck shouting for us to wait. Raul had surfaced and was ready to go fishing. I helped him onboard and thought we were finally ready to go.

Once they were all onboard, I untied the stern lines as Raul demanded to have breakfast. I looked over at Riley, who had passed out on the deck on the far side of the cockpit, and I knew I had to solve the problem. When Rachael saw me enter the galley, she picked up a meat cleaver and held it over her head. After some very tense moments and a little sweet talk, I explained I would fix some eggs and toast so we could finally go fishing. She put down the cleaver, picked up a medium-size paper bag, and headed for the garbage area.

After a bit of digging, she found some scrambled eggs and scraped up a handful with her fingers. She carefully put the wad of eggs in the bottom of the paper bag. She went to another garbage can and found three pieces of stale toast; she wrapped them in a paper napkin and added them to the bag. She handed me a knife, a spoon, and a fork and told me, "I want these back!" On the way to the galley door, she saw a small box of Wheaties, which she added to the bag. As I was closing the galley door, I heard her say, "Tell Raul to enjoy his fu**ing eggs."

As Peter ran the boat toward the marlin grounds and I got the baits ready to go, Raul ate every bit of his eggs and toast. I never told him that what he thought was pepper on his eggs was actually cigarette ashes. Later I was lucky to see Raul throw something overboard, and I made Peter circle back around to pick up the paper bag as it floated in our wake. Sure enough, it contained the promised knife, fork, and spoon. If I did not return them, Rachael might have brought the meat cleaver with her when she visited my cabin that night.

When Peter slowed the boat to start fishing, it was after one o'clock, and conditions were perfect for black marlin fishing. Harry was going to be our first angler, and he was fast asleep on the starboard engine box. Raul was asleep on the port engine box. Riley was still curled up in the corner of the cockpit, with salt spray caked over his shirtless back.

The first black marlin strike was a five-hundred-pound fish that I hooked. All I could do was laugh at Peter as he jumped up and down on his favorite hat, screaming for Harry to get into the fighting chair.

Finally Raul stumbled out and crawled into the fighting chair as I snapped the harness to the 12/0 Fin-Nor reel.

Riley was now up, and he and Raul both looked like death. Ten minutes into the fight, Raul could not hold his breakfast back any longer. He vomited on the deck and then on his knees and then on his chest. Riley took one look at the scrambled eggs and toast all over the deck and vomited over the starboard side of the boat.

Peter had a two-inch ID (inside diameter) wash-down hose attached to a JABSCO pump, which looked like a fire hose in action. It did not take long to hose the eggs and toast off of Raul's chest, stomach, and legs. Cleaning the deck was easy, with everything running out the scuppers in the back of the boat. Since I had to do Riley's job and mine, I had lost patience with him. He crawled forward and slept on the bunk for the rest of the day.

We released the five-hundred-pound marlin and were back trolling when another black ate the small bait on the left outrigger. We fished a scad on the left outrigger. A scad is about the size of a big mullet or average mackerel. When I could not wake Harry, Raul affectionately said to him as he slept, "F**k Harry" and jumped in the chair to catch the small marlin. We turned a two-hundred-pound black loose in a couple of minutes, since the 130-pound test tackle overpowered the fish. The next bite was a seven hundred pounder that Raul missed. The next bite was about four hundred pounds, which Raul also missed. The next was a small black marlin that ate the scad, and Raul stuck him. The small fish lasted about two minutes before we released him.

Harry came out in the cockpit holding his head and found out that Raul had released three marlin. He was furious. Moments later a seven-hundred-pound black marlin grabbed the three-foot mackerel we were fishing from the right outrigger, and Harry hooked the marlin and was in the chair and fighting the fish. It took about one hour of our valuable fishing time for Harry to catch and release his first marlin of the day. Harry blamed his poor performance on his bad knee. The injury was from all the years he'd played football in his college years. We all knew he was lying.

Harry felt he deserved the next marlin. Raul agreed, and Harry missed a three hundred pounder on a big mackerel. Although the day was almost over, Raul agreed again to let Harry try to hook the next fish, but only if Raul got to have the following marlin strike, which would probably be the last strike of the day.

All of us saw the four-hundred-pound black try to eat the big scaly mackerel on the right outrigger. Harry missed the marlin and gave both rods to Raul for the last bite of the day. Being fair to Harry, hooking a small marlin on a big bait is very difficult.

The day was getting late when I saw a big shadow under the right outrigger. Up came the largest marlin of the day, and Raul stuck him on his first try. Once Peter saw the marlin jump, he told me to lay the gaffs out on the deck and wake Riley. I had Harry steer the chair while I went forward and got Riley up, telling him we really needed him.

After about fifty minutes of great boat handling, Peter had the marlin in a perfect position for Riley to grab the leader wire and hold on. The added pressure caused the marlin to stop swimming and to turn straight up, sticking the front half of his fourteen-foot-long body out of the water. Peter instantly backed the Avalon alongside the vertical marlin, and I reached out and gaffed the big fish in the right shoulder as it hung momentarily in midair. As the black fell back toward the boat, I put the gaff rope loop over the stern cleat, so the marlin could not go down.

Everything went as perfect as it could, and we had a one-thousand-pound black marlin alongside the boat. The thrashing fish caused the white water to cover the cockpit, soaking everyone. Soon the marlin gave up, and we started the process of pulling the big fish into the cockpit of the boat. Peter attached the block and tackle to the nose of the marlin, and the four of us started to pull. Once the fish was in the boat, Peter headed toward the mother ship, and I shut the transom door. The other three fell asleep.

As I steered the boat through the reef, Peter called Dirk on the radio, advising him to get the scales out and the lifting davit ready. The two girls were to have champagne and glasses ready for the celebration if the marlin weighed over a thousand pounds. Raul's dream in life was to catch a marlin that weighed more than a thousand pounds.

Peter docked the *Avalon* under the davit, and Dirk lowered the lifting hook down so I could put the nylon loop over it. Up went the fish till it was high enough to be suspended in the air. Dirk activated the scales and waited. Soon the numbers flashed, and everyone could read the 1,025 pounds that showed on the face of the scales. I first shook Peter's hand because he had made the call to gaff and kill this fish. He was sure it would weigh over one thousand pounds. I then shook Raul's hand. He had gotten off to a bad start but did a great job of catching the fish.

The champagne was poured, and all the other crew members and anglers celebrated with us. I took my glass of champagne and went forward, where I could sit on the side rail of the *Manta Ray* in the twilight darkness and look out over the famous Great Barrier Reef. I thought how lucky I was to have grown up in South Florida and end up here, fishing on the world's largest and most famous Great Barrier Reef. Reality set in when Rachael came up behind me and put her arms around my waist and her chin in the back of my neck saying, "You'd better have my silverware."

CHAPTER 36

St. Thomas, US Virgin Islands, September 7, 1987
The Great Captain Mike Benitez

Blue marlin painting, Hooked Fury by Marine Artist Mike Hoffman

I was running Estabon Byrd's boat from Puerto Rico to St. Thomas. Bobby Jenkins was our mate, and my two anglers were Ralph Christiansen Jr. and Mike Benitez. Mike had fished out of San Juan since he was a kid and owned two charter boats, both named the *Sea Borne*. Ralph and I had fished together for almost twenty years, and Mike, Ralph, and I were the best of friends. Estabon's boat was an Ocean-built boat called the *Aguha*. We planned on running to the St.

A YOUNG FISHERMAN'S DREAM COME TRUE

Thomas North Drop, and then I would slow down the boat and put the baits out to fish for blue marlin.

Bobby was one of the best mates I had ever seen, since he had worked the cockpit for the legendary Captain Buddy Carey for thirteen years of charter boat fishing out of Miami. He was looking forward to fishing with Mike because Mike had caught more than two thousand blue marlin and was a legend in the Caribbean area as the best blue marlin captain ever.

Approaching the North Drop, I slowed the boat down to trolling speed. Bobby took the right side of the cockpit, and Mike took the left. They put mackerel in the long outriggers and R+S lures in the short outriggers.

Ralph liked to fish a special black lure with a cupped head he had designed while Mike, now my second angler, brought a special lure he called the "purple beauty." Ron Schatman, owner of R&S Lures in Miami, was making custom lures for Ralph, Mike, and me.

Since Mike had not worked the cockpit in a long while, Bobby had his side of the boat fishing, with the mackerel flopping behind the boat in the long rigger position, and Ralph's special black lure in the short outrigger position long before Mike could get one bait out. Even with Bobby dropping back the mackerel and lure for Mike, it took a while for him to run the mackerel and lure up to the proper position in the outrigger. Ralph brought this to everyone's attention several times that afternoon, as he pointed out Mike's increasing age and body weight.

We started off the short fishing day with a doubleheader—a 375-pound blue marlin for Ralph on the left long outrigger and a 250-pound blue for Mike on the other long rigger. Ralph jumped into the fighting chair to catch his fish, and Mike kept his rod in the right covering board. Bobby always wore wire-cutting pliers for safety and gave Mike an extra pair just in case. Bobby also put a National Marine Fisheries Service tag on the tag pole, hoping Mike would be able to use it.

When catching a doubleheader, I like to keep both fish in a straight line behind the boat, so I can release the closest marlin first and then go after the other. Mike's marlin did just what I had hoped. It stayed on top of the water, thrashing its bill back and forth violently. Bobby grabbed the leader wire when I backed the boat up while Mike tagged the blue marlin and cut the leader wire, releasing the fish in great shape.

Ralph's marlin swam down sea for about a mile and then went straight down for about two hundred yards. Ralph had thirty years of marlin fishing experience and was great in the fighting chair with a 9/0 Fin-Nor reel and one-hundred-pound test monofilament line. He stood up in the chair and used his body weight in the fishing harness to his advantage. It was not long into the standoff before Ralph started to gain line. He was raising the marlin. First he gained only one crank of the fishing reel, then he turned it into two cranks. Bobby was watching as Ralph's years of experience were paying off.

Bobby had his wiring gloves on and got the leader wire while Mike tagged the blue marlin in the shoulder and cut the leader wire. Ralph went inside the boat and filled out all the information on a National Marine Fisheries Service tag card. Before he finished, Mike was screaming, "We have another doubleheader." We had one blue on the right long outrigger and another on the right short lure. Ralph, since he was paying the bills, got the fighting chair, and Mike left his rod in the right covering board rod holder.

Both marlins stayed on the surface and jumped enough times for me to maneuver the Aguha to the closest fish and tag and release it.

A YOUNG FISHERMAN'S DREAM COME TRUE

Ralph had the larger of the two marlin on, and it rocketed down sea and eventually went down, taking three hundred yards of monofilament line. It was not long till Ralph had pumped the fish up to the surface, and Bobby wired the blue while Mike tagged and released it. Ralph's marlin looked to be about 325 pounds, and Mike's fish was under two hundred pounds. Ralph went inside and logged the info. Mike and Bobby high fived each other! A lasting friendship had been formed.

It was about a one-mile run back to the North Drop. Mike and Bobby had new rigged mackerel snapped on the long outrigger rods and a black lure and a purple lure ready to go on the short outrigger rods. Bobby had his two rigs fishing quickly, and Mike was getting faster every time we put the baits back out. Bobby and Mike both shouted at the same time, and as I turned around I saw two rods bent over and a third fish halfway out of a wave crashing the left long outrigger mackerel. I stomped on the flying bridge deck to get Ralph out of the saloon. As he came out of the door, one of the marlin came off. We still had our third doubleheader of blue marlin on and jumping.

Just like before, Ralph got to use the fighting chair, and Mike fought his fish from the rod holder in the covering board. Bobby wound in the left long outrigger bait and held up the destroyed mackerel for me to see. Ralph was hooked up to the largest fish of the day, and it was tearing up the ocean with wild jumps. We were in the middle of a group of marlin boats, so the radio was alive with comments about our two fish.

Both marlin headed down sea at different speeds, with Mike's smaller fish going much slower. This boat did not handle nearly as well as Ralph's *Pescador* did, so it took much more time to swing the bow around and chase the two marlin. Bobby turned the fighting chair to the right side of the cockpit so Ralph could gain line from us running forward, and Mike moved his rod to the right covering board rod holder and pointed the rod forward.

Ralph was giving Mike verbal jabs about making an out-of-shape boat captain work too hard, and Mike returned with a comment about how the day's fishing was exactly like their nightclub experiences throughout the years. According to Mike, Ralph always got the big heavy ones while Mike got the young skinny ones. Bobby and I laughed for ten minutes while the exchanges continued.

Once Mike had the double line on the reel, there was silence in the cockpit. Mike pushed the drag lever up to full, and the marlin, feeling the much heavier pressure, did a crazy turn away from the boat, making me put one engine in reverse. I roared back toward the fish, which was struggling to pull line off of Mike's reel, which he had on full drag. Luckily the marlin was small and tired, so Bobby grabbed the leader wire while Mike quickly tagged and released the fish. Meanwhile Ralph's fish had pulled much more line off the 9/0 Fin-Nor reel than I realized, causing a barrage of verbal complaints from Ralph. I spun the bow of the boat down sea, and off we went trying to regain line as fast as possible.

It took a long time to catch up with this blue marlin because it kept swimming hard down sea. I finally saw its black back and tail out of the water on a down sea roll of a big wave. Seeing the fish made it much easier for me to chase it, since I had a visual reference.

The double line was on the reel, and Ralph stood up in the chair, putting as much pressure on the marlin as he could. Mike patted Bobby on the shoulder and said, "I'm glad you're wiring this hot fish and not me." Bobby had wired thousands of all kinds of fish during his charter boat days but never anything as large as this six-hundred-pound blue marlin. When Bobby took a wrap of the heavy leader

A YOUNG FISHERMAN'S DREAM COME TRUE

wire, the angry fish got hotter and leaped out of the water on a down sea charge.

As I pushed the throttles forward to catch up with the fish again, I heard Bobby say, "I hope you have my wife's phone number." He was referring to one of my mates, who had been dragged over the side of the boat and deep into the ocean. Again Ralph was in the air with the double line on the reel and putting full pressure on the reel.

The swivel was almost close enough for Bobby to get the leader wire, but the marlin accelerated down sea. We repeated this several more times until the marlin became visibly tired. Mike looked up at me and said, "She has had it." I was happy to hear this, since he had caught well over two thousand blue marlin, and I had caught only about nine hundred at that time.

Mike was right—the fish started to struggle and needed to use the down sea waves to help it keep ahead of the boat. I soon had the bow of the *Aguha* close to the marlin, and it was having great difficulty staying ahead of us. Once Ralph had the double line on the reel, he went to full drag, and the tired marlin rolled over and gave up. Bobby wired the fish while Mike tagged it in the shoulder. Bobby then held the tired blue marlin close to the boat while I took pictures of Ralph, Mike, and Bobby with the tag clearly visible. This picture was used on the cover of Ralph's fishing club magazine several years later.

Ralph helped Bobby and Mike put the baits out and up in the outrigger pins, and we were trolling for marlin again. It wasn't long till we had a late afternoon strike on the right short outrigger and missed the marlin. Two minutes later we had a strike on the left long and pulled the hook. I noticed the humor in the cockpit had evaporated. No one was saying a word. We were now in the corner, and I asked Ralph if he was ready to call it a day as the mackerel on the left long outrigger popped out of the rigger pin and came down. Ralph dropped back and hooked the marlin. Everything went back to normal as far as the humor, and the tagging and releasing of the blue marlin showed perfect teamwork.

As I was running the boat toward the dock, Ralph and Mike came up the bridge ladder to talk. Bobby stayed below, cleaning up and organizing things for the next day of fishing. Ralph's first question to Mike and me was, "Have either of you ever gone three doubleheaders in a row catching blue marlin?"

Mike looked at me, and I said, "Never."

Mike then said, "I've never gone two doubleheaders in a row."

When I backed the boat into the dock, there was a big group of captains and mates waiting to congratulate Ralph and Mike for flying seven blue marlin flags. Releasing three doubleheaders in a row and a single was unheard of. Since that day I have caught a lot of blue and black marlin, but I have never gone three doubleheaders in a row.

Ralph ended his blue marlin fishing career having caught somewhere around eight hundred. Mike ended his charter boat captain career having caught about three thousand blues.

Unfortunately neither can tell me the exact number because both of my good friends have sailed on.

CHAPTER 37

THE GREAT BARRIER REEF, AUSTRALIA, OCTOBER 31, 1989 SAM'S WINNING BLACK MARLIN

Halloween Jackpot Tournament winning black marlin with angler Sam Jennings. Caught on the Avalon with captain Peter Bristow and mates Bill Harrison and Jay Reiber. Great Barrier Reef, Australia October 31, 1989

I was fishing the Great Barrier Reef of Australia. Peter Bristow was running the *Avalon*, which he had built himself as a charter boat, and I was working the cockpit mating, as was Jay Reiber. Our angler was Sam Jennings, who was one of my fishing charters from Miami. We had fished together in many areas, including the Bahamas and St. Thomas. I had been living on the Island Club mother ship, which had anchored at different places on the reef for most of the month.

We'd had several days of windless weather, with flat, calm seas, and this day was going to be the same. We would be competing in a one-day tournament held every October 31 called the Halloween Jackpot Tournament. It was open to all fishing boats on the Great Barrier Reef as long as the captain had the entrance money in his hand before eight in the morning.

The rules were simple. An angler could kill only one black marlin. Once the first fish of the day was in the boat, the measurements were called by radio to all the boats fishing the tournament. If another marlin was caught, the measurements had to be at least one inch larger to qualify, and the marlin could then be put in the boat. If the marlin was equal in size or smaller, it had to be released.

It didn't matter what tackle was used or where you were fishing. Fishing was to stop at five in the afternoon. Most mother ships had scales onboard to weigh the marlin. Everyone pretty much knew which boat won because the lengths and girths had been radioed to all boats. However, no one knew the exact weight of the winning fish.

The big steel *Flamingo Bay* was anchored at Number Ten Ribbon Reef, where our mother ship was also anchored, and the *Flamingo Bay* had scales set up for all the boats in the area to use.

A YOUNG FISHERMAN'S DREAM COME TRUE

I liked fishing the ocean side of Number Ten Ribbon Reef because Peter and I had caught a lot of big blacks there in years gone by, but the calm seas were not my favorite condition to fish. When the wind blew out of the southeast, the black marlin frequently got up near the surface and could be seen gliding down the waves. This was called "tailing," since the marlin's big black tail was visible for a long distance sticking out of the face of the wave. It was like a surfboard rider except the marlin was beneath the surface of the water.

My days started at five in the morning. I got the charter boat *Avalon* ready to go fishing and then got some masks and fins so the stewardess, Jay, and I could go diving and get some exercise. There was a great spot close to where we were anchored called the Cod Hole. In this small area of beautiful coral lived a dozen or more huge potato cod that could be hand-fed.

A potato cod is like an Atlantic black grouper except larger. A cod weighing 150 pounds was very common to see at this location. We saved the marlin baits that had been damaged while trolling. The wahoo and dog tooth tuna frequently attacked and ruined twenty or more marlin baits a day. We saved these baits and cut them into one-pound pieces to hand-feed our friends.

On an incoming tide, which brings in the clear water from the ocean side of the reef, visibility goes to over one hundred feet. The reef had huge elevated structures of twenty feet covered with corals of every color. Schools of tropical reef fish knew that the game boats would bring enough food so all the fish, large and small, could have a feast.

I had a favorite potato cod that I named King Potato. He was the biggest and fattest fish in that part of the reef. Whenever I entered the water wearing a tank or free diving, he recognized me and swam over to greet me. He knew the five-gallon bucket I was carrying would be filled with yummy pieces of fish.

Of the three or four moray eels that lived in this area, Mona was my favorite. She knew me but hid in the coral passages for her safety. I made an effort to feed her sometime during each of my dives. I had a big problem with King, because he was the dominant guy of the reef, and he would grab Mona in the middle of her long, skinny body and swim her off to a distant part of the reef and then spit her out. Since she had to slither from coral head to coral head, it took her a long time to return.

King Potato had a posse of six smaller but loyal potato cods that followed whatever he did. If a whitetip reef shark smelled the fish scent and blood from the food I had brought, King would teach the shark a lesson it would never forget. If a shark would swim up the scent trail to me, knowing I had fish, King would attack with a vengeance while the other hundred-pound cods bit the shark's stomach, fins, and tail. The terrified shark never returned.

After forty or fifty minutes of feeding the fish and diving, we climbed back into the *Avalon* and cruised to the Island Club. I always showered and put on clean clothes before I entered the galley and asked the chef if she needed any help putting breakfast on the table at nine or so.

By the time we had finished a great breakfast and were ready to go fishing, the tournament had already started. Luckily no one had hooked a marlin. Peter liked to troll a big bait from one outrigger and a smaller scad from the other. He used two 12/0 Fin-Nor reels filled with 130-pound test Dacron line. He liked heavy leader wire and big hooks. I think Peter dreamed of big marlin in his sleep. At that point in Peter Bristow's career, he had weighed in fifty-two black marlin that were over one thousand pounds. Quite an accomplishment!

A YOUNG FISHERMAN'S DREAM COME TRUE

After I put the baits out and ran the marks up in the outriggers, I looked out over the surface of the ocean, which resembled a huge mirror. There was not a breath of wind. By high noon a few boats fishing in the tournament had reported having a couple of small marlin strikes, and two rats had been released. A rat is a small black marlin weighing in at less than the two-hundred-pound range. These fish were fun to catch and release but not as much fun as a marlin larger than eight hundred pounds.

At exactly one in the afternoon, we had our first strike, and Sam hooked the black on a large mackerel we fished from the right outrigger. Peter Wright was running the charter boat *Duyfken* with Carl Anderson onboard filming the fishing tournament. Once Peter ran over and got in position behind the *Avalon*, our marlin started jumping, right on schedule, toward Carl's camera. As Peter Wright moved the *Duyfken* away, the fish jumped closer and closer to it. While Peter Bristow backed the *Avalon* at full throttle, Sam wound the Dacron line on the Fin-Nor spool. We were getting very close to the jumping fish.

Peter Bristow told me to take a gaff shot if I could get one, so I picked up the flying gaff and moved to the corner of the cockpit. I looked over at Jay, our wire man, and smiled. Grabbing the leader wire as an eight-hundred-pound black marlin jumped away from the boat took a lot of skill and guts. Compounding our problem was Carl and his ever-running camera, which would capture everything we did. If one of us made an error, the world would see it over and over for the rest of our lives.

Sam had as much pressure on the fish as was possible as Peter backed the boat toward the leaping marlin. Once Sam had the swivel to the tip of the rod, Jay grabbed the wire, took a double wrap, and pulled. The added pressure from Jay caused the marlin to turn a small amount to its right as it made its next jump. This gave me a possible shot with the flying gaff. I leaned out as far as I could and managed to get the tip of the flying gaff over the airborne marlin's left shoulder.

With Jay pulling as hard as he could from the right corner of the cockpit and me pulling on the flying gaff rope from the other side, the marlin fell back against the transom of the *Avalon* and crashed down into the water. Luckily I got the loop of the flying gaff rope around the stern cleat, and the marlin could only thrash on the surface, since the rope on the stern cleat would not allow the fish to get its head beneath the water. Peter Wright backed the *Duyfkin* close against our transom as Carl filmed the exciting encounter. Everyone on our boat had done a great job, and it was now on film for the world to see.

After Peter Bristow radioed the measurements to the rest of the fishing fleet, we went back to trolling for marlin. During the next two hours, several other boats caught black marlin that were not as long as ours and released them. At five o'clock we wound in our fishing lines and ran toward the *Flamingo Bay* to weigh our marlin. Sam Jennings had caught several hundred blue marlin in the Atlantic Ocean, but this was going to be the first black marlin he would weigh in.

The *Flamingo Bay* was a big steel-hulled expedition type boat. Several fishing boats were using it as their mother ship that season. Peter put the stern of the *Avalon* to the stern of the *Flamingo Bay* as the engineer lowered the lifting hook and loop of the winch to Jay, who attached a nylon loop to the marlin's tail. I had the engineer lift the marlin just high enough to get some good pictures of Sam, Jay, and Peter standing in the cockpit of the *Avalon* with the winning fourteen-foot marlin.

I took over driving the *Avalon* and put Sam, Peter, and Jay off on the *Flamingo Bay* for the official weighing of Sam's marlin. Peter read the scales at 882 pounds. We had known we had caught the winning fish, but we had not known exactly what it weighed.

I ran the *Avalon* back to our mother ship, the *Island Club*, and tied it up. The mother ship captain, mate, stewardess and chef were waiting in Halloween costumes to ride in our small skiff to the party on the *Flamingo Bay*. After I took a quick shower and gathered up six bottles of rum, I grabbed my camera., and off we all went. It was dark, and the red, blue, yellow, and green party lights gave the *Flamingo Bay*'s deck a strange glow.

The crews from all the mother ships and game boats anchored in our area were there for the big Halloween party. A lot of the crew members, like me, had not set foot on dry land for a month. With all the singing and dancing and the alcohol flowing, it did not take long for us to get three of the young stewardesses up on a table. After some encouragement they started raising their T-shirts for the cheering crowd.

After celebrating our victory with a couple of glasses of champagne and photographing the three topless girls, I had the engineer run me back in our skiff to the *Island Club*. Peter, Sam, and Jay stayed on the *Flamingo Bay* to enjoy the rum. I had the entire mother ship to myself, so I went to the back deck and angled a big comfortable chair toward the *Flamingo Bay*, which was anchored a half mile away. It did not take long for me to fall asleep as the big boat gently rocked back and forth.

After four hours of sound sleep, I heard the hooting and howling of our crew approaching in the skiff. I knew it was time for me to sneak down to my cabin, which was located under the bow deck. As I laid in my bunk, I could hear singing and dancing feet pounding on the teak deck above where I lay. I rolled over and went to sleep.

I woke up early in the morning to a silent boat. Once I entered the galley, I saw lots of empty glasses and wine bottles and the remains of a dozen sandwiches. The ham, cheese, and roast beef were still on the counter. Finally I found the coffeepot and plugged it in. The day's breakfast for me was a cold muffin and a hot cup of coffee.

The chef was the first up, and she was as mean as a snake. Apparently she had tried to get Peter to go to his cabin, but he'd had other ideas. Peter looked a lot like a Leprechaun, with a full dark beard and a mustache. His hair at that time was also full and dark. He always went barefoot and seldom wore a shirt. He was slim and slight, so the Leprechaun look-alike was easy to see.

As Rachael had chased him toward the bow, grabbing his shirt, he had twisted away, leaving her holding it. Her next grab was his deck shorts, which he gladly slipped out of and was quickly dancing again. The stewardess later told me the last thing she had seen was Peter, totally naked, dancing an Irish jig on the bow deck, with the chef spraying him with the wash-down hose.

When I went looking for Peter, who was not in his cabin, I headed to the bow and found his clothing on the teak deck. Seeing the uncoiled wash-down hose and no trace of Peter made me remember what the stewardess had said. I then started a further inspection and heard moaning coming from the belowdecks rope locker.

When I lifted the deck hatch and looked down, I saw Peter. He was curled up, totally naked, and holding his head. He had slept on a bed of one and three-quarter inch wet, stinky anchor line. I finally managed to wake him up, and he crawled out of the rope locker and over to the right side of the bow, where he threw up into the water. I handed him a big bath towel to wrap around his body, so when he walked by the breakfast table no one would see the deep marks caused by his sleeping on the wet, stinky anchor line.

At noon Dave Presnel, the pilot of the *DeHavilland Beaver*, landed in the water behind the *Island Club* with our next group of fishermen. Sam Jennings said good-bye, and the plane took off, headed for Cairns. Sam flew out from Cairns that night, headed for the United States. Dave would fly in and land on the water behind our mother ship every few days to bring us our new anglers or to bring fresh food and the many new cases of great wine we were going through. The *Island Club* was owned by a winery, so we got the best wine they produced at a rock-bottom price. Peter and I had spent months discussing which mother ship we were going to charter that year, and we'd ended up with a great choice.

Right at sunset Peter walked out on the back deck, rested and ready to pick up from where I had left off telling stories of catching giant marlin while everyone drank the best wine and ate great appetizers the chef had just baked. This time our two anglers had each brought a gorgeous lady.

CHAPTER 38

Captain Buddy Carey

A typical good one day catch by captain Buddy Carey on his charter boat Sea Boots with mate Pete. The Old Pier 5 Miami, Florida

During the sixty years that Buddy Carey charter fished out of Miami, he had many great mates. All of them have their own Buddy Carey stories that are true but still hard to believe.

A YOUNG FISHERMAN'S DREAM COME TRUE

When a friend and I would sneak off and take the bus from Coconut Grove to downtown Miami in the mid-'50s, our destination was always Pier 5. Even though we were way too young to drive, we would get there in time to see the charter boats come in at the end of the day with their variety of fish caught by tourists. Buddy Carey had the first slip on the left (the north side of the dock), and that was where people would gather waiting for him to dock at three thirty every afternoon.

When you are young, the bigger the fish the better! We would run from boat to boat looking for sharks, amberjack, sailfish, and grouper. Once the entire dock was surveyed, it was back to the *Sea Boots* to see the volume of different fish being unloaded. What always amazed me was the huge number of fish Buddy would catch every day. The standard summer catch seemed to be a line of bonitos laid side by side that went from dock cleat to dock cleat. Next came a row of kingfish, some small snakes, others gaffing size. Then came a pile of dolphin, two or three wahoos, two or three puppy sharks (this is any kind of shark that was less than four feet), and a couple of sailfish. In the winter the bulk of the catch would be groupers, with a mix of barracuda, cero mackerel, jacks, mutton snappers, and sometimes a shark. In the spring the bulk would be amberjack, with a few sails, sharks, and big dolphin and sometimes a white marlin or blue marlin.

Today's charter boats sure have changed. They have become larger and larger, changing from wood to fiberglass and from gas to diesel. But as we wandered the dock in the old days, there was one thing that never changed: some boats caught lots of fish while others caught only a few. It was common to see a boat back in with a good catch and the boat next to it had only a shark and a jack or two. Back then there were twenty-six boats at Pier 5, and some of the questionably maintained ones were lucky to make it to the Gulf Stream and back. A good day for them was when they actually caught a fish!

Buddy Carey was the most consistent captain who ever fished. His boat ran day after day. Good weather and bad weather. Some days he would be outfished by other captains, but on a weekly or monthly basis he not only outfished them, he buried them in fish carcasses.

He ran his charter boat as a business. He would leave early in the morning and was always back by to the dock by 3:30 p.m. Sometimes he would get back even earlier if the people would get tired of cranking in fish. He loved fishing but hid from the glory. He had no desire to travel. Pier 5 produced many great captains who traveled the world, but Buddy was not one and never cared to be one. He did make two trips to Bimini during the spring bluefin tuna northern migration and successfully caught one bluefin each trip. His love was arriving at the dock before daylight and getting the boat ready for fishing, then going out Government Cut early in the morning to fish a full day and returning to the dock to sell fish to the loyal customers who gathered every afternoon behind his boat.

Captain Ronnie Reibe, who went on to run a private boat, fished with Buddy for five years. He started mating on the *Sea Boots* the day he left high school, and the next day off wasn't for thirty-five days. The *Sea Boots* would run for seventy days straight and then have one day off, and Buddy would be at the boat before 6:00 a.m. with sandpaper in his hand, wondering where Ronnie was. The *Sea Boots* would then run the next fifty or more days in a row. Ronnie had to love fishing to keep the pace Buddy set.

One winter day when Ronnie was wire line trolling for grouper with Buddy, and they had trolled south on the reef to Beacon A (about twelve or so miles) with only one grouper and two barracuda, he went to the bridge of the *Sea Boots* and asked Buddy, "How much longer are we going to stay up here in the dead zone?"

Buddy looked over and said, "The groupers will start to bite in twenty minutes. Would you like my extra piece of cheesecake?" Buddy's wife would always include an extra dessert for the mate.

Ronnie returned to the cockpit, and when the groupers started to bite he could barely keep the pace of gaffing fish and rigging grouper baits. The *Sea Boots* returned to Pier 5 with thirty-five black groupers and the usual numbers of barracuda, mackerel, kings, and jacks. Ronnie still swears the groupers started to bite in eighteen minutes, not twenty.

Tommy's Boat Yard, which was just west of the Brickell Avenue Bridge on the south side of the Miami River, was the yard all the charter and commercial fishermen used to pull and paint their boats. One fall day when I worked for Buddy, he had scheduled three days to pull the boat and paint the sides and bottom. Luckily we were able to sand the transom and both sides by five thirty the first afternoon. The next day I arrived at the boat yard at 5:00 a.m. and found the gate open. I was greeted by the guard dog, Killer, which was a big black and brown lovable mutt. Walking to the scaffolding that surrounded the *Sea Boots*, I was surprised to see a clean china bowl with two just-opened cans of dog food on top of todays clean rags that were on the ground. I was even more surprised to see what was next to Killer's breakfast bowl: an open can of Z-spar paint, a quart of mineral spirits, four paintbrushes, and a box of rags.

From above me on the scaffolding, Buddy said, "I woke up, and the weather looked perfect to paint, so I came down and started without you." He had painted the entire port side of the boat in total darkness! Then he said, "While you're drinking coffee, why don't you pick up a brush and see if there are any spots I missed?"

Only people who knew Buddy could understand he was not being demanding or pushy; he was just being himself. He loved to work.

Whether it was five o'clock in the morning or five in the afternoon, Buddy assumed everyone else shared his hard work ethic and enjoyed working.

I folded up my egg sandwich and put it somewhere high enough to keep Killer from sniffing it out and adding it to his healthy breakfast. I then picked up a paintbrush and walked to the bow with a can of blue paint. My morning coffee had already been found and enjoyed by you know who—Killer the guard dog. I could only laugh at Buddy for being in a boatyard painting the port side of the *Sea Boots* in the middle of the night and truly thinking this was nothing out of the ordinary.

Buddy was always thoughtful. When he picked up his lunch bag in the early morning and headed for the boatyard, he would also select one of his wife's nice china bowls and two cans of dog food. At break time Buddy and the guard dog would sit down for breakfast. I would look over and see him with a brown bag in his lap and Killer, with his tail wagging, having his morning meal out of a clean bowl.

Red Hagen worked for Buddy from 1953 until 1957. The *Sea Boots* at that time was a forty-five-foot wooden charter boat built by Norseman Ship Yard in Miami, with three Chrysler Crown gas engines. When Red left Buddy, he went to work for the Jack Tar Hotel at West End, Grand Bahama Island. Red liked the *Sea Boots* so much that he persuaded the hotel to buy it. Buddy kept the Norseman until his Charlie Allygood Carolina boat was finished.

I worked for Red a lot when he fished the Bahamas. Our favorite thing to do when marlin fishing was slow was to swap Buddy Carey stories. Red liked to tell me about one particular spring day while fishing off Miami with Buddy. The wind was out of the northeast. Two men of the charter party that day had previously caught and

A YOUNG FISHERMAN'S DREAM COME TRUE

mounted sailfish with Buddy. They both expressed a desire to catch and mount a white marlin for their office.

When Buddy passed the jetties of Government Cut, he turned north, which was very rare for the Pier 5 boats to do. Once he reached the edge of the Gulf Stream, he started to troll in and out of the current (Buddy called this "sawing" the current). Lo and behold, one hour later there were two white marlin lying on the deck of the *Sea Boots*. Once the task at hand was accomplished, Buddy returned to his normal routine of going down the edge of the Gulf Stream catching dolphin, kings, and bonitos like every other day.

Red and I would laugh about things that happened regularly, like this, onboard the *Sea Boots*. Catching two white marlin was very uncommon, but doing it upon request was a different matter altogether. When you asked Buddy how he knew he could catch two white marlin in one hour, he could not give an answer.

One day while I was working for Buddy, I had some friends charter the *Sea Boots*. The one thing my friends wanted most was to catch a big grouper. We went all day catching dolphin and kings along with the usual barracuda and mackerel and a couple of sailfish. I knew that afternoon when we passed the Miami Sea Buoy that the day's charter was coming to an end. I went up to the bridge and reminded Buddy I had promised my friends we would at least try for a warsaw grouper. He told me to cut a fillet off one of the barracuda and rig it on one of our big rods and reels that was filled with Monel wire. We normally used this outfit for deep dropping for amberjack and groupers.

Knowing we had only fifteen minutes till Buddy would be running for the barn, I rushed to make the rig. When the engines slowed, I knew we were over what we called the main hole. As Buddy nodded, I sent the barracuda slab to the bottom in 350 feet of water. As I cranked the weight off the bottom, the wire line rod bent over the transom with an angry 286-pound warsaw grouper. It all happened so fast, I felt I must have hit the grouper on the forehead with the bait.

When most of the crowds left that afternoon, I asked Buddy how he knew a big warsaw grouper would be waiting and hungry on that particular spot. He just shrugged his shoulders and avoided answering me by saying, "Wrap the fish customer's dolphin fillets 'cause we have to get going."

Buddy and an old snowbird from Canada by the name of Mr. Shepherd had been good friends through the 1960s. When Mr. Shepherd sold his boat, the *Hazel S*, in 1965, he made a deal with Buddy to charter the *Sea Boots* four days a week from November 1 through March 31. The only thing Mr. Shepherd liked to do was troll the reefs for groupers. Buddy was the best in the world at trolling for groupers with wire lines.

Mr. Shepherd chartered the boat for seven years in a row. When he first started, Ronnie Reibe was the mate. Later on Ronnie was replaced by "Machine Gun" Gavin, who fished for three years on the *Sea Boots*. Bobby Jenkins then took over as mate and fished with Bud for thirteen years.

About halfway through Machine Gun's career as mate, a young runaway showed up living somewhere on the dock. Once Buddy got to know him, Geronimo, as Buddy nicknamed him, soon was living onboard the *Sea Boots*. He started as the boat washer and worked his way up. As more of us on the dock got to know him, we all became aware of how smart Geronimo was and how much fun he was to have around.

Once Mr. Shepherd met him, he hired him to ride on the boat to wind in the "junk fish"—kingfish, amberjack, mackerel, dolphin, wahoos, sailfish, and marlin. The only fish that were not junk fish to Mr. Shepherd were groupers. One of the great sights I will always remember seeing was the *Sea Boots* trolling next to me down the reef in the winter, with Geronimo in one wire line chair and Machine Gun in the other as the seventy-year-old Mr. Shepherd stood there shaking his finger at both anglers because they were not winding in the doubleheader of groupers as fast as he thought they should.

One March day when Buddy took a very rare day off, he asked me to run the *Sea Boots* for Mr. Shepherd. This was frightening for me, since no one could catch as many groupers as Buddy, and Mr. Shepherd was meaner than a snake if the groupers weren't biting. On that day I spent too much time down south on the reef, trying to catch a few extra groupers, so I had to get offshore to get the boat in the north-flowing Gulf Stream for the extra four knots of speed it would take to make it home by three o'clock. As we raced home in the blue water, we caught several big dolphin and a couple of wahoos.

Geronimo had just come up the bridge ladder to talk to me about his favorite subject, sports, when suddenly the long outrigger popped out of the pin, and I dropped back the ballyhoo and wound down on one of the 9/0 Penn Senators that we fished from our two long outrigger bridge chairs. The rod bent over, and up jumped a hooked sailfish. Geronimo moved to the chair and caught the fish like a real star. After Machine Gun had thrown the sail into the fish box, I commented to Geronimo about his new career as an angler. He looked over at me strangely and said that in the last four months with Mr. Shepherd, he had caught twelve sailfish, four white marlin, and two blue marlin. At that early point in Geronimo's life, I truly believed he thought this was average for one of Buddy's wash-down kids.

Bobby Jenkins became mate just after Buddy built a fifty-four-foot Padilla boat. It was solid fiberglass and had three 370-horsepower Cummins diesel engines. Mr. Shepherd immediately liked Bobby for his great personality and sense of humor. I think every charter boat captain or mate fishing out of Miami was jealous as they watched the *Sea Boots* go by that winter with Mr. Shepherd's group onboard. Where else can you get paid to go fishing, catch lots of fish, and have fun all day?

Buddy had started mating for his dad, Oliver, before he was a teenager. He would steer the boat while his dad would make baits and gaff fish. Not having any idea where to steer the boat, Buddy would watch his dad in the cockpit and learned that a quick glance to the right meant turn a little right, and a long look to the left meant the boat was too shallow, and he'd better turn it hard left and do it fast. Without a Fathometer Buddy quickly learned that if you trolled over the shallow reef the boat caught groupers, and if you trolled just inside the Gulf Stream the boat caught kingfish, and if you trolled in the blue water the boat caught dolphin.

With the help of his dad, Buddy bought his first boat in 1932. He painted the name *Sea Boots* on the transom. Buddy's mother told me that when he had first learned to read and write, Buddy would draw boats and print "*Sea Boots*" down their sides. According to Buddy the only problem with his first boat, outside of the fact that it broke down every third day, was the car transmission he used to link the gas engine to the propeller. When the boat was put in reverse, the engine had to be raced to make the prop turn fast enough to stop the boat and go backward into the slip. Most of the other boats had the same problem, so it was common to have the charter party and other captains and mates help pull a boat back down the dock to the right slip. In those days most of the men who chartered the boats wore coats and ties. How things have changed!

The commander of the coast guard base on Miami Beach knew Buddy well. There was a sandbar just off Fisherman's Island, now called Dodge Island, where coast guard boats regularly went aground. Frequently, on his way out to go fishing in the early morning, Buddy would pull these coast guard patrol boats off the shallow sandbar and tow them to the base, which was only a short distance across Government Cut. Buddy was polite enough not to tell the base commander that the real reason the patrol boats ran aground was actually Crawfish Eddie, who had a shack built on the south side of Fisherman's Island. So as not to be seen, the coast guard boats would turn off their running lights and sneak over to Crawfish Eddie's shack. Eddie was known to have an endless supply of cold beer that could be purchased only if he knew you. Eddie knew every young coast guard recruit and all the officers as well by their first names. The Miami Beach coast guard base had the distinction of leading the nation with the highest number of volunteers for the late-night patrols.

When World War II started in 1939, the commander of the coast guard base went to Buddy's house and asked him if he would run a patrol boat between Key West and Miami Beach. He knew that Buddy Carey could name every rock, sea fan, and conch shell in that area. Buddy tied up his charter boat and started running a patrol boat to Key West, staying one day and then running back to Miami Beach the next day. The commander was very proud of Buddy's patrol boat because Buddy and his crew would show up hours before the other crews. They were also very eager to work late on the nights when they returned from Key West.

It took a while for the base commander to get suspicious, but he finally decided to come to the base very early one morning and sit in his office with the lights off, so he could watch Buddy and his crew ready the patrol boat to defend their nation. Soon Buddy arrived in his truck under the streetlights next to the patrol boat. The crew quickly unloaded four huge boxes and a thousand pounds of ice and bait. Several days later the commander watched Buddy and his crew tie the boat up just after dark. As soon as the other crews had left for the evening, Buddy's old pickup truck came speeding down the alley and stopped alongside the patrol boat. It took the entire crew to get the heavy boxes off the patrol boat and into the bed of the pickup. The old, overloaded truck filled with groupers then raced up the alley, heading for the downtown fish market with Buddy at the wheel.

One of Buddy's good friends from Pier 5 also signed up with the coast guard to fight in the war. Captain Walter lived in a small wooden house with his mother, and after a month of showing up at the coast guard base on time and in uniform, Walter decided to go back to lobster gigging, which was what he had done for a living before he'd signed up. The commander of the base went to Buddy and said this was a time of war, and Captain Walter could not just walk off. If Walter refused to show up at the base, the commander was going to put him in jail.

Buddy went to Walter's house and talked to Walter's mother. She said Walter didn't like the uniform and didn't like getting up early. She also said Walter worked hard all night carrying that light, gig, and big bag of lobsters, and the soonest she could get Walter to the base would be about noontime.

Buddy went back to the commander and explained the problem. The commander assigned Buddy the difficult job of going again to Walter's house and solving this problem.

Two nights later Buddy had dinner with Captain Walter and his mother. When Buddy left the small, run-down wooden house on the north side of the Miami River, Captain Walter had become the official fish provider for the Miami Beach coast guard station. It was Walter's job to catch enough fish, lobsters, turtles, conch, and stone crabs to keep the base stocked with fresh seafood. In return Walter wasn't required to wear shoes or a uniform or even show up on time for work. Walter took his new position very seriously and commanded great respect from all those men who enjoyed the fresh seafood Captain Walter brought in daily.

Of the above-mentioned mates, Red Hagen went on to fish the Bahamas for the rest of this fishing career. He has since sailed on. Ronnie Reibe became a very successful charter boat captain in the Florida Keys. He is now retired. His son, Ron, went into fishing and is now a very successful captain in Central America.

Geronimo, with his great smile and good nature, has moved on to larger boats and now wears a white starched shirt with gold epaulets on his shoulders. "Machine Gun" Gavin took a job in Texas running a private sport fishing boat and is still there. Bobby Jenkins stayed with the fishing boats till he and his family of four beautiful daughters and a lovely wife moved to Stuart, Florida. None of his pretty girls decided to become fisher-people. And I went on to travel the world, fishing wherever the ocean was blue, above and below the equator.

Buddy took thousands of people on their first fishing trips. He enjoyed sharing his knowledge about the sea and about the fish that live in it with everyone. Buddy Carey is sadly missed by all.

CHAPTER 39

Captains Who Have Influenced My Life

I started fishing in my early teens and have worked with or docked next to so many truly famous captains from around the world. The captains who most influenced me were all charter boat captains or had charter boat backgrounds. When you build a boat that you are going to run and make a living with, you are far less likely to give up, because you have committed your own time, money, and effort to make it work.

I was a product of the Florida public school system and learned, while attending the fourth, fifth, and sixth grades, that I could ride my bike down to the waterfront of Coconut Grove, which was a half mile from my school. There were a few charter boats and one head boat docked in the county-owned slips. There were also a dozen lobster, stone crab, mullet, mackerel, and shrimp boats docked there.

Through the years I have come to believe true charter boat people enjoy seeing young kids like me and many others walk up and stare at all the different fish lying behind the boats on the dock. My wide-eyed excitement at seeing and listening to the fish stories associated with charter boats drew me to this area several afternoons during each week.

After a couple of weeks of staring, talking, and, mostly, listening, the special afternoon came when one of the older captains looked up as he backed his boat into the slip, and said, "How are you doing, matey?" As a fourth or fifth grader, being recognized was very special. By that time I could talk to the tourists and answer most of their questions about the kinds of fish or the price of a charter.

It did not take me long to learn how to tie knots and bend leader wire. Sharpening hooks and setting drags followed. When I was still in the public school system, I was fishing every weekend I could on private or charter boats. When my gym teacher learned how much money I made on an average weekend, he was amazed. Fishing out of Miami, we made our day's pay, sold fish, sometimes got a tip, and, if we were lucky, made something off mounting a fish. It all added up to a good day's pay.

Jimmy O'Neille was the first real charter boat captain I worked full-time for. He built a forty-eight-foot boat he and Tweed Hunter designed strictly for chartering out of South Florida. I went to work for him a year or so after he launched the *Queen B*. He ran a very professional operation and made money because he had to. He had his money in the boat and needed to pay the bank every month.

Jimmy was probably the first captain I worked for who did not keep a bottle of Scotch under the helm on the flying bridge. When I caught several of the old salts drinking as we fished, I believed them when they said, "It steadies my nerves." I thought this was true till I was probably sixteen. Finally it dawned on me that the Scotch was the reason the captain could not back the boat into the slip or why he crashed the boat into the dock. It wasn't the wind or the current after all.

I liked working for Jimmy because he was a good fisherman, and we caught lots of all kinds of fish every day. Most of his rules were easy to live with, because I was taught to brush my teeth, shower, and put on clean clothes every morning. I didn't like having to cut my hair, but my girlfriend at the time took care of that because she loved the cash I brought home every night. We had a good retail fish market behind the boat and a bunch of loyal customers.

I learned so much from Jimmy. He was the first captain I worked with who talked to the charter parties and listened to what they had to say. When we were catching big amberjacks two at a time, Jimmy would sometimes say, "Hold that one up so we can see it." Someone sitting in the flying bridge mentioned I was gaffing and throwing the fish in the fish box so fast, they never got to see the fish. Jimmy heard this and spoke to me. I always wanted to be the fastest mate. At the end of the day, the guy who wanted to see the sixty-pound amberjack handed me a tip, and I knew why Jimmy had asked me to hold the fish up.

Jimmy was willing to pass down what he had spent his lifetime learning. When we were on our way to the Bahamas, he would talk about running a successful charter operation. We talked about all the small things that add up and make it so difficult to get started and stay in business. I listened carefully, because I had dreams of one day building a boat and chartering. The fishing skills always came to me like fleas to a dog, but the people skills were learned by watching.

I moved to Pier 5 because that was where the real money could be made. Buddy Carey was a second-generation charter boat captain and had built a boat just like Jimmy's *Queen B*. The main difference between the two boats was that Bud left the back bulkhead open and put engine boxes for seats in the saloon. Buddy's boat was far more utilitarian and basic than Jimmy's.

I first worked on Buddy's forty-seven-foot Charlie Allygood Carolina-built boat named *Sea Boots* and then moved to the newer boat by the same name and captained it most of the time. Both boats were sky blue and set up exactly the same. Bud always put a steering station on the port side of the cockpit that was lower than the covering board and had a clutch, throttle, and helm three feet ahead of the transom. This was the best thing ever because I could come down from the flying bridge controls and help the mate gaff fish as I steered the boat from the cockpit. When we fished the many wrecks off the South Florida area, I could drop live baits or big grouper baits on the electric reels at the same time as the mate. Catching two big amberjack or warsaw groupers at the same time helped fill the fish box twice as fast.

Periodically I would mate for Buddy if he had a special customer, or I would captain his Carolina boat because I knew it so well and he had to take the day off for some appointment. Although I rarely had time, I enjoyed talking to Bud as we ran out to fish, because he was a fisherman like no one else on earth. He would fill the boat with every kind of fish every day. He never bragged about his skills. He could rarely tell you why he knew where to go to produce the great catches we brought in every day.

Everyone knew how to live bait for sailfish, but Buddy knew exactly when to put two live small bonitos overboard and hook two sailfish five minutes later. After a ten-minute fight, we had our two sailfish mounts in the boat and were back trolling, catching kingfish two at a time on the electric reels.

Everyone knew how to troll the reef with wire lines, but Bud would catch thirty groupers a day when most other captains hooked only bottom. He taught me his fifteen or twenty secret barracuda holes, where he would circle and catch a dozen barracuda and be back trolling for groupers ten minutes later. I learned his eight gag grouper areas where we would catch ten or twenty gag groupers a day when they were spawning.

He showed me areas on the shallow reef where mutton snappers schooled. He had me rig mutton snapper baits, and then he would troll through these areas and catch three doubleheaders of eight- to ten-pound muttons. He never circled, so it was easy to keep these small areas secret from the other boats.

The greatest thing Bud taught me was utilizing my time and making money. Pier 5 had a fish market like nowhere else on the Florida coast. Every afternoon it was common for us to sell twenty amberjack, twenty groupers, plus all the kingfish, snappers, blue runner, bar jack, and mackerel we caught earlier that day. When you worked for Bud on the *Sea Boots*, you worked fast and hard. He wanted to sell his fish and get home to his wife, Sevilla.

Fishing out of Pier 5 gave me the opportunity to bring in giant sharks, huge warsaw groupers, and lots of jewfish (Goliath groupers) that weighed three or four hundred pounds. I put thousands of amberjack and groupers on the dock after the end of a fishing day. But learning how to drive a fishing boat in order to catch blue marlin, black marlin, and giant tuna came from mating with guys who were the real big-game professionals.

I was so lucky to mate for Captains Bill and George Staros, catching giant bluefin tuna out of Cat Cay and blue marlin off Chub Cay. Together they had caught over two thousand giant bluefin tuna. I worked four seasons on the charter boat *Avalon*, fishing Australia's Great Barrier Reef with Captain Peter Bristow. When I started with Peter, he had caught more than 1,900 giant black marlin, and I helped add a couple hundred more to his lifetime achievement. All three of these captains knew how to run a boat once a big fish was hooked. I watched, and I learned.

Looking back at those years, I am so thankful I had the opportunities to fish with these five greats of the fishing world. I came away as a much better fisherman and a better person because of them. My values, ethics, morals, business skills, and fishing skills were influenced by each of these captains to some degree.

CHAPTER 39-A

Dude Perkins

My first memory of Dude was him working at his aunt's business, called Commercial Fishing Supply Company, which was located near the Miami Avenue Bridge in downtown Miami. According to him I would do chin-ups on the front counter. He was in the tackle business all his life and knew thousands of captains and mates through his sixty-some years of retail sales.

Some of the early greats that bought fishing tackle from Dude and who shaped the fishing world were Bill Fagan, Tommy Gifford, Eddie Wall, Red and Bob Stuart, Buddy and Allan Merritt, and the entire Voss family.

There is no way to calculate the numbers of jobs Dude helped create by knowing the many captains and mates who were looking for work at the time and having an instant recall of who was available whenever a boat owner or captain asked. With his photographic memory, Dude put people into boat and fishing jobs that lasted for decades and longer.

I watched old-timers from under the bridge ride up on their bicycles and lean them against the front wall as a stretch limo would pull up and let someone out accompanied by two bodyguards. The Miami waterfront at that time was no different from the waterfront of

Shanghai, New York, or Hong Kong. Dude knew all the shady characters because they loved to stop by the shop, as the tackle store was called, and talk to him.

Long before Miami had a professional football or basketball team, Dude would talk about dog racing with one customer and sailfishing with another. He knew how many groupers were caught yesterday and if the marlin were biting off Bimini. People called from New England for fishing tackle for bluefin tuna and would pass on info about the fishing up there. People would call from Las Vegas and tell him how much money one of his friends had just won or lost.

Like a lot of Miami people, he moved to different locations during his many years. His following was massive. People wanted to stop by and learn what was happening in the fishing world, and no one knew better than Dude. At one time he had a single-sideband radio put behind the tackle counter and would talk to the fishing boats all throughout the Bahamas and the Caribbean.

When I was fishing St. Thomas in the US Virgin Islands during the summer, he would call my mate, Bobby Jenkins, and ask him how many blue marlin we had caught that morning. When a customer walked into the shop, he enjoyed mentioning that we released a four-hundred-pound blue twenty minutes ago. Bobby would always ask Dude to call his wife and tell her Bobby loved her. He did this willingly.

If one of his customers at the tackle shop wanted some fresh fish, Dude would call the Pier 5 dock and ask me or whoever was tied up about getting some fresh dolphin, wahoo, tuna, or grouper. If we had what the customer wanted, Dude would pass the phone to the amazed person. He generated dozens of fish customers who did not know about the fish sales that took place behind the Miami charter and commercial boats.

What this man willingly did for the boatyards, retail shops, and charter boats was monumental. Sadly he is now retired but is still uniting captains with owners and finding mates to fly out on a moment's notice. He contributes to the Facebook page of the Crook & Crook tackle shop and comments on anything political that will outrage the general public.

Not only did Dude give me an untold amount of work, he influenced my life in so many ways I could never repay him.

www.ingramcontent.com/pod-product-compliance
Lightning Source LLC
Chambersburg PA
CBHW071251160426
43196CB00009B/1245